The Arnold and Caroline Rose Monograph Series of the American Sociological Association

The shape of culture

Judith Blau's book is based on an investigation of cultural institutions and activities in 125 cities in the United States. Rather than theorizing in speculative terms, it makes an empirical study of the development of a universal culture as a result of increasing urbanization and rising levels of education. Professor Blau's analyses include an examination of changes in cultural demand over time, which leads her to suggest that a taste for the avant-garde and experimental in art and culture has largely been confined to the "sixties generation." Her study of cultural organizations looks at their interrelationship, their internal structure, and relations with their metropolitan environments. Other questions addressed include the importance of the critical mass, and qualitative characteristics (style, traditionalism, and innovation) in the arts, as found in diverse media: rock music, museum collections and the theater. In addition, the author analyses long-term changes in artists' job opportunities and in cultural conditions determined by urban characteristics and federal art funding. This study will be of interest to sociologists, geographers, economists, and historians addressing themselves to contemporary culture, and its conclusions will be relevant to public policy on the arts.

The shape of culture

**A study of contemporary
cultural patterns in the United States**

Judith R. Blau

University of North Carolina, Chapel Hill

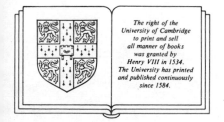

The right of the
University of Cambridge
to print and sell
all manner of books
was granted by
Henry VIII in 1534.
The University has printed
and published continuously
since 1584.

Cambridge University Press

Cambridge
New York   Port Chester
Melbourne   Sydney

Published by the Press Syndicate of the University of Cambridge
The Pitt Building, Trumpington Street, Cambridge CB2 1RP
40 West 20th Street, New York, NY 10011, USA
10 Stamford Road, Oakleigh, Melbourne 3166, Australia

First published 1989

Printed in Great Britain
at the University Press, Cambridge

British Library cataloguing in publication data
Blau, Judith R., *1942–*
The shape of culture: a study of contemporary
patterns in the United States. – (The Arnold and
Caroline Rose monograph series of the American
Sociological Association).
1. American culture. Anthropological perspectives
I. Title   II. Series
306′.0973

Library of Congress cataloguing in publication data applied for

ISBN 0 521 370981

VN

Contents

Figures and tables

Acknowledgements

Any research undertaking of this scope involves contributions from and the support of many others. Sometimes people who play a critical role in shaping research questions are not even aware of their influence. The late Joshua C. Taylor, who taught me as an undergraduate, played such a role, as did Arthur C. Danto, Norbert Elias, and Stanley Lebergott. My graduate statistics teacher, Leo Goodman, influenced the direction of my work far more than he or I could have predicted at the time I took his courses.

Other people have played a more direct role as they responded to various early ideas and provided general interest in this research. Of the many, I particularly thank Paul DiMaggio, Harold Horowitz, Elihu Katz, Richard Peterson, and especially Peter Blau, who has been my toughest critic and most supportive colleague throughout this and earlier projects.

I am very grateful for the research support from the National Science Foundation (grants SES-8319074 and SES-8320420). Some additional funding was provided by the National Endowment for the Arts and, in the final stages of manuscript preparation, by the American Council of Learned Societies. A Rockefeller Foundation fellowship that supported a month's residency at its Bellagio Conference Center is gratefully appreciated.

Peter Blau was a co-principal investigator on the National Science Foundation project, and the results of our earlier collaborative work is described in chapter 8. The statistical consultant for this project, Joseph E. Schwartz, provided me with clear and helpful advice.

Every chapter was read by at least one person prior to revisions. For their extremely useful criticisms and suggestions I thank the following: Howard Aldrich, Judith Balfe, Ronald Burt, Paul DiMaggio, Herbert Gans, Norvell Glenn, Wolf Heydebrand, Noah and Pauline Sherman, Scott South, and Kathy Trent. To the editorial committee, to Ernest Campbell, the editor of the Arnold and Caroline Rose Monograph Series, and to the reviewers, Diana Crane and David Brain, I owe a most special debt of gratitude. The reviews were exceptionally thorough and the suggestions for the revisions especially helpful. Ernest Campbell not only helped to evaluate the reviewers' suggestions but also provided solid support through the last stage of revisions.

Many students were involved with data preparation, coding, and analysis that were carried out in connection with this undertaking. Special acknowledgement is given to Laurie Newman and William E. Hall for computer analysis and data management, and I would also like to thank Gail Quets, Tetsuya Tada, Chris Betts, Wen Xie, and Reid Golden for assistance with the computer work. William Hall, who tragically died in 1989, was also closely involved in the development of a section in chapter 7.

Other people assisted with data collection: Mitchell Chamlin, Ian Cole, Dawn Leger, Guillermo Melendez, Helen Myers, Donald Nitchi, David Shulman, and Greg Stevens. Dozens of individuals affiliated with arts associations, such as the American Association of Museums, the American Symphony Orchestra League, the Central Opera Service, and many others, were extremely helpful during this stage of the research. The staff of various libraries, including the Lincoln Center Library for the Performing Arts and the Documents Service Center of Columbia University's Lehmann Library, helped to locate obscure materials. Particular individuals who should be personally thanked for providing access to data are: Joe Anderson, William Behanna, Thomas Bradshaw, Beatrice Handel, and Dave Verdery. I owe a special debt of gratitude to Karen Abbott for her patience with me as she skillfully transformed poorly typed pages into final clear typescript.

When I started this research in 1984, homebase for me was the Sociology Department of the State University of New York at Albany and my colleagues provided me with support and intellectual challenges. A year's leave to teach at New York University made it possible to consolidate teaching, research, writing, and family life, and I am grateful to Al Liska who approved my leave. My colleagues at New York University asked good questions; like most good questions, they require some thought and are not all answered here. My thanks, especially, to Eliot Freidson. Some of the research and much of the writing was carried out at the Center for the Social Sciences at Columbia University. Its assistant director, Pnina Grinberg, was a steadfast friend, easing the problems of grant and budget management and recognizing the importance of a secluded haven in which to work.

Reva and Peter know how much I have appreciated their support and forbearance; I also want to thank my stepdaughter, Pammy, who put up with my eccentric working schedule and helped with her great cheer and delightful charm to keep up the quality of household life for many months while I was commuting and working on this book. It is appropriate that I dedicate this book to my parents, Theda and Harold, who always exhibited more faith than now seems reasonable in their incorrigible eldest daughter.

1 Culture as structure and meaning

Twenty men crossing a bridge,
Into a village,
Are twenty men crossing twenty bridges,
Into twenty villages,
Or one man
Crossing a single bridge into a village.
> Wallace Stevens, "Metaphors of a Magnifico" (1918)

Wallace Stevens makes an observation here that is simultaneously perplexing and profound. What is in certain terms considered to be complexly structured with intricate patterns and multiple meanings is, in other terms, considered to have a simple shape and singular meaning.

The relevance of this apparent paradox for the queries I raise here about culture is that it is shaped by many different objective conditions: spatial, social, economic, and organizational. Moreover, my conclusion draws attention to the contradiction that is intended: the very social conditions that shape institutionalized culture also erode distinctive cultural meanings as these meanings have become universal and are widely shared in modern society.

These considerations also raise questions about the conventional assumptions made in the social sciences about the nature of social and cultural patterns and the processes that govern them. Social scientists have emphasized one world view at the expense of others. We stress differences over uniformity, the multiple over the singular, structure over disorder, progression over retrogression. Whether understanding is sought through empirical study, theoretical explanation, or meaningful interpretation, the intricacies of the social fabric and the complexity of the processes that underlie change are relentlessly emphasized.

Wallace Stevens urges us to consider instead the possibility that complexity and singularity are two sides of the same coin, or that they are in a dialectical relation that is governed by contradictory conditions. In other words, we need

1

to entertain questions about structure and indeterminacy, stasis and transformation.

Cultural meanings in modern societies seem to be messy and disordered, since preferences for culture – liking the Beatles and disliking Bach – are highly personal and idiosyncratic.[1] Cultural interests are shaped by early family experiences, schooling, neighbors and acquaintances, how close one lives to a concert hall, and very many trivial events and experiences. Culture has no shape to it, one supposes, because it is such a personal affair. As a friend and colleague once told me, he could not imagine going to a public concert: listening to a Brahms violin concerto is much too intimate an experience to share with other people.

But if we assume the meanings of culture have little shape, what about those structures in which they are embedded? Among those "structures" are cultural products (paintings, dance performances, films, musical recordings) and cultural institutions (museums, concert halls, cinemas, night clubs). It is generally believed that cultural products and institutions exhibit order and pattern. On the one hand, cultural products are much like other consumer goods; regardless of the meanings people attach to them, they are distributed more or less systematically in the population according to individuals' accessibility, leisure time, disposable income, life style, age, and so forth. Cultural institutions also exhibit meaningful patterns, and like all institutions, are subject to political, economic, and social forces. The number of theaters in a city is, one might expect, a function of population size and other urban characteristics, such as the city's location, and what other kinds of entertainment are available.

Contrary to such expectations, this investigation of cultural institutions and products in U.S. cities concludes that in a variety of ways they exhibit little structure and order. That is, there are few fundamental differences in the ways that high and commercial cultural products and institutions relate to their urban environments. Much social and economic inequality impairs the development of both, despite our commonsense view that cultural consumption and display are generated by differences in social rank, education, and the economic resources of individuals. This study suggests that large-scale social forces promote a decline in the differences in the conditions that account for the distribution of both high and popular arts, and also a decline in the differences in the opportunities that individuals have to enjoy them.

High entropy refers to a process that produces messy configurations and random distributions, whereas low entropy is one that leads to highly structured configurations and nonrandom distributions. Entropy can be employed analogously to describe an historical process – which is inferred from the conclusions of this study of contemporary patterns in culture – and also, metaphorically, to capture such contrasts as those between the potential for divisiveness created by differences in class and other structural aspects and the integrative possibilities inherent in common cultural understandings.

Background

This investigation is based on the relationships between social conditions and culture in large contemporary American cities, specifically the largest 125 Standard Metropolitan Statistical Areas (SMSAs). About two-thirds of the American population lives in these urban locales, and undoubtedly, a much higher proportion of most cultural institutions is located within them. This study considers the significance of various urban conditions for the supply of culture, as indicated by the numbers of cultural institutions and of cultural workers, and it looks at the contrasting features of art institutions and how these features can be understood in terms of their cultural products and urban environments. Attention is also paid to the linkages among arts organizations and to the qualitative characteristics of the arts they produce. Such analyses lead to inferences about developmental processes and historical changes in American culture and about sources of aggregate demand.

Major theories in sociology that deal with individual preferences for culture, as well as historical interpretations of the development of art, attach great importance to class distinctions in explaining cultural development. A version of the current perspective in sociology is clearly summarized by Pierre Bourdieu: elite or esteemed cultural products are appropriated by dominant classes, which augments and reinforces the prestige of members of these classes and at the same time provides an extra measure of authoritative legitimacy to these cultural products.[2] This view is not inconsistent with historical scholarship that places great emphasis on the role of patronage for the elite arts and on the symbolic significance of culture for maintaining distinctions between classes or estates.[3] In short, it is generally considered that class differences are exceptionally important for the traditional or "legitimate" arts.

Similarly, it is generally assumed that standardized and inexpensive commercial arts are especially popular with "the masses." Some argue that the working and lower classes readily take to "kitsch" because low education hinders their appreciation of classical forms of culture and low incomes preclude their access to them in any case. Others claim that the class-based observation is correct but the reason why the producers of commercial culture are successful with the working and lower middle classes is that escape in mindless entertainment provides relief from boring and exploitative work.[4] Thus, the general assumption is that class differences maintain the distinction between traditional and commercial culture. These conclusions about social class and cultural preferences seem to be substantiated in surveys of individuals. Yet, survey data or other individual-level observations can only be used to speculate judiciously about the relation between class structure and cultural development at the societal level.

At the same time, however, there is irrefutable historical evidence that the origins of commercial, popular, and elite arts are very different. In traditional European societies and in the early stages of the industrialization of America, urban traditions were conspicuously different from one another as were the traditions of different groups, largely defined by class. For example, only cities like New York and Philadelphia supported the theater, while puritanical traditions retarded development of the performing arts in places like Boston. The south was precocious in its acceptance of early forms of live entertainment, but with few exceptions did not support the development of museums and galleries. Places with considerable concentrations of immigrants became the centers of cultural entertainment that did not require much education, while wealthy elites engaged early in ambitious and highly exclusive cultural undertakings – societies for the presentation of artists' works, concert series, and museum construction.[5]

In the early stages of industrialization, not only cultural institutions, but cultural products and group preferences as well, were much more conspicuously different from one another than they are now. Thus, by most accounts, well into the twentieth century, class, regional, and ethnic differences were greatly magnified when they found expression in cultural practices.[6]

My empirical results suggest that owing to rising levels of education and urbanization, a universal culture has been spawned, and the process of modernization has eradicated the consequences of class differences since the various institutionalized arts are now rooted in more or less the same social-economic matrix. To be sure, there are differences between elite and commercial culture in their base of production, modes of dissemination, and cost. And there is variation in the ways in which individuals prefer to use their free time. But at the societal level the differences one expects to find in the social conditions of elite and popular art are not very great – at least insofar as I am able to discern with data on the supply of cultural institutions and the characteristics of cities.

Culture stands in fundamental juxtaposition to the social context, which is to say that societal or institutional complexity is found to engender diffuse cultural patterns. For example, most forms of high culture are transmitted by a single cohort (namely those between the ages of 35 and 44 in 1980) and generally fail to be in great demand by other groups not in this cohort. In contrast, most forms of popular culture are in demand by a single age group but for only brief periods of time. These patterns are different since they suggest that items of high culture are in evident jeopardy while those of popular culture exhibit a regular turn-over.

Regardless of the mutual benefits that art establishments allegedly derive from each other's presence, I find that suppliers of cultural products adhere relatively weakly in cities. For one reason the demand for culture of all kinds is so spatially ubiquitous that there is very little concentration of cultural suppliers in any part of the country. (Surprisingly, the little concentration that can be detected is for commercial cultural suppliers, not for the suppliers of elite culture.) For another, there is little evidence that similar types of cultural institutions exhibit ties of interdependence within cities. One could call organizational suppliers footloose, except that at very high population thresholds they begin to occur together and to establish bridges in ways that are not intuitively obvious.

Organizations of all kinds face problems of co-ordination, deadlines, balancing efficiency with quality, and of raising revenues. Nevertheless, performing arts organizations differ in important ways from other types of organization. While they are inordinately dependent on their environment – on funding agencies, on fickle consumers, and the good will of local government – they respond in paradoxical ways to environmental conditions. Specifically, they become less bureaucratic – not more – in munificent and complex urban environments, as they apparently become assimilated into larger structures (or are co-opted by them). Organizational success, we also learn, accompanies the appreciation, or the relative decline, of artists. This, too, can be described, metaphorically, as an entropic response to complex circumstances.

There is evidence throughout this study that public funding policies have benefited the arts. Public subsidies, for example, promote innovation and contribute to the democratization of American culture by stimulating arts activities in places that earlier had relatively few. Some results suggest that the private efforts of wealthy art devotees have a limited impact on the arts, and what impact they do have is counter to the overall trend towards increasing equity of cultural opportunities.

Caveats

It must be stressed that my conclusions are generally at odds with the original hypotheses. I initially expected that variegated social systems would be implicated in complex cultural systems. The assumptions on which this was based are altogether plausible: producers compete for markets, there are local traditions of cultural specialization, great inequalities in income and in education would appear to generate demands for cultural and art products of different kinds, the social and moral worth of high culture and popular culture varies from one social group to another; and, cultural organizations operate on ad hoc lines and not on the models of organizations that are geared to production and efficiency, which would suggest great variability in organizational structures. The design of the study fully permitted – even biased – the outcome in that direction. That is to say, the broadest and most diverse indicators of culture available were employed to study their relationships with organizational and population diversity. The findings are consistently contrary to the initial assumption that cultural complexity and structural complexity go hand in hand.

It is impossible in this study to have elicited people's reactions and evaluations of culture, but to some extent it is possible to juxtapose the results of this study with those of analyses of individuals to make inferences about the meaning of culture. It is also possible to infer meaning from the types of groups that are likely to appropriate cultural products. To be sure, it was impossible to obtain detailed information on arts organizations when the questions being asked required some information on many thousands of them. However, crude information on organizational structure, the nature of the arts they support, and the numbers of staff make it possible to derive tentative conclusions about the relations these organizations have with the public and with other organizations, and about the variation in the roles that artists have in different types of settings.

I do attempt to examine various qualitative dimensions of culture – traditionalism, innovation, and distinctive styles of popular music – in an effort to decipher plausible connections between identifiable aggregates of people and the symbolic codes of cultural products. There is evidence, for example, that museums with traditional collections are on the decline with the increasing population diversity of cities, and that avant-garde conventions in theater are not explained by the unique values of particular locales (notably, New York City), but rather by the relative affluence of cities (and New York City happens to have quite rich people). But other places do as well, and their theaters compete with those in Manhattan by launching innovative productions.

Methodology

The basic unit of study is the metropolitan place. Specifically, the largest 125 Standard Metropolitan Statistical Areas (SMSAs) are under consideration and they are described in terms of the social conditions that influence their cultural supply, cultural organizations, and cultural workers. The SMSA was selected as the unit of analysis because it is defined as an integrated economic and social unit, unlike cities whose boundaries are defined partly in response to political, administrative, and fiscal pressures and sometimes change slowly in response to population and economic expansion. In general terms, an SMSA consists of a county or group of counties containing at least one city with a population of 50,000 or more, plus adjacent counties that are metropolitan in character and economically and socially bound to the central city.[7] The 125 SMSAs are listed in Appendix A.

Two time periods are examined. Virtually all social and economic characteristics of SMSAs are from the 1970 Public Use Sample and the 1980 census of population, and most of the data on culture are for the early 1970s and when possible for the early 1980s. Detailed discussions of methodology and statistical techniques are confined largely to the notes and also the methodological appendix of chapter 8, which provides the information that is necessary for the reader who wants to understand the details of the change analysis. Descriptions of the cultural indicators (including sources, means, and standard deviations) are summarized in Appendix B.

A brief outline

In a conventional and linear fashion, I will now summarize the organization of the materials. Chapters 2 and 3 deal, respectively, with the spatial and temporal dimensions of cultural supply. In chapter 4, I examine the extent to which culture depends on a large population base and the extent to which cultural suppliers are themselves linked in an urban place. Cultural organizations – their internal configurations and their relations with their metropolitan environments – are the topics of chapters 5 and 6. Qualitative dimensions of culture – the extent to which an art genre has traditional or wide public appeal, the degree of innovation, and differences in style – are issues considered in chapter 7. Chapter 8 presents the analyses of secular, ten-year changes in artists' job opportunities and labor markets and the prevalence of cultural institutions. The main arguments are broadened in chapter 9 to examine historical processes that help to explain the patterns observed for the twentieth century in terms of earlier developments.

The basic theme that underlies the various topics is that there are trivial differences between the social forces that govern elite and popular culture since they are both explained by virtually the same social conditions. While one could argue that this means that culture has lost its historical roots, its social relevance, and therefore its distinctive meanings, I prefer to consider this an indication that a relatively universal culture modulates social complexities and provides a common framework of meaning and experience.

Notes

1 Methodologically, culture is treated throughout most of these analyses as a "structural" factor, in that it is measured as an aggregate or global indicator of cities, regions, time periods, or as derived from pooled data on aggregates of organizations, and cultural suppliers. In this sense, from the analysis of cultural patterns, inferences can be made about cultural markets and demand exerted by large identifiable groups, but this is reasonable when there is sufficient theoretical reason to do so since group preferences are not known. The main purpose, thus, is to explain cultural patterns in terms of larger social and urban factors and the emphasis is on a macro analysis of culture. (Additional methodological issues concerning ecological relationships are discussed in chapter 7.)

2 *Distinction*, trans. Richard Nice (Cambridge, MA: Harvard University Press, 1984).

3 See for example: Neil Harris, *The Artist in American Society* (New York: Simon and Schuster, 1970); Meyer Schapiro, "Style," pp. 137–171 in Morris Philipson and Paul J. Gudel, eds., *Aesthetics Today* (New American Library, 1980); Frederick Antal, *Classicism and Romanticism* (New York: Basic Books, 1966).

4 A recent summary of these positions is provided by Patrick Brantlinger, *Bread and Circuses* (Ithaca: Cornell University Press, 1983).

5 See for example: Arthur Meier Schlesinger, *The Rise of the City, 1878–1898* (New York: Macmillan, 1933).

6 See for example: Russel Nye, *The Unembarrassed Muse* (New York, Dial Press, 1970); Foster Rhea Dulles, *America Learns to Play* (New York: D. Appleton-Century, 1940).

7 Recognizing the greater cultural attraction of particular places, an alternative to using SMSAs would have been to use Standard Consolidated Areas (SCAs) as the units of analysis. Two metropolitan complexes – one that includes New York, Newark, Jersey City, Paterson–Clifton–Passaic, and Middlesex and Somerset counties in New Jersey and the other that includes Chicago and the Gary–Hammond–East Chicago SMSA – were designated in the 1970 census as SCAs. By 1980 there were 23 such metropolitan complexes defined by the Bureau

of the Census. Using the broader geographical definitions would have offered the advantage that the full potential market for cultural facilities that are primarily located within particularly important core cities could be taken into account. While it is true that the cultural facilities of New York and Chicago, as well as those of other very large metropolitan centers, attract many visitors, there is evidence that these visitors are not more likely to be suburbanites. In spite of generally high levels of education, somewhat low rates of cultural attendance (such as attending live classical music performances, opera, and nonmusical plays) are observed for people on the fringes of central cities (see Judith R. Blau and Gail Quets, *The Geography of Arts Participation. Report Prepared for the National Endowment for the Arts*, Washington, DC: National Endowment for the Arts, 1987). The conclusion is that while interest in the cultural facilities of New York City, Chicago, Los Angeles, Philadelphia, Washington, and Boston is not purely local, it can be better understood as national or international rather than as narrowly regional.

2 The American cultural landscape

I visited all of the exhibits in New York. The Medici of the Republic must exert themselves a little more before these can become even respectable . . . Often where a liberal spirit exists and a wish to patronize the fine arts is expressed, it is joined to a profundity of ignorance on the subjects almost inconceivable.

Mrs. Frances Trollope (1832)

Probably a century after Mrs. Trollope's visit to the United States, and certainly by the middle of the twentieth century, American arts and culture had earned an unqualified recognition in international circles. Yet it is still taken as a matter of course in our times, as in those of Frances Trollope, that most forms of institutionalized high culture in the United States, such as opera, museums, orchestras, and art galleries, are highly concentrated in a very few large cities located in the east, such as New York City, Washington, Boston, and Philadelphia. It is true that midwestern cities, notably Chicago, and some older cities in the west, such as San Francisco, have fostered important high culture institutions, and more recently southern cities, such as Dallas and Houston, have intensified their efforts to establish their cultural worth. Still, the undisputed centers for the visual and performing arts are considered to be on the eastern seaboard.

The historical record supports these assumptions. Simply put, east coast cities had an early start. The concentration of wealth in Philadelphia, Boston, and New York City in the nineteenth century facilitated patronage of the arts. The farflung commercial interests of these eastern cities promoted intellectual and artistic ties as well, which encouraged public figures and families of means to express their social worth and good taste.[1]

While early academies established by artists in Philadelphia and New York initially floundered for lack of support, by the mid-1850s, the monied elites of Philadelphia, New York, Boston, and also Chicago, recognized the social, moral, and symbolic importance of the arts. Class interests were undeniably implicated in cultural entrepreneurship. Patronage served to justify the claim made by early capitalists that they were as cultured as European aristocrats, and, therefore, superior to the vulgar masses. Nevertheless, the masses were perceived as not entirely beyond enlightenment and the arts were perceived to play a useful role in quelling their frustrations, instilling civic values, and fostering personal virtues. As Harlow Higinbotham, a Bostonian philanthropist and successful financier, pointed out, when museums are made available to the public they divert workers' attention from their sorry economic lot, and also broaden the horizons of the aspiring middle classes.[2] In the decade between 1870 and 1880, four major museums opened: the Metropolitan Museum of Art in New York and the Boston Museum of Fine Arts, both in 1870, the Philadelphia Museum of Art in 1876, and the Art Institute of Chicago in 1879.

Theater, in fact, had very early origins in the New World; initially introduced as part of religious pageantry, Spain brought plays to its colonies. But the history of North American "art theater" is largely the history of English influence on east coast cities and was, until about 1900, very much based on ceaseless revivals of Shakespearean and Restoration plays. The first professional company with its own building opened in Philadelphia in the 1750s, and companies established roughly at that time toured in major cities both in the northeast and in the south. By 1800 a great many places had their own permanent theaters, including New York, Philadelphia, Baltimore, Washington, Providence, Newport, Albany, and Boston (Although its theater was disguised as a hall for moral lectures). Still, the major competition was between Philadelphia and New York until 1900, by which time New York had the unquestionable lead over Philadelphia with 43 theaters. New York's dominance was so great that Jack Morrison termed developments outside of New York as the "little" theater movement.[3] It was not until the late 1950s that major theatrical productions were launched in "provincial outposts," primarily under the auspices or with the support of universities, including John Houseman's Theater Group at the University of California at Los Angeles, the Olney Playhouse at Catholic University, and the Guthrie Theater affiliated with the University of Minnesota.

The pattern is virtually identical for music, with small associations formed during the early 19th century: Boston's Philharmonic Society in 1810, Philadelphia's Musical Fund Society in 1820, and the New York Philharmonic Society in 1842. All three became major musical institutions by the end of the century. Compared with the visual arts, theater, and orchestral music, opera initially followed a different path, perhaps owing to the lack of a strong operatic tradition in northern European countries. Opera took root first in New Orleans and San Francisco, only later appearing in New York City.

Except for occasional tours, dance also came relatively late to America but when it did arrive it followed virtually the same geographical route as that of classical music, theater, and the visual arts. By the end of the 1930s dance companies were concentrated in New York, Philadelphia, San Francisco, and Chicago.

Thus, the historical record suggests that the early cultural superiority of New York, Philadelphia, Boston, Chicago, and San Francisco would ensure their lasting pre-eminence. These cities were the custodians of "high art": they supported prominent cultural institutions that had been organized and funded by elites who had great stakes in linking their personal wealth and power with those of the cities in which their financial empires were built. Contemporary impressions support this conclusion for the present as well: critical reviews of theater productions in all newspapers feature Broadway productions, nationwide public TV and radio stations broadcast concerts from Boston and Philadelphia and not from Hoboken or Cincinnati, blockbuster art exhibits tend to appear in the same few major metropolitan museums.

There is also some social science literature that can account for the apparent concentration of cultural institutions in a few major cities. Research in both geography and sociology provides ample support for what we commonly believe to be the case. According to one theory in urban geography there is, over time, an increasing differentiation of urban centers, with the emergence of a hierarchy among them with respect to functional dominance. A variety of methods has been used, with varying degrees of success, to classify places by their ranking on one of several hierarchies. For example, an early attempt by Aurousseau led to the following classification of urban functions: administration, defense, culture, manufacturing, economic extraction, export, and recreation.[4] In principle, all places have a ranking on each of these functions but for each there is a primate city or more prominent place in the rank ordered hierarchy. For example, there are many cities in the United States that are large centers for administrative activities, but in each state the capital city has more administrative activities than do other places, and the center of administration for the nation as a whole is Washington DC. On the other hand, New York City is unquestionably the financial center of the United States; it has only about 7 per cent of the population, but 30 per cent of all major manufacturing concerns have their headquarters located there,[5] and New York is the hub of the nation's banking and stock market activities.

The principle of metropolitan dominance is more firmly rooted in assumptions about demand for services and goods than in their supply. However, complementary concepts from central place theory also help to explain patterns of dominance in terms of both supply and demand. It is also a more complete theory, for it takes into account networks and transactions involving organizations and capital, the importance of urban scale as it relates to a critical mass, and also the factor of competition among establishments in cities and regions of varying sizes.

For example, services and establishments that serve a very large number of people, such as drug stores, post offices, and dry cleaners, are found in places of all sizes, whereas services and establishments that can either benefit from economies of scale or require large populations to attain a critical mass are only located in very large places.[6] The latter includes, for example, wholesale supply outlets, specialized governmental services, and large teaching hospitals. Recent studies in central place theory emphasize that regional dominance as well as urban dominance results from the interdependencies of producers and the advantages of agglomeration economics.[7] Thus, the middle west is dominant in agriculture and manufacturing and the east in commerce and industry.

This theory seems to account for the apparent regional variation with respect to cultural enterprises, since we assume that the west coast has a monopoly on the production of films, television programs, and musical recordings, and that the east coast megalopolis includes most of the large cities that have a disproportionate amount of high culture, such as opera, dance, and theater. Central place theory also appears to account for the observation that very large places support esoteric and very expensive cultural activities but that places of all sizes support cultural activities that are in high demand and relatively inexpensive.

Such inferences as these are also consistent with the assumptions of urban ecology, which draws attention to the importance of dominant centers that control the terms of exchange in economic, political, and social transactions with lesser centers. And urban ecology that is informed by world system theory posits that prevailing hierarchies among contemporary cities can be traced to historical patterns of their relations of power and dependence, and that core cities in a national (or world) system exert power and control over communications, goods, fashions, and services.[8] Thus, it is consistent with theories in geography and in sociology to expect that large cities or particular regions are able to control cultural production and maintain hegemony and are thereby able to shape national tastes and standards. These theories help to account for the apparent virtual control that New York City has in dictating standards for the elite arts and also for the power that Los Angeles exercises over the production of much popular culture.

Popular culture compared with high culture

To a far greater extent than elite culture, many products of commercial culture (film, television programs, radio programs) are not "consumed" where they are produced. Moreover, many establishments that provide popular entertainment and leisure activities (bowling alleys, health clubs, golf courses, nightclubs, and cinemas) are entrepreneurial in nature, and while many of them rely on the centralized production of a commodity, they distribute products and sponsor events on a local level. Thus, the American landscape of commercial culture is perceived to be one in which the opportunities are more or less uniformly distributed, in contrast with the opportunities to enjoy participation in high culture, which are highly concentrated. That is, the consumption of high culture is closely linked with its locus of original production. The extent to which these assumptions are widely shared is illustrated by our common understanding of what the New Yorker or the Bostonian means when referring to a place as a "cultural wasteland" and our expectation that wherever one travels in the country, it is possible to see the same evening news as one sees at home, and to easily find a cinema or disco.

The ubiquity of the consumption of much popular culture (as distinct from its production) is not inconsistent with central place theory since it is assumed that widespread demand for a service, such as a post office or a pub, means that a low threshold of population is required to support such a service. It is also consistent with mass culture theory that has its origins in the nineteenth-century writings of Tocqueville and Matthew Arnold.[9] Although versions of mass culture theory are best known for either their vitriolic attacks on popular culture,[10] or their moralistic defenses of it,[11] all versions share one assumption, namely that popular culture pervades modern society and is fairly uniformly distributed if not among social classes, at least among cities, states, and regions. This legacy of mass culture theory is eminently plausible. Not everyone, of course, is expert at breakdancing, goes to the cinema, or even watches television, but these forms of popular culture pervade American society and are universally available for those who are interested in them. Moreover, profitable enterprises seek as large a market as possible, and there is no a priori reason to believe that cinemas, nightclubs, and burlesque theaters involve greatly varying amounts of capital investments from one city or region to another. As mass culturalist van den Haag notes, "As society becomes fully industrialized, popular culture becomes the most universally shared type of culture," whereas high and folk culture "are isolated and dry up in institutions or regions cut off from social development."[12]

The argument for specialization of place

While a plausible argument can thus be made that the elite arts are concentrated in a few cities and that the popular arts are uniformly distributed throughout the country, some social science theory and research suggest a far more complex pattern that minimizes the significance of geographical differences and emphasizes the fact that cities specialize in particular forms of culture. To establish symbols of distinctiveness and to attract tourists, urban planners and policy makers capitalize on their cities' economic resources and their potential for corporate investment. Both high culture and popular culture have benefited from alliances between wealthy families or corporations and municipalities, as illustrated by the City of Rochester and Eastman Kodak, Pittsburgh and the Mellon family, and Los Angeles and the Disney Corporation. A city can also turn local traditions to good account to amplify its cultural standing. New Orleans' Mardi Gras, Louisville's Kentucky Derby, and Nashville's Grand Ole Opry are instances of the success of cities of institutionalizing local traditions to make them important tourist attractions. Of course, these are distinctive types of cultural activities, founded on unusual local traditions, but such instances nevertheless suggest that there may be great variations among urban places with respect to the kinds of culture they support.

Economists and sociologists have examined the quality of life in urban places, using indicators from the U.S. population census and other sources that pertain to health, crime, housing conditions, costs of living, income, and employment. However, very few have attempted to incorporate indicators of culture in these comparisons of cities. An interesting exception is Ben-Chieh Liu's study of 243 metropolitan areas.[13] It includes over 120 indicators, three of which pertain to cultural activities. Whereas the sources for health, crime, and other indicators are official government documents and subject to relatively little error, the source for the cultural indicators is a questionnaire completed by Chamber of Commerce representatives from each metropolitan area. Liu recognizes that biases may result from relying on individuals whose job is, after all, to publicize their cities' cultural contributions and who may also have to hazard estimates in the absence of official records. Nevertheless, this is an important study, for it is probably the first that systematically examines cultural indicators as well as those traditionally used in research on the quality of urban life. The tables in Liu's study suggest that the variation among large urban places with respect to fairs, festivals, sporting events, and radio stations per capita – forms of popular culture – is greater than one would expect, while the variation among them with respect to dance, drama, and music events is much less. These patterns are contrary to those described by mass society theory.

Liu's study examines the supply of cultural activities and their facilities. Those who have studied the demand for culture, that is, audience interest and participation, report marked regional differences, at least for the United States. Raymond Gastil in *Cultural Regions of the United States*[14] and research by Peter Marsden and his colleagues[15] report that southerners are less likely than people from other regions of the country to attend artistic events or to engage in artistic activities generally.[16] Although the relationship between demand and supply, especially for culture, is not a perfect one, these audience (demand) studies suggest that the south has fewer cultural institutions (supply) compared with other regions.[17]

These different conclusions for variations among cities and among regions are based on empirical studies, but there are also theoretical reasons to suppose that urban places may be differentiated from one another in many ways, including the cultural activities they are likely to support. The "grass roots" decision model of urban growth and development proposed by Amos Rapoport posits that decisions are made, accumulate, and become embodied in institutional forms not only at the highest political and economic levels but also at the local neighborhood, or "vernacular" level as well.[18] Thus, a city's cultural, social, and economic patterns emerge from a highly localized decision-making process.

Another theory that explains organizations' locations posits that there are economic interdependencies among subsystems of a local market, and, therefore, that related firms and industries tend to develop together as the result of explicit transactions in a given locale. The film industry in California, as Robert A. Faulkner describes it, depends on close relations among occupational groups (scriptwriters, musicians, filmmakers, designers) and among industries (studios, orchestras, schools of acting).[19] Although the "grass roots" decision model and the organizational model rest on quite different assumptions, the conclusion is the same: because transactions of all kinds emerge as an orderly process at the local level, there will be marked differences among urban places, including differences with respect to the kinds of art and culture they support. This conclusion is consistent with the observation of Gunther Barth, a cultural historian.[20] He notes that the unique historical experiences of America gave rise to a set of cultural institutions that rest on local tastes, traditions, and values. The result, according to Barth, is that America has a variegated cultural landscape rather than a uniform one. Barth and other cultural historians[21] often refer to culture in its most pristine forms – local ethnic saloons, county fairs, the Mummers' parade, and ethnic festivals. These are cultural forms that, unfortunately, cannot be considered here for many of them are unique and few are recorded. But it is plausible that folk culture, even in an industrialized society, is rooted in local traditions.

Bluegrass music, jazz, many local crafts, and country dancing were initially tied to styles of life or subcultures as, we assume, many forms of folk culture still are. However, when such lifestyles become very successful they are usually captured by commercial producers or become legitimized as high culture. Shaker furniture is copied by commercial companies but the originals are collectables; while police arrest youngsters for painting on subway cars, a few of them are able to sell their works in SoHo galleries; some jazz sounds have entered the popular mainstream while jazz has also been incorporated into the repertoires of experimental avant-garde music. On the whole, however, we expect that in its vernacular versions, folk culture is confined to particular places and to certain regions of the country, just like elite art.

Urban variation*

The great range of cultural institutions for which data are collected permits comparisons both at the metropolitan and at the regional level. Any comparison of the numbers of institutions or events without regard to potential demand would be misleading. The smallest of the nation's 125 urban metropolitan areas in 1970 had a population of 248,000 (Salinas–Monterey) while New York City had a figure of about 11 million. To take population size – or the number of cultural consumers – into account, the comparisons are based on the number of institutions or events per capita.[22] Since it is metropolitan prominence that is of interest, information is provided only on the three highest ranking SMSAs for each cultural indicator. These results for virtually all cultural indicators on which data are available are reported in table 2.1.

The perception that New York City is the pre-eminent cultural center is somewhat justified by these results. Even when taking into account its large population size, it has the highest number of specialized galleries, theater premieres, chamber music groups, and modern dance companies of all large metropolitan places, and it also does exceptionally well in supporting many nonprofit theaters[23] and ensembles. But surprisingly it does not appear in the top ranked places with respect to other major elite art indicators, including

*A brief summary of this section was published in my essay, "High Culture as Mass Culture," *Society* 23 (1986), 65–70.

Table 2.1. *High culture: metropolitan places*
with highest rankings: number of institutions
per 100,000 population[a]

Art museums – D2	
Jackson	3.83
Springfield–Holyoke	1.31
Appleton–Oshkosh	1.09
Specialized museums – D1	
Providence	5.62
Springfield–Holyoke	4.37
Boston	3.32
Art galleries – F2	
Tucson	5.15
Santa Barbara	4.56
Albuquerque	4.08
Specialized galleries – F3	
New York City	4.77
Wilmington	2.00
Tulsa	1.68
Opera companies – K	
Charleston	.33
Tucson	.29
Charlotte	.24
Dance premieres – I	
Charleston	3.90
Youngstown	3.36
Norfolk	3.24
Ballet companies – J2	
Augusta	.78
Austin	.67
Tucson	.57
Modern dance companies – J3	
New York City	.66
Salt Lake City	.39
San Francisco	.29
Theater premieres – G	
New York City	35.7
New Haven	12.1
Boston	5.1
Nonprofit theaters[b]–H	
Canton	.81
Tucson	.57
New York City	.49

Opera workshops/festivals – L
Jackson	1.53
Spokane	1.39
Binghamton	1.34

Chamber music groups – N
New York City	1.22
Binghamton	.67
Washington	.60

Contemporary ensembles – O
Baton Rouge	1.40
New York City	1.23
Syracuse	1.10

Major orchestras – M2
Augusta	.39
Orlando	.24
Tulsa	.21

Nonmajor orchestras – M3
Madison	1.38
Jackson	1.15
Des Moines	1.05

[a] Sources reported in Appendix B.
[b] See note 23, this chapter.

ballet, opera, major orchestras, and art museums. What is also surprising is that the other presumed giants of culture, such as Boston, Washington DC, Philadelphia, and San Francisco – are not, in fact, especially prominent in these rankings. It is noteworthy that Jackson, Mississippi, has disproportionately many art museums and opera workshops, that Charleston has the highest ranking for both dance premieres and opera companies, and that Augusta, Austin, and Tucson are the leading cities for ballet.

With the possible exception of New York, which does rate high on several cultural indicators, there is little evidence for the concentration of elite arts in a few major metropolitan areas. Indeed, most metropolitan areas tend to rank high on only one cultural indicator; for example, Appleton–Oshkosh has many art museums per capita, but is not among the three highest ranking SMSAs on any other cultural indicator. This tends to suggest that there is little interdependence among art establishments. Since a high ranking on the number of orchestras per capita does not mean that a place will rank high on chamber or ensemble music or opera companies per capita, this indicates that cultural activities of one type do not affect the locational advantages of closely related types. (An exception is observed for some kinds of music in the city of Binghamton, as it ranks high both on contemporary ensembles and on opera workshops.) The more complex analysis of the extent to which art institutions tend to "adhere" will be discussed in chapter 4, but suffice it to say that a notable pattern of coherence among similar cultural establishments cannot be discerned here.

Of course, these comparisons do not take into account the quality or the size of institutions. For example, Washington does rank in the top 15 per cent of the SMSAs in the number of art museums per capita and in the top 10 per cent of SMSAs for specialized museums, although it is not in the top ranking three on either. Springfield, which ranks second on art museums, has six art museums that are available to approximately 500,000 people, whereas Washington's 13 art museums are available to a population of nearly three million. No museum in Springfield or Jackson, which has the most art museums per capita, has the scope of the Smithsonian's comprehensive store of art or the quality of the relatively specialized collection at the Hirschhorn. Nevertheless, when we also take into account the fact that Washington's museums serve an extraordinarily large number of tourists, it might be concluded that from a Springfield resident's point of view her or his museums are far more accessible compared with a Washingtonian's. In the particular instance of museums, another early source, *Museums USA*,[24] provides evaluations of what the authors consider to be noteworthy museums, which they describe as "excellent" or "good." The SMSAs that rank the highest on the number of highly rated museums (with the two ratings combined) relative to population size are Providence, Newport News–Hampton, and Tucson – again, hardly cities that we consider to be the main centers of the visual arts.

These results suggest that the traditional dominants in elite culture – Philadelphia, Boston, New York, Chicago, San Francisco, and Washington – have narrowly focused economic resources and symbolic attention on a relatively small number of very large, prominent institutions, and have not encouraged the establishment of many small ones.

In sum, many cities not especially recognized as noteworthy artistic centers have higher concentrations of institutions sponsoring high culture relative to their population sizes compared with other cities conventionally believed to be major centers. For example, the leading cities for major orchestras are Augusta, Orlando, and Tulsa – not, surprisingly, New York, Chicago, Boston, or Philadelphia. Also, related cultural forms (such as different types of music institutions) do not tend to be concentrated in the same places. More generally, the distribution of high culture institutions appears far more random than we would expect on any a priori basis, especially one that is informed by an understanding of the historical record and of theories of central place and urban ecology.

The information on folk culture is hardly as rich as that on either elite or commercial, popular culture, but two fairly good indicators of it are available – country music festivals and craft fairs. As table 2.2 indicates, the leader in 1970 for both was Newport News–Hampton.

The major source of information on commercial culture is the U.S. Bureau of the Census' tabulations based on employers' tax records,[25] but to supplement these data information on the numbers of formatted music radio stations, television viewing,[26] and rock concerts were obtained. Table 2.2 indicates that commercial, popular culture is more concentrated in a few places than is elite culture. Nashville, Salt Lake City, and Little Rock are major centers for cinemas, bands, commercial orchestras, commercial theaters, dance halls, and variety entertainment (such as nightclubs, burlesque and vaudeville). Charlotte, which ranks among the top three for opera companies, is also a major center for cinemas and dance halls. Still, the leading metropolis for commercial culture is Las Vegas, ranking first on four of the nine indicators, namely, commercial theaters, bands, orchestras, and variety entertainment.

These indications of popular culture are not free from unknown sources of bias, but the scope of coverage is large and estimates of stability over time indicate that the bias is random, not systematic. In contrast to the pattern observed for elite art institutions, commercial popular culture establishments are far more concentrated in two regions, namely in the south and the west. There are, however, a few exceptions. For example, Milwaukee has more than its share of bands, and New York City is among the top three for commercial theaters per capita.

Live popular music concerts are also prevalent in southern SMSAs, including Charlotte, Baton Rouge and Little Rock, and television viewing is also highest for three southern SMSAs: Baton Rouge, Augusta, and Charleston. Of some interest, perhaps, is the greater popularity of television in warm southern places, while cities with very cold winters – Utica, Erie, and Johnstown – have the highest number of radio stations. (This perhaps indicates the use of radio for weather reports and the time northerners spend listening to the radio while warming up their cars in the mornings.)

In general, there is more than casual evidence that there are regional differences for popular culture but not for elite culture, but this can be tested by comparing regions' SMSA means on each of the cultural indicators.

Table 2.2. *Popular and commercial culture:*
metropolitan places with highest rankings:
number of institutions per 100,000
population[a]

Country Music Festivals – Q	
Newport News–Hampton	17.1
Huntington–Ashland	10.7
Corpus Christi	10.5
Craft fairs – P	
Newport News–Hampton	1.03
New Haven	.94
Lancaster	.94
Commercial legitimate theaters – S	
Las Vegas	2.54
New York City	2.32
Nashville	1.47
Cinemas – R	
Charlotte	11.29
Greenville	9.61
Salt Lake City	9.60
Bands – U	
Las Vegas	19.59
Milwaukee	6.93
Kansas City	6.59
Commercial orchestras – T	
Las Vegas	2.54
Nashville	1.47
Little Rock	.92
Variety entertainment – V	
Las Vegas	20.00
Nashville	12.16
Honolulu	7.59
Dance halls – W	
Salt Lake City	3.79
Charlotte	3.19
Fort Lauderdale	3.08
Popular music concerts – X	
Charlotte	5.89
Baton Rouge	5.59
Little Rock	5.23
Television ratings[b] – Y	
Baton Rouge	40
Augusta	37
Charleston	37

Radio – Z
Utica	12.43
Erie	8.81
Johnston	8.78

[a] Sources reported in Appendix B.
[b] See note 26, this chapter.

Regional variation

The urban comparisons of elite culture suggest a pattern of national ubiquity that is confirmed in the regional comparisons using analysis of variance (see table 2.3). With two exceptions – specialized museums and modern dance companies – nonprofit high culture institutions exhibit no significant variation by region. While in some instances one region may exhibit a higher mean than the other regions, there is sufficient variation within regions to make the differences among the four regions insignificant in all cases except for the two instances (specialized museums and modern dance). Unlike art museums, which are not concentrated in any region of the country, specialized museums, such as national history and science museums, are prevalent in the northeast. A good case could be made that these are not institutions that support high culture, but rather serve recreational and educational purposes. But in spite of New York City's prominence in modern dance, on average, western SMSAs have more modern dance companies per capita than do northeastern SMSAs.

A cursory inspection of interrelated cultural forms – for example, opera and opera workshops – does not suggest there is much institutional interdependence at the regional level. For example, on the average there are more opera workshops in eastern metropolitan places than elsewhere, but this is not the case for opera companies, of which there are more per capita in southern SMSAs.

Of the two forms of folk culture, one exhibits regional variation. There are relatively more craft fairs in northeast metropolitan places than elsewhere. And most types of popular cultural establishments exhibit quite strong regional patterns, with relatively more cinemas in the south and west, more bands and commercial orchestras in the west, and more variety entertainment in the south. Commercial theaters, on the other hand, exhibit no marked regional variation. Live music concerts are events, not establishments, which might help to explain why they are relatively uniformly distributed throughout the four regions' metropolises. Rock groups and the music that they perform

Table 2.3. *Cultural indicators by region*[a]
SMSA means (per 100,000)

	Northeast	South	Northcentral	West
High culture				
Art museums	.28	.39	.23	.18
Specialized museums	1.22	.68	.63	.63
Art galleries	.46	.90	.47	1.03
Specialized galleries	.32	.31	.14	.21
Opera companies	.016	.047	.014	.040
Opera workshops/festivals	.39	.37	.21	.23
Chamber music groups	.18	.07	.10	.14
Contemporary ensembles	.20	.15	.18	.21
Major orchestras	.023	.060	.044	.029
Nonmajor orchestras	.25	.29	.31	.28
Dance premieres	.14	.51	.20	.45
Ballet companies	.11	.20	.14	.19
Modern dance companies*	.063	.023	.10	.071
Theater premieres	2.36	.62	.29	.65
Nonprofit theaters	.12	.06	.10	.09
Folk culture				
Country music festivals	2.73	4.20	2.68	2.33
Craft Fairs*	.22	.092	.086	.090
Popular culture				
Legitimate theaters	.32	.35	.26	.50
Cinemas**	3.89	5.60	4.53	5.71
Bands**	.82	1.55	1.92	2.96
Commercial orchestras*	.13	.22	.17	.36
Variety entertainment*	.31	.96	.70	2.06
Dance halls*	.80	1.44	1.17	1.30
Popular music concerts	1.59	2.22	1.46	1.84
Television**	27	31	29	25
Radio	3.37	2.93	2.63	2.81

[a]See notes to tables 2.1 and 2.2.
 * ANOV; p < .05
** ANOV; p < .01

create demand and then satisfy it fairly quickly, whereas institutions are dependent on particular markets that are quite stable over time.

Since concerts have been classified by type, it is possible to examine regional variation for different styles of music. Most styles, including country, rhythm and blues (R&B), jazz, blues, and reggae exhibit no regional variation, but some are more prevalent in the south – hard rock, generic rock, and southern rock.[27] Neither is radio a regional phenomenon, although undoubtedly the reasons why it is not are different from those for rock music. It can be assumed that there will be as many radio stations as the Federal Communication Commission's licensing regulations will permit, but that considerations of regional equity play a role in maintaining geographical uniformity. Radio stations, however, are formatted in different ways to attract both listeners and advertisers, which makes it possible to examine regional differences in the numbers of music stations of different kinds. Of all the radio formatted music stations, the following exhibit no regional differences: memory, classical, middle-of-the-road (MOR), rock, and hard rock. In contrast, jazz radio stations are more frequent in the northeast, ethnic stations in the northeast and west, soul music in the northeast and south, and country in the south.[28] Thus, demand both for live popular music and for broadcast music is relatively uniform from one part of the country to another, but tastes for particular kinds of music apparently do vary.

Television viewing does differ significantly from one region to another, with higher rates for southern SMSAs than for other regions of the country. This certainly does not imply, however, that the south is deficient in other forms of culture, including high culture. The south ranks high on cinemas per capita and variety entertainment establishments per capita and though it is not significantly higher than other regions on forms of elite art establishments, it has especially high means for art museums, art galleries, opera companies, and nonmajor orchestras.

Discussion

In spite of the observed tendency for popular culture to be prevalent in the south and west and to be concentrated in particular places, and for high culture to be generally ubiquitous, at the city level all combinations are possible. It could be said, for example, that Nashville residents have a taste for many kinds of popular culture, but residents of most SMSAs tend to have more specialized tastes. Popular and elite arts are not substitutes for one another. Tucson is a center for several elite art institutions, but it also ranks in the top 10 per cent of urban places in numbers per capita of rock concerts and dance halls. Other places, such as Jersey City, rank relatively low on all types of culture, perhaps because of their proximity to much larger centers. Some metropolitan areas are particularly strong in many kinds of high culture but weak with respect to their supply of popular culture. Jackson, Mississippi, for example, ranks in the lowest 10 per cent on bands, commercial orchestras, and dance halls, but is pre-eminent in a variety of high culture institutions. There are also major centers for the popular arts that have little elite art. A notable example is Charlotte, North Carolina, that ranks in the top 10 per cent on radio, dance halls, and commercial orchestras, but ranks low on nearly all the elite art indicators.

Thus, the concern of the mass culture theorists that the "bad" (that is, commercial popular culture) would drive out the "good" (that is, traditional elite culture) appears to be unfounded. There is considerable variation among urban places with respect to their cultural strengths and weaknesses and that variation is not a function of any compatibility or of any antagonism between elite and popular culture. The largest cities in the United States do have more elite art establishments than smaller ones, which supports common prejudices, but they have no more than their large populations would predict, which is to say, they generally have no more per capita than other cities.

Eminence is another matter. It is incontestable that New York City is the dominant leader in the visual arts, as trends and prices are set by its galleries, auction houses, and museums. Similarly, without question the leading symphonies in the United States are located in New York, Philadelphia, Cleveland, Chicago, and Boston. Yet art work in New York is enjoyed by a tiny proportion of its residents and a substantial number of museum visitors are not local residents. Relative to the size of the population base, there are more major orchestras in Augusta than there are in Boston, more art museums in Appleton than in Washington, Boston or New York, and more opera companies in Charleston than in San Francisco. This means that there are at least as many opportunities for the residents of Salt Lake City, Appleton, and Charleston to enjoy certain types of cultural events as do the residents of much larger metropolitan areas. Perhaps Charleston's opera company does not have the reputation that the San Francisco opera does, but given the comparisons in per capita supply, it is probably easier to get a season subscription or a single ticket in Charleston than it is in San Francisco.

The ubiquity of elite art and the concentration of popular art run counter to what would be predicted by theories of urban dominance, central place theory, mass culture theory, and by common observations. The overall pattern for the elite arts supports the thesis for much specialization of place but with near uniformity from one region of the country to another. In contrast, popular culture exhibits marked regional variation and many cities have disproportionate amounts of several types of popular culture. How can it be that those forms of culture that have commercial backing and, presumably, universal appeal, are not uniformly distributed throughout the United States while many forms of traditional elite culture are?

New work in cultural history by, among others, Alan Trachtenberg and James Sloan Allen,[29] provides some clues for understanding these patterns. High culture, they argue, has great symbolic value for a particular place and also enhances its attractiveness to private enterprise. Beginning in the nineteenth century, the period in which the gap between the rich and the poor began to widen, high culture was perceived, as it still is, as an instrument of social reform and a means whereby working people's tastes could be shaped according to bourgeois standards. High culture, Janet Minihan notes,[30] provides a base of legitimacy for government and for elites because the arts symbolize a bridge between the rich and the poor, and exert moral and educational influences. They also have economic value as they are presumed to attract tourism and play a role in the efforts of cities everywhere to stimulate commercial growth and reverse the flight of the middle class to suburbia.

For these reasons, it is not so surprising that high art has been dislodged from its traditional enclaves and widely disseminated throughout the United States. Because it transcends the traditions of the local community and dignifies the activities of political and economic actors, art is a safe investment. "Buying art is an indication of making it," F. D. Klingender[31] wrote of the capitalist in the nineteenth century. The same could be said of any growing city, and when political and economic elites act in concert to develop cultural resources they can ignore local tastes and overcome initial handicaps.

On the other hand, popular culture is shaped according to free market principles. Competition among cultural industries within a given locale will set an equilibrium based on what the market will bear, and market research is carried out with an eye to local demand and taste. The demographic and lifestyle characteristics that prevail in the sunbelt cities of the southern and western regions are probably major factors that explain the prevalence of forms of popular culture in these regions. Thus, high culture has become more popular in the sense of being more widely distributed than what we call "popular culture." Although high culture institutions have not continued to proliferate in those places where they originated and were once entrenched, high culture has become quite common elsewhere, and, consequently, has not much shape.

Notes

1 Primary sources consulted include: Lillian B. Miller, *Patrons and Patriotism* (Chicago: University of Chicago Press, 1966); Neil Harris, *The Artist in American Society* (New York: Clarion, 1970); Phyllis Hartnoll, ed., *The Oxford Companion to the Theatre* (London: Oxford University Press, 1967); Marion Bauer and Ethel R. Peyser, *Music Through the Ages* (New York: Putnam's Sons, 1932); George Freedley and John A. Reeves, *A History of the Theater* (New York: Crown, 1941); Richard Kraus, *A History of the Dance* (Englewood Cliffs NJ: Prentice-Hall, 1969); Walter Terry, *The Dance in America* (New York: Harper and Row, 1956); Vera Mowrey Roberts, *A History of the Theater* (New York: Harper and Row, 1962).

2 See Helen Lefkowitz Horowitz, *Culture and the City* (Lexington: University of Kentucky Press, 1976), p. 207.

3 Jack Morrison, "The Theater Outside New York," pp. 975–977 in Phyllis Hartnoll, ed., *The Oxford Companion to the Theatre.*

4 M. Aurousseau, "The Distribution of Population: A Constructive Problem," *Geographical Review* 11 (1921), 563–592. See also Chauncy D. Harris, "A Functional Classification of Cities in the United States," *Geographical Review* 33 (1943), 86–99.

5 R. J. Johnston, *The American Urban System* (New York: St. Martin's Press, 1982).

6 The model of central place was initially advanced by W. Christaller, *The Central Places of Southern Germany*, trans. C. W. Baskin (Englewood Cliffs NJ: Prentice-Hall, 1966). The most extensive efforts to test the model have been carried out by Brian J. L. Berry, *Geography of Market Centers and Retail Distribution* (Englewood Cliffs NJ: Prentice-Hall, 1967).

7 See A. R. Pred, *The Spatial Dynamics of U.S. Industrial Growth, 1800–1914* (Cambridge MA: MIT Press, 1966); H. W. Richardson, *The New Urban Economics and Alternatives* (New York: Academic Press, 1977).

8 For a study demonstrating the extent to which core urban centers dominate peripheral cities in financial transactions see David R. Meyer, "The World System of Cities," *Social Forces* 64 (1986), 553–581. The major theoretical work on world system theory has been carried out by Immanuel Wallerstein, a summary of which appears in his book *The Modern World System* (New York: Academic Press, 1974).

9 Alexis de Tocqueville, *Democracy in America* (New York: Random House, 1945); Matthew Arnold, *Culture and Anarchy* (Cambridge: Cambridge University Press, 1950).

10 Edward Shils, "The Theory of Mass Society," pp. 30–50 in Philip Olson, ed., *America as a Mass Society* (Glencoe IL: Free Press, 1963); Ortega y Gasset, *The Revolt of the Masses* (New York: W. W. Norton, 1932).

11 Leslie A. Fiedler, "The Middle Against Both Ends," pp. 537–547 in Bernard Rosenberg and David Manning White, eds., *Mass Culture* (Glencoe IL: The Free Press, 1957); Herbert Read, *Art and Society* (New York: Schocken Books, 1966).

12 Ernest van den Haag, "Of Happiness and Despair We Have No Measure," pp. 504–536 in Bernard Rosenberg and David Manning White, eds., *Mass Culture.*

13 Ben-Chieh Liu, *Quality of Life Indicators in the U.S.* (New York: Praeger, 1976).

14 Raymond Gastil, *Cultural Regions of the United States* (Seattle: University of Washington Press, 1975).
15 Peter V. Marsden, John Shelton Reed, Michael P. Kennedy, and Kandi M. Stinson, "American Regional Differences in Leisure Time Activities," *Social Forces* 60 (1982), 1023–1049.
16 The south's lower standing on indicators of residents' interests in the arts persisted through 1985, but one sub-region of the south, namely the east south central, is primarily responsible for the south's low standing. See Judith R. Blau and Gail Quets, *The Geography of Arts Participation* (Washington DC: National Endowment for the Arts, 1987).
17 Audience or participation studies usually do report variation by region as well as by city size. In an unusual investigation of both supply and demand Elihu Katz and Michael Gurevitch (*The Secularization of Leisure*, Cambridge MA: Harvard University Press, 1976) report that for Israel there are more cultural events per capita in smaller communities, which is due to the high interest in kibbutzim in culture. They also report that the distribution of types of noncommercial cultural activities is about the same for places of different sizes.
18 Amos Rapoport, "Culture and the Urban Order," pp. 50–75 in John A. Agnew, John Mercer and David E. Sopher, eds., *The City in Cultural Context* (Boston: Allen and Unwin, 1984).
19 Robert A. Faulkner, *Music on Demand: Composers and Careers in the Hollywood Film Industry* (New Brunswick: Transaction, 1983).
20 Gunther Barth, *City People* (Oxford: Oxford University Press, 1980).
21 See, for example, Warren I. Susman, *Culture as History* (New York: Pantheon, 1973); Richard Wightman Fox and T. J. Jackson Lears, eds., *The Culture of Consumption* (New York: Pantheon, 1983).
22 As Harold Horowitz ("Comment, High Culture/Mass Culture," *Society* 24 (1986), p. 2) correctly points out, the number of institutions per capita has some difficulties as a supply variable. Some SMSAs have a high proportion of residents who live in the central city where most cultural institutions are, whereas other SMSAs have large suburban rings and suburban residents do not have easy access to centrally located institutions. Nevertheless, Horowitz reports in a paper with Carol Keegan and Barbara Kempnich ("Cultural Participation and Geographic Population Schema," presented at the Fourth International Conference on Cultural Economics and Planning, May 1986) that the attendance rates by region and city size for cultural activities tend to replicate the findings on supply reported here.
23 The source for nonprofit theaters (H) includes only the members of the Theater Communications Group, which are virtually all large resident theaters in the United States. This does not, however, exhaust the number of nonprofit theater companies. For this reason the list was supplemented for the purposes of the analysis presented in this chapter with listings in the following sources: John Willis, *Theater World* (New York: Crown, 1978), Catherine Hughes, ed., *American Theater Annual 1978–79* (Detroit: Gale, 1980); Donald W. Fowle, ed., *Notable Names in American Theater* (Clifton NJ: James T. White, 1976).
24 Herbert Katz and Marjorie Katz, *Museums USA* (Garden City NY: Doubleday, 1965).

25 There was some concern about the consistency of the reporting procedures for establishments reported in the Census of Selected Services. Since the data are collected as part of a five year cycle by the Bureau of Economic Analysis for the purpose of estimating revenues and not for the purpose of identifying establishments, a given set of organizations can be subsumed under one umbrella organization. Some analysis of the variation in average reported number of employees suggests, however, that this does not create serious bias at the metropolitan level. Furthermore, some nonprofit establishments are included in the total counts, which may be a problem for orchestras but is less of a problem for commercial theaters and cinemas. Tax exempt orchestras were optionally included for the first time in the 1972 reports, but the vast majority of orchestras listed apparently play on a commercial basis, and the other producers (cinemas, bands, legitimate theaters, dance halls) are for-profit ventures. See Harold Horowitz, "The Arts in the National Income and Product Accounts," pp. 14–22 in W. S. Hendon, N. K. Grant, D. V. Shaw, eds., *The Economics of Cultural Industries. Proceedings of the Third International Conference on Cultural Economics* (Akron: University of Akron, 1984).

26 The Nielsen ratings indicate the proportion of households regularly tuned in to television network programming. While it is unfortunate that cable viewing is not included in these reports, cable was relatively rare in 1982, the year for which data are reported, and, in fact, it was only after that year that the Nielsen reporting procedures included cable viewing. The Nielsen data on audience size are presented for Designated Market Areas, which were re-estimated for SMSAs. Procedures are described in Steven F. Messner and Judith R. Blau, "Routine Leisure Activities and Rates of Crime," *Social Forces* 65 (1987), 1035–1052.

27 The means for hard rock are: NE, .03; S, .06; NC, .03; W, .03; for generic rock, NE, .02; S, .04; NC, .02; W, .03; for southern rock, NE, .01; S, .02; NC, .01; W, .01. Analysis of variance reveals significant regional differences.

28 The means for jazz are: NE, .03; S, .01; NC, .01; W, .01; for ethnic, NE, .08; S, .03; NC, .04; W, .06; for soul, NE, .03; S, .04; NC, .02; W, .03; for country, NE, .07; S, .10; NC, .08; W, .07. Analysis of variance reveals significant regional differences.

29 Alan Trachtenberg, *The Incorporation of America* (New York: Hill and Wang, 1982); James Sloan Allen, *The Romance of Commerce and Culture* (Chicago: University of Chicago Press, 1983).

30 Janet Minihan, *The Nationalization of Culture* (New York: New York University Press, 1977).

31 Francis D. Klingender, *Art and the Industrial Revolution*, ed. and rev. Arthur Elton (New York: Schocken, 1970), p. 26.

3 Reproduction and decline

Voltaire tells this story about change and decline:

When the two travellers [a French councillor and a Brahmin] arrived in Asia Minor the councillor said to the Brahmin: "Would you believe that a republic was once established in a corner of Italy that lasted 500 years, and that possessed this Asia Minor, Asia, Africa, Greece, Spain and the whole of Italy?" "So it quickly turned into a monarchy?" said the Brahmin. "You're right," said the other, "but that monarchy fell, and every day we publish fine dissertations to discover the causes of its decline and fall." "You take too much trouble," said the Indian; "this empire fell because it existed."[1]

Art is self destructive, at least under contemporary conditions, because artists often reject the past to create something new. It can be said that culture and cultural styles – abstract expressionism, punk rock, ragtime – eventually do fail and the explanation may be (in the spirit of Voltaire's account) that cultural producers and the public become bored with something that has existed too long. Nevertheless, some cultural forms persist longer and are more resilient than others.

Resiliency and persistence are themselves problematic. When a cultural form becomes universally accepted – such as Levi jeans, a song from a Broadway musical, or the current widespread revival of Chaplin films by third world countries and by IBM – should we not conclude that such a form has become a meaningless component of the cultural life of a period, rather than a distinctive cultural product that carries original social and symbolic meaning? As Mary Douglas suggests, when there is no unique niche or social context for an artistic or other cultural activity, this is an indication that collective assumptions about it have dissipated and that it has lost its salient meaning. Specifically, patterned rituals, communication, and referent codes previously associated with the activity become meaninglessly ritualistic and disordered; and thus they atrophy.[2]

The persistence or disappearance of cultural items can be traced through time and a good indication of persistence is the enduring evidence of viable markets defined by particular groups, for without such viable markets a

31

cultural item can be said to have disappeared (which, paradoxically, may be the same as becoming universally acceptable). Historical continuity, then, is evident when identifiable groups transmit their tastes to younger groups, or at the very least hold on to their own tastes throughout their own life cycles.

The nature of cultural change

Two dimensions can be distinguished here by which approaches to an understanding of cultural change can be described. One is substantive and refers to the attributed cause of change and the other is formal and accounts for the dynamic of change.

One substantive approach is social psychological; David McClelland's work nicely illustrates it.[3] He finds in his study of ancient cultural artifacts that just preceding a major economic expansion the designs on pottery become increasingly geometric and linear, but accompanying a period of slow economic growth and stability pottery designs are ornate and curvaceous. It is, according to McClelland, an achievement orientation that expresses itself at the level of the society that is responsible for the dynamic relationship between art and the social order. Some art historians, including Abell and Van den Meer[4] account for changes in artistic style as the result of transformations in the psychological predispositions of members of a society, which in turn become expressed as social norms or values.

A major alternative substantive focus is on certain aspects of the objective social structure, such as changing social class relations[5] or economic factors.[6] Institutionalized producers and markets play an increasingly important explanatory role in the sociology of culture since the publication of Richard A. Peterson's edited volume *The Production of Culture*.[7]

The production of culture

The second dimension that can be used to distinguish approaches to understanding cultural change is purely formal and it refers to the specific mechanism of change that is posited. There are four major perspectives on change in cultural practices: convergence, increasing diversity, functional correspondence, and cyclical change.

The assumption that culture is becoming increasingly uniform – that convergence guides the process – is usually made on normative grounds. Critical standards are clearly at stake as there exists both a leftist and a rightist view on the matter of what the consequences of convergence entail. On the left it is argued that high culture and popular culture are becoming alike as both serve therapeutic purposes in an increasingly exploitative and dehumanizing society.[8] While forms of indigenous popular culture lose their distinctiveness as they are dislodged by the promoters of cheap and banal substitutes, high culture, too, has become highly standardized through commercialization. Having co-opted the artistic and intellectual fringe, economic elites appropriate culture and in turn establish the criteria by which culture is to be defined and evaluated. Standards degenerate because commodified, produced culture – high brow and low brow – placates, pacifies, and entertains; commerce buys the masses off.[9]

From the right, the intellectual heirs of de Tocqueville, Ortega y Gasset and Matthew Arnold, argue instead that the blame for the deterioration of standards and cultural uniformity rests not with the rich and the powerful (or the conditions of modern post-capitalism) but rather with an unenlightened mass audience whose unsophisticated tastes have created vast markets for ticky tack or high toned pastiche.[10]

Thus, most who view culture as undergoing convergence – whether their assumptions are pulled from the rhetoric of the right or the left – maintain that culture is becoming increasingly uniform and banal. Juxtaposed to this conclusion is Norbert Elias' contention that culture is becoming increasingly homogenous because it is more diffused or widely shared, not that it is necessarily becoming worse.[11] Manners are the specific issue, but Elias' analysis of the evolution of manners can be treated more generally, as he himself puts it, as part of the "civilizing process," or slightly more to the point here, as the diffusion in cultural practices. Decorum and tastefulness, Elias purports, filter through the class structure – from top to bottom – until virtually all people and all classes are well mannered and well cultured. For instance, during the Middle Ages, the same revolting manners were shared by everyone, but gradually members of the nobility, the landed gentry, and then the peasantry – each in their turn – abandoned convenient habits (such as urinating practically where or when one wished, or spitting in the dining hall) in favour of what became defined as more civil habits. This articulation and diffusion of conventions about what was right and proper, or what cultural choices were most and least appropriate, served to unify disparate strata, groups, and classes. Elias indicates that codes of civility are themselves rather arbitrary; what is important is that they help to break down social barriers; and in Niklas Luhmann's terms, help to thematize an increasingly complex society.[12] This version of convergence maintains, in any case, that it is immaterial whether culture and cultural tastes "improve" or "degenerate" over time. More to the point, they become universal.

Conversely, the notion that culture exhibits increasing diversity is posited by Herbert J. Gans. He contends that evident proliferation of many different interests and tastes is the expression of a pluralistic society. Moreover, owing to a weak relationship between the meaning of cultural products and group membership, individuals themselves will often express widely discrepant preferences.[13] That is, concerti and comic books may be linked with class differences, but they are loosely linked, and in a pluralistic society some people will like both. However, as Gans recently notes, the basis of cultural diversity is itself fragile.[14] When a given cultural product – square dancing for example – loses its traditional source of legitimacy, it becomes *déclassé* and then extinct. On the other hand, recent studies by English social scientists suggest that working class culture has great vitality when it serves as a vehicle for political and social protest.[15] The thesis is that class and racial antagonisms will continue to generate new cultural forms and in this way sustain cultural diversity.

The idea of functional correspondence is that social and economic problems will generate a need to express problems symbolically, but when the problems are solved – or simply go away – their symbolic expressions will also disappear. For example, in a functionalist interpretation of the operetta, Arnold Hauser writes,

[it] was the product of the world of *laissez faire, laissez passer*, that is a world of economic, social and moral liberalism . . . The rise of the operetta marks the penetration of journalism into the world of music. After the novel, the drama and the graphic arts, it is now the turn of the musical stage to comment on the events of the day.[16]

Joshua Taylor, former curator of the Smithsonian's modern art collections, traces in his book, *America as Art*,[17] the sequence of social and economic problems in United States history and the cultural responses that ensue: establishing a national identity, conquering the frontier, and facing the dilemmas posed by industrialization, immigration, and urbanization. For example, the challenge of establishing a unique national identity following the American revolution led to the Greek revival in art and architecture. Its cultural function was to capture the spirit of a universal truth, to express the ideals of equality and democracy, and to establish deep historical roots that could be traced back to an era pre-dating despots, monarchs, and barbarism. In his treatise on nineteenth century American culture, Russell Lynes notes that styles help mend ruptures in social life but they reach a dead end when they no longer have a functional relationship to prevailing conditions.[18] The assumption made here, in contrast to those made in theories that posit convergence or increasing diversity, is that history does not move in a particular direction, but rather is an unfolding sequence of a series of large scale predicaments, each of which is met in turn by an appropriate cultural response. With the solution to the predicament, the cultural response loses its meaningfulness and its appeal.

The cyclical model of change is probably the most ambitious of the four, owing to its implicit dependence on some version of a dialectical process. It is well known that fashions, such as skirt lengths, growing beards, the popularity of certain colors, or a taste for the exotic, tend to follow cyclical patterns.[19] Such periodicity can be interpreted in demand terms as the result of aggregates of individuals of a particular generation rejecting the fashions of their parents' generation and rediscovering the values of their grandparents' generation.[20] Or they can be interpreted in supply terms as the outcome of artists rebelling against outworn traditions. It is argued that there are compelling constraints, particularly in modern times, for cultural workers to attempt to offer something new and exciting, although very often it contains retrograde elements, as post-modernism clearly illustrates.[21]

Periodicity in culture can also be explained in terms of production. For example, Peterson and Berger, in an analysis of the popular music recording industry, discover a cyclical pattern oscillating between the concentration of ownership (oligopoly) to decentralization, and note that such fluctuations in the patterns of product control accompany fluctuations in music style; that is, concentration tends to accompany conventionality in musical styles whereas market competition accompanies great musical diversity.[22]

In art generally, style has been described as a swinging pendulum, from minimalism to expressionism, from classicism to romanticism, from naturalism to theatricality,[23] or, in Pitirim A. Sorokin's view, a more complex pattern from ideational to ideal to sensate culture.[24] Raymond Williams suggests that the underlying dynamic is a dialectical one, driven by societal contradictions:

In a society as a whole and in all its particular activities the cultural tradition can be seen as a continual selection and re-selection . . . Particular lines will be drawn, often for as long as a century, and then suddenly, with some new stage in growth, these will be canceled or weakened, and new lines drawn.[25]

Such diverse understandings of cultural change provide a perspective on the task at hand, namely, an analysis of the shifts between 1970 and 1980 with respect to metropolitan supply and group demand. The approach employed here is demographic, and it is assumed that the strength of the relationship between the relative size of an age stratum and the supply of a cultural item is an indication of demand exerted by the aggregate that comprises that stratum, and that temporal changes in these relationships reflect changes in demand. More importantly, such changes also help to interpret the dynamic principles that govern cultural transformation, at least for a very short period of time.

It is reasonable to think of each stage in the life cycle as a proxy for a host of factors including past and present collective experiences in school, work, and families. Again, SMSA is the unit of analysis since the demand for local cultural activities and the support of local institutions are assumed to be generated at the metropolitan level.[26]

The cultural boom of the 1970s

The great expansion of culture, as indicated by the increase in participation in cultural activities by the American public and by the greatly augmented levels of public and private spending on the arts and culture in the 1970s, makes this decade particularly interesting to study. The evidence is clear that greater numbers of Americans were enjoying cultural activities by 1980 than in previous times. For example, in the period between 1975 and 1980, the number of people who attended live theater performances increased from 41 to 59 per cent; the attendance at art museums increased from 44 to 60 per cent; the number playing an instrument jumped from 18 to 30 per cent; and those who sang in a chorus or musical group nearly doubled from 11 to 21 per cent.[27] By 1980 there were over a million artists, as least as self-identified in the census, which represents an increase of more than two-fifths from 1970.[28] For the same decade, the funding and philanthropic picture looks very much the same. Total corporate giving increased fourfold from nearly $800 million to nearly $3 billion in 1981,[29] and combined federal and state support grew from $18 million to $145 million in 1980.[30]

The analysis of age, cohort, and period effects

The age structure is a powerful predictor of the demand for schools, health services, jobs, and sundry government services. Diachronic data on individuals distributed by their ages makes it possible to draw inferences about change over time, including, for example, the shifts in demand for schools and day care facilities, profiles of wages and earnings over time, and the nature of changes in political identification and involvement in work roles.

In principle, such data make it possible to separate the sources of change, that is, age related change, cohort transmission, or historical experiences that affect all individuals or only those in certain age categories.[31]

Similarly, by disentangling those instances when the demand for a cultural product is exerted by one age group regardless of time from those instances when the demand for a cultural product is exerted by a given cohort or cohorts over time, it is possible to draw conclusions about the resiliency of the cultural product. It is also recognized that some cultural forms or styles, like the jitterbug, are very short lived – fads or fashions, really – while others, such as the big dance band or art deco furniture, come and go. A cultural flash in the pan might be called, in sociological idiom, a period effect.

Here, what is typically employed to identify the source of change – the effects of aging, transmission by cohorts, or historical change – is a cohort table with data obtained from a panel survey reported in a way that age categories appear in the rows, years in the columns, and cohorts in the diagonals. Instead of using information on individuals, this analysis is based on the correlations between the relative sizes of various age strata in SMSAs and the prevalence of culture of various kinds. Only a ten year interval between 1970 and 1980 is being considered, but, as noted, given the dramatic changes associated with this period, it is an important decade for the changing nature of American culture.[32] Thus, what is under consideration is the demand for culture when demand is specified in terms of age, period, and cohort.

Methodological issues

A critical problem in any cohort-age-period effects analysis arises when the pattern of variation in the table is linear (that is, there is consistent change on all three dimensions), which is to say that two effects are a function of the third. Under such conditions there is no way of disentangling the influences of age, cohort, and historical period as a one or two variable model. The possibility of misinterpretation when the data are linear is discussed by Norval Glenn.[33] Fortunately, the patterns for these data are largely nonlinear in form, which makes it possible to dissect effects, and in those cases where effects are confounded, tentative conclusions are possible by drawing on a priori knowledge about the nature of recent cultural history and some understanding of the experiences and the life styles of various age strata.

There is an important caveat that must be noted. Because these are ecological correlations, there are the usual problems of inference. To give a fictitious yet plausible example, it is likely that there are more little league baseball and softball teams in southern and southwestern communities, owing to the extended periods of warm weather compared with colder climates in the northern United States. The higher proportion of senior citizens in these sunbelt cities might very well produce a positive correlation between little league teams and the proportion of people who are over 65, suggesting the implausible conclusion that seniors are spending much of their time playing on scaled-down diamonds. Thus, any interpretation must be sensitive to factors that promote cultural interests that are typically associated with age. Fortunately, we have sufficient understanding of cultural participation at the micro-level – that is, audience characteristics and predictors of individual leisure activities – to assess the validity of inferences based on a macro-level analysis.[34]

An important consideration for assessing the validity of the macro analysis is the age distributions observed in studies of individuals' cultural choices. In research based on individual level data, the rate of participation in cultural activities is curvilinear with age. To give a precise example, the likelihood of attendance at musical events increases at a decreasing rate, until about the age of 54, and thereafter participation decreases with age at an increasing rate.[35] Dividing age into ten year intervals, Robinson and his colleagues report that the highest rates of attendance for classical music, musicals, plays, ballet, and art museums are between 35 and 44. Attendance at jazz concerts is an exception with higher percentages of those under 35 reporting that they attend jazz concerts than those in older groups. And, surprisingly, the relationship of age with opera going is nearly flat.[36]

In general, age structure is used here more as a heuristic device to study cultural change and not as an explanation of individual preferences, although it is necessary to posit that the relative sizes of age groups make a difference for the demand of culture and that members in each age group have common past and present experiences which bear on their cultural interests. It is assumed that the reproduction of tastes and interests is only assured if cultural preferences are successfully transmitted from one generation to the next or are in continuous demand by certain age groups; when cultural preferences are not transmitted over time or are so only by a single cohort, there is little assurance of a permanent dynamic of reproduction.

Many indicators of cultural supply are considered. Cultural institutions include art museums, cinemas, and establishments for commercial theater. Groups include dance company, symphony orchestras, nonprofit professional theater companies, and music ensembles that specialize in contemporary music. Events include craft fairs and live popular music concerts. Two major types of dance companies – ballet and modern dance – are considered separately. In the analyses total numbers are transformed into natural logs (as described in Appendix C).[37] Since popular music concerts have been categorized by the type of music performed (such as hard rock and punk) and radio stations are classified by the type of music they play, it is also possible to analyze the relations between age strata and music genre. Music styles provide a particularly interesting basis for comparison, owing to their volatility and the extent to which they are presumably linked with distinctive age specific life styles.

Pure age effects

In support of the research on cultural preferences and participation by individuals, the relationships between age strata and indicators of cultural supply are all curvilinear. These age effects can be observed in each of the tables in this chapter. The markets for nearly all forms of culture are composed of young to mature adults; the relationships of these cultural supply indicators with the relative size of younger strata (ages 15 to 19 and 20 to 24) are negligible or negative; with that of the middle age cohorts (25 to 34 and 35 to 44) they are usually positive and often significant; and the relationships of the indicators with each successive older stratum are increasingly small, and are usually negative for the oldest strata.[38]

Evidence of a *persisting* age effect is a stable association over time for an age stratum; that is, both correlations for the same age group in both 1970 and 1980 must be significant and they cannot be significantly different from one another. As we shall see, age effects often accompany cohort and period effects, but pure age effects are extremely rare. Of the eleven major types of cultural indicators and eight types of music styles considered, only one – commercial theater – exhibits a pure age effect, a stable and lasting appeal to a given age group, as reported in table 3.1. Theater has a relatively broad appeal, however, since it is related to two age groups, those between 25 and 34 and between 35 and 44, for 1970 and 1980. The rarity of pure age effects over time is interesting, given the pronounced age effects reported in cross-sectional studies of individuals and given that the cross-sectional patterns in these data also show that age is curvilinearly related to cultural supply. Age has an important influence on cultural demand, but not, it appears, a persisting one.

Across time, age effects are not very meaningful, which is to say that the life style and experiences of given age groups explain very little about the sustained demand for the supply of given cultural products. For only one out of the eleven major cultural indicators (and for none of the musical genre) does it appear that age exerts significant influence. However, it is true, as we shall see, that there are other age effects but that they are confounded with period or cohort effects.

Table 3.1. *Markets expressed as pure age effects: simple correlations*[a]

Commercial theaters – S, SS

Age strata	1970	1980
20–24	−.04	.02
25–34	.32**	.26*
35–44	.22*	.33**
45–54	.07	.11
55–64	.01	.01

[a]Sources of cultural indicators –
Appendix B; log transformation –
Appendix C.
*p < .05
**p < .01

Pure cohort effects

When the correlational patterns indicate that a collective taste is acquired by an age group and maintained through time as that stratum ages, it is interpreted as a cohort effect. A pure cohort effect is one that is not confounded with age or period effects. The typical pattern is for the age stratum between the ages of 25 and 34 to exert a demand for the supply of a particular type of culture in 1970 and to continue to exert demand for the supply of the same type in 1980, when they are between 35 and 44.

Instances of pure cohort effects are far more common than pure age effects. Whereas a pure age effect, as noted, is only observed for relatively conventional, institutionalized, cultural institutions – commercial theaters – pure cohort effects are observed for three relatively innovative, even esoteric, cultural forms – avant garde music played by small ensembles, performances by resident professional theater, and modern dance. These results are shown in table 3.2. For each of these three the same cohort is involved: specifically, that group whose members were between the ages of 25 and 34 in 1970 and who entered the 35 to 44 age range in 1980. The correlations are in all instances higher in 1980, which might suggest that with increases in leisure time and higher incomes, members of this aggregate became increasingly able to translate their tastes into a consolidated market demand. This tends to suggest that period effects are operating selectively on this cohort, which is to say that the cultural boom of the 1970s had a specially important impact on this

Table 3.2. *Markets expressed as pure cohort effects: simple correlations*[a]

Age strata	Contemporary ensembles – O, OO 1970	1980	Nonprofit theater H, HH 1970	1980	Modern dance – J_3, JJ_3 1970	1980	Ethnic radio – Z, ZZ 1970	1980
20–24	.08	−.02	.01	−.06	−.03	−.15	−.17	−.16
25–34	.28**	.13	.26*	.20	.23*	.16	−.11	−.12
35–44	.10	.31**	.09	.30**	.16	.37**	−.10	.01
45–54	.08	.17	.11	.12	.17	.19	.21*	.19
55–64	−.01	.05	.03	.04	.06	.08	.19	.28*

[a] Sources of cultural indicators – Appendix B; log transformation – Appendix C.
*p <.05
**p <.01

cohort. (However, this is only a conjecture since the differences in the correlations are not quite significant.)

I will later develop an explanation as to why members of this age stratum, born between 1936 and 1945 and attending universities or entering the labor market during the 1960s, have aesthetic preferences for the unconventional that are sufficiently organized that they become translated into cultural markets. It can be noted here that the next-older stratum (age 35 to 44 in 1970) were youngsters during the Depression and grew up or were young adults during World War II. In contrast, many members of the cohort aged between 25 and 34 in 1970 were – if not fighting in Vietnam – the prime beneficiaries of unprecedentedly expanding college opportunities in the 1960s. And compared with the members of older strata, they entered professional careers in their mid to late twenties in extraordinarily large numbers. The conditions of education they experienced, combined with the relative affluence of the times in which they grew up, help to explain, I shall argue, why this cohort has, surprisingly, much consolidated market power for cultural institutions, events, and performances.

Results for the cohort aged between 25 and 34 in 1970 can also be contrasted with those for another cohort – those between the ages of 45 and 54 in 1970. The proportion in this older group is positively related to the numbers of ethnic radio stations in an SMSA in 1970 and in 1980. Moreover, as we shall see, this same cohort exerts market demands for craft fairs, which perhaps reflects the interests of older people in maintaining culture that has traditional significance.

Table 3.3. *Markets expressed as pure period effects: simple correlations*[a]

Age strata	Country radio		Classical radio		Hard rock radio		R&B concerts		Pop soft concerts		Progressive rock concerts		Hard rock concerts	
	1970	1980	1970	1980	1970	1980	1970	1980	1970	1980	1970	1980	1970	1980
20-24	-.02	.09	.02	.11	.03	.02	-.09	-.10	-.05	-.01	.13	.04	-.01	.04
25-34	.13	.23*	.13	.31**	.08	.17	.23*	.02	.20	.22*	.06	.27*	.16	.22*
35-44	-.03	-.02	.02	.24*	.08	.21*	.22	.10	.15	.24*	.10	.22*	.05	.19
45-54	-.13	-.26*	-.00	-.07	.17	.03	.10	.14	.13	.04	.07	.03	.07	.04
55-64	-.03	-.28*	-.01	-.16	.04	.05	-.00	.05	.13	.07	.03	.00	.06	-.03

[a]Sources of cultural indicators – Appendix B (concerts, X, XX; radio, Z, ZZ); log transformation – Appendix C.
*p <.05
**p <.01

Age-specific period effects

None of the major cultural supply indicators (institutions, groups, or events) exhibits pure period effects, but many styles of music exhibit period effects for given age groups. The musical styles examined here include both formatted music radio stations and live popular concerts.

Of the total of nine types of music played on radio stations, five reveal no substantial correlation with any strata for either period. These include very prevalent ones, such as MOR (middle-of-the-road) and rock, and relatively rare ones, including memory, jazz, and soul. Aggregate demand for ethnic radio music, as we have already seen, is expressed by a cohort composed of relatively older people. The remaining three – country music, classical and hard rock – exhibit age-specific period effects with significant correlations for 1980, as shown in table 3.3. The mean number of stations playing classical and hard rock increased dramatically between 1970 and 1980 and in both cases the demand was absorbed by those between the ages of 35 and 44 in 1980 and in the case of classical radio, those between the ages of 25 and 34 in 1980. The overall supply of country music, in contrast, though relatively stable between 1970 and 1980, exhibits period effects in 1980 only for those between 25 and 34.

An explanation for these findings is that there are genres of music, such as rock and MOR, that have universal appeal, and, therefore (paradoxically) have no distinct appeal, as they provide background music in elevators, grocery stores, and for "holding patterns" in telephone waiting queues. Ethnic music, as already reported, has a very distinctive and stable appeal to an aggregate of aging Americans. In contrast, there were other musical genres that were either new or repackaged during the 1970s. Country music was redefined increasingly in terms that would appeal to urbanites – raucous and rebellious, merging with rockabilly towards the end of the decade; classical music became crowd-pleasing and acceptable to people who considered themselves "well-rounded;" and hard rock, heavy metal, and glitter rock all underwent a series of transformations. The main point to be made here is that the three types of music played on radio that exhibit age-specific period effects are the ones that became increasingly distinctive and identifiable as authentic styles.

Of the eleven types of musical styles into which the performers of live popular concerts could be classified in 1970, only eight remain essentially unchanged by 1980.[39] Of these eight there are four for which demographic or temporal effects can be identified. In all four cases – R&B, pop/soft rock, progressive rock, and hard rock – age-specific period effects are observed (table 3.3). In the case of R&B there is a focused age market in 1970 but not in 1980; one suspects that the reason is that R&B lost its distinctive social identity and its musical (Motown) emphasis. While in the 1970s R&B performers – such as the Blackbyrds, War, Gladys Knight and the Pips – were singing about the plight of poor blacks and the persistence of social and economic problems, by 1980 much R&B music was absorbed into mainstream rock, disco music, and acid rock. The symbolic moment that the soul music of Motown lost its clear focus was probably when B. B. King sang at Lincoln Center. In effect, too many crossovers diluted the purity of R&B and it lost its appeal to a specific age group.

Except for R&B, age-specific period effects are evident for live music only in 1980 and not in 1970. These music styles include pop/soft rock, progressive rock, and hard rock. For progressive rock, which experienced a steady fusion with jazz, classical, and funk, and for hard rock, which became increasingly bolder and more distinctive, the case can be made that the assertive and dynamic musical identities they achieved helped to generate large followings by 1980. Both forms of live popular music that were captured by identifiable age group followings – progressive rock and hard rock – are similar to the three types of radio music already discussed in that they are styles that have been successful in creating distinctive images and clear forceful directions. Why is it then that pop/soft rock concerts, which could be defined as Top 40 music in the early 1970s, also exhibit age-specific period effects in the early 1980s? Pop/soft rock, it can be argued, became increasingly sophisticated, incorporating country, classical, and even camp themes. It was also fairly experimental during this time, as illustrated by the collaboration of Linda Ronstadt and Philip Glass. Other innovators included Peter Allen, Paul Simon, Bette Midler, and Lionel Richie. Unlike easy listening, generic rock, or MOR, pop/soft rock, it can be argued, became less standardized during the decade.

It can be concluded that so long as musical styles have a distinctive identity and a sense of direction, they do make an historical impact on given age groups. It is, nevertheless, a short-lived historical impact. In contrast, bland and nondescript musical styles have no historical or demographic impact whatsoever. And with the single exception of ethnic music, no matter how important a genre of music is at a given point in time for a particular cohort, it does not continue to appeal to its members for very long.

Combined effects

When period, cohort, and age effects operate together in any combination, there is typically a splaying out of the relations in the comparison of the 1970

Table 3.4. *Markets expressed as both age and cohort effects: simple correlations*[a]

Age strata	Art Museums – E, EE 1970	1980	All dance – J_1, JJ_1 1970	1980	Ballet – J_2, JJ_2 1970	1980	All popular concerts – X, XX 1970	1980
20–24	.04	.00	.13	.01	.16	.05	.03	.06
25–34	.27*	.21*	.30**	.30**	.30**	.33**	.23*	.28*
35–44	.12	.31**	.14	.41**	.12	.40**	.07	.26*
45–54	.04	.12	.06	.09	−.01	.05	.05	.06
55–64	.02	.03	−.04	−.05	−.06	−.11	.02	−.01

[a] Sources of cultural indicators – Appendix B; log transformation – Appendix C.

*p <.05
**p <.01

and 1980 periods. That is, when a narrow demand is exerted by one age stratum in 1970, there is a broader demand exerted by two or several age strata in 1980. The most typical pattern is an interaction of cohort and age effects, which is exhibited in the cases of museums, dance, ballet, and the total number of popular concerts (table 3.4). To take a typical instance, the group composed of 25 to 34 year olds exerts a significant demand in 1970 for a cultural product – for instance, ballet – and it still does in 1980, when its members have aged 10 years. But the group whose members enter the 25 to 34 year old category in 1980 also exhibits a significant demand for the cultural product. The potential market, in other words, consists of a broader age group in 1980 compared with 1970, suggesting perhaps that the members of one cohort hold onto its cultural interests and that their younger sisters and brothers follow suit.

The highest correlation in most cases is between the cultural indicator and the proportion of people between the ages of 35 and 44 in 1980, which is consistent with the strong cohort effects already discussed. People who were born between 1936 and 1945 appear to have more than a mere taste for the arts; they have an increasingly strong habit.

The patterns for cinemas, craft fairs, and commercial orchestras are more complex than those already discussed. As table 3.5 indicates, the results for each of them can be explained as a combination of period effects and either age or cohort effects. The increasing sophistication of film, combined with the tendency of those who were in their young twenties in the 1970s to constitute a sustained market for the the cinema, helps to account for the observed high correlations between two age strata (those aged 25 to 34 and those aged 35 to 44) and the number of cinemas in 1980. Such results as these suggest that the film industry, perhaps spurred on by the competition of television, has been

Table 3.5. *Markets expressed as period and other effects: simple correlations*[a]

Age strata	Cinemas – R, RR 1970	1980	Craft fairs – P, PP 1970	1980	Commercial orchestras – T, TT 1970	1980
20–24	.27*	.04	−.14	−.20	−.13	−.12
25–34	.18	.28**	.02	.00	.29**	.12
35–44	.09	.37**	.10	.22*	.25*	.21*
45–54	.05	.09	.31**	.29**	.09	.15
55–64	.19	.03	.23*	.23*	.05	.10

[a] Sources of cultural indicators – Appendix B; log transformation – Appendix C.
*p <.05
**p <.01

successful in creating a differentiated product that has become popular with a broad spectrum of the adult population.[40]

Across both time periods, craft fairs appear to be especially popular among older Americans. Two age strata, which together span the ages of 45 to 64, are significantly related to the numbers of craft fairs in a metropolitan place in 1970 and in 1980. However, by 1980 this group broadens still further to encompass those between the ages of 35 and 44 as well. The splaying out of the market between 1970 and 1980 is the result of demands for craft fairs being exerted by increasingly younger groups of people as well as by demands being exerted by an increasingly broadly defined older age group. The success of crafts is not dissimilar from that of films and in both cases there is impressionistic evidence of greater sophistication as well as greater diversity in the products being brought to the public's attention.

The final cultural indicator considered here is orchestras. The category is assumed to include primarily commercial orchestras for both time points, although a change in the category's definition by the Bureau of the Census results in some undercounting in 1977, which is unfortunately confounded with an actual decline in big dance orchestras. However, for the purpose of a cross-sectional comparison where the interest focuses on age groups rather than the supply of commercial orchestras, this is unlikely to greatly bias the results.[41]

An initially broad demand, exerted by those between the ages of 25 and 44 in 1970, is narrowed by 1980 to those between 35 and 44. In this case, age, period, and cohort effects are difficult to disentangle. The diminished popularity of live orchestral music may be responsible for the barely significant correlation between commercial orchestras and a relatively small group of 35 to 44 year olds. This result may either reflect age or cohort effects. For example, it is possible that 35 to 44 year olds in both periods enjoy the music of the Artie Shaw Orchestra and the Boston Symphony Orchestra (reflecting age effects) and it is just as likely that those aged 25 to 34 in the 1970s – and who are cultural addicts anyway – constituted the only cohort who still were unsatiated by orchestral music by 1980.

Discussion

In principle it would be possible with observations spanning several decades to test the conflicting empirical consequences of the four versions of dynamic change considered, namely, the models of convergence, increasing diversity, functional correspondence (the dead end theory), and cyclical change.

The trajectories for particular genres of music tend to highlight an explanation that centers on the functional significance of culture. There are distinctive audiences at a particular time for live concerts by such performers as the Wall of Voodoo, AC/DC, and Doc Watson. There are also clearly defined markets at any given time for radio broadcasts of Beethoven symphonies and Bach cantatas. But the patterns that are observed for these genres of music, whether performed live in concert or broadcast on the radio, suggest that distinctive market demand is short lived and will, sooner or later, dissipate. Music exhibits the features of faddism.

But does this mean that when the generational demand for a musical style disappears it no longer has any significance? Or, does it mean that it thereby acquires general significance? I suspect it can mean either depending on the perspective one takes. The melodic rock and diluted versions of "An American in Paris" piped by dentists and doctors into their waiting rooms signal the universality of musical tastes and also the compromise of authenticity. Such music fails to provide prominent symbolic codes of meaning and of group identity, but is, nevertheless, as much a part of the large collectivity's stock of knowledge and symbolic codes of meaning as are, say, pizza, shopping malls, and the Golden Gate Bridge, or even the Mona Lisa.

Whether we all have become enlightened because we can discern the difference between the background music to "Star Wars" and Mozart's Concerto for Piano and Orchestra #21 (Elvira Madigan), or whether we all have become the consumers of adulterated and vulgar commercial music is a matter of personal values. Herein lies the difference between the views of the mass culturalists and those of Elias. The premise of the former is that when any cultural item becomes standard fare, it is debased and social distinctions are further eroded. It is Elias' view that the wide dissemination of cultural products provides a basis for social integration.

If the trajectories of music tend to support two different versions of change – functional correspondence and convergence – is there any evidence to support the contention that culture is becoming increasingly diverse or that culture exhibits cyclical change? If we mean by a cycle a pattern in which there are antithetical cultural preferences expressed by successive generations – for example, a particular age group expresses a strong interest in, say, ballet, while their grown children actively dislike it – there is no evidence that aggregated preferences follow antithetical cycles. (However, an unequivocal test of the model of cyclical change would be based on more than two time points.)

When markets broaden over time to encompass more age groups this indicates that public tastes are becoming more diverse. This is the case when a combination of period and other effects are observed (cinemas and craft fairs, but not commercial orchestras for which markets are shrinking), and in all instances in which a combination of age and cohort effects are observed (art museums, modern dance companies, ballet, and total popular concerts). These results are consistent with Gans' conclusions about cultural pluralism and support research findings for individuals that demonstrate that there has been a steadily increasing interest in cultural actitivies on the part of people with diverse backgrounds.

For what might be considered mainstream high culture – art museums, dance, ballet – there is one particular cohort that is especially important. This cohort, whose members were aged 25 to 34 in 1970, constitutes a significant market for total popular concerts, commercial orchestras, and by 1980, cinemas as well. These consistent cohort effects for young adults, compared with the single instance for which age effects alone appear to be operating for young adults – as in the case of commercial theater – indicate that it is not the life style of this particular age group that is important but rather the life style of a particular cohort when its members were young adults.

We also learn that this single cohort, which in large measure constitutes the significant one for mainstream high culture, is also particularly important for understanding patterns of demand for unconventional and innovative culture, including contemporary music, professional theater, and modern dance. The experiences of this cohort, the average member of which would have been about 20 years old in the mid-1960s, are important to recall. The 1960s are, of course, best remembered for political upheavals, the assassination of Kennedy, the Vietnam War, the marches on Washington, civil rights activities, and the killings at Kent State. There was also general prosperity, as

Johnson's unfortunate remark "both guns and butter" recalls. At the same time, those who would constitute potential organized markets for avant-garde culture in the 1970s had had in the 1960s a thorough socialization in the avant-garde, which as the poet John Ashbery observed, only was "sure proof in existence" by the 1960s.[42] The 1960s were the years of intellectual and aesthetic experimentation, "happenings," the proliferation of literary journals, the strong reaction to McCarthyism, the "discovery" by the United States media of the Holocaust, further refinements in abstract expressionism, the appearance of pop art, and the creation of Off-Off Broadway. These were heady days for everyone, but such intellectual, aesthetic, and political conditions as these probably intoxicate mostly the young.

The next older group were on the average 30 years old in the mid-1960s and were young adults in the 1950s, many having experienced as children the recession and all of them having lived through World War II. The historian Warren Susman has described the conditions of this generation as those of adjustment and conservatism: "fear and shame drove its members back into conservative postures" as they employed "cultural forms that worked as temporary responses to the problems the experiences of the period demanded."[43] This cohort, consistent with Susman's observations, does exhibit sporadic interest in culture that is sufficient to constitute a market effect in the case of commercial theaters, craft fairs, and symphony orchestras, but this interest is insufficiently organized to be expressed as a cohort effect over time for any cultural indicator.

The youngest stratum that could potentially exert market demands on culture is the one that is composed of 20 to 24 year olds in 1970 or, considered as a wider interval, of 25 to 34 year olds in 1980. Cohort effects for this group are isolated only in the case of cinemas, although by the time the people in this group enter their late twenties and early thirties they constitute a sufficient market for a variety of forms of culture, including virtually all types of radio music, nonprofit theaters, art museums, dance, ballet, and live popular concerts. This might be viewed as a sufficient expression of interest to sustain this group's demand for culture into the next decade. However, given this group's relative low impact in the 1970s, the cautious interpretation is that this cohort will have short term effects on cultural supply, not long term ones.

Only to the extent that there are successive groups whose members acquire an early interest in culture and that these groups express aggregate demands for a great variety of forms of culture over time, can we infer with some degree of certainty the continued lively and vital cultural life of a society. If the cultural boom is in fact simply the result of the maturing interest and financial stability of a single cohort, members of which became addicted early to art and culture, there is no reason to be greatly optimistic about the future of stable and enduring markets for the arts.

In this chapter we discovered that groups that have a keen interest in cultural products of particular kinds often do not sustain that interest for very long. We also discovered that one particular cohort is especially important as a source of demand for many kinds of culture, but it has largely failed to kindle in younger cohorts those same interests. It was also suggested that some types of institutionalized culture and musical genre have no particular following at all, which is to say, they are in ubiquitous demand.

Culture is shaped, exhibiting clear and distinct patterns when its institutions are distributed in some prominent way according to social, geographical, or economic differences, or – as considered here – according to age and historical differences. If cultural institutions are not so pronouncedly patterned according to differences in age, cohort, and time, it might suggest the insignificance of culture. Alternatively, such shapelessness may signify the profound significance of a culture that is widely shared.

It could be argued that when a cultural product no longer has a firm and particular foothold in the social order, it may very well have lost its claim for a position in the classificational realm of history. But, simultaneously, it has secured for the time being a ubiquitous presence without which interpersonal relations would be quite unmanageable.

Notes

1 Voltaire, *Philosophical Dictionary*, ed. and trans. Theodore Besterman (Harmondsworth: Penguin, 1972 [1764]), p. 193.
2 *Natural Symbols* (New York: Pantheon, 1970).
3 David C. McClelland, *The Achieving Society* (Princeton: Von Nostrand, 1961).
4 Walter Abell, *The Collective Dream in Art* (New York: Schocken, 1966); F. Van den Meer, *Early Christian Art*, trans. Peter Brown and Friedl Brown (New York: Faber and Faber, 1967); see also Vytautas Kavolis, *Artistic Expression – A Sociological Analysis* (Ithaca: Cornell University Press, 1968).
5 See, for example, Arnold Hauser, *The Social History of Art*, 4 vols. (New York: Vintage, 1951); Nikolaus Pevsner, *Academics of Art* (Cambridge: Cambridge University Press, 1940).
6 See, for example, Ernst Fischer, *The Necessity of Art*, trans. Anna Bostack (Harmondsworth: Penguin, 1963).
7 (Beverly Hills: Sage, 1976).
8 For versions of this argument see: Louis Harap, *Social Roots of the Arts* (New York: International Publishers, 1949); Richard Wightman Fox and T. J. Jackson Lears, *The Culture of Consumption* (New York: Pantheon, 1983); Roy Rosen-

zweig, *Eight Hours for What We Will* (Cambridge: Cambridge University Press, 1983).

9 See Peter Dobkin Hall, *The Organization of American Culture* (New York: New York University Press, 1984); Alan Trachtenberg, *The Incorporation of America*.

10 See Edward Shils, "Mass Society and its Culture" pp. 129–32 in P. Davison, R. Meyersohn, and E. Shils, eds., *Literary Taste, Culture and Mass Communications*, Vol. 1 (Teaneck NJ: Somerset, 1978).

11 *The Civilizing Process: The History of Manners*, Vol. 1 (New York: Pantheon, 1978 [1939]).

12 *The Differentiation of Society*, trans. Stephen Holmes and Charles Larmore (New York: Columbia University Press, 1982).

13 *Popular Culture and High Culture* (New York: Basic Books, 1974).

14 "American Popular Culture and High Culture in a Changing Class Structure," pp. 40–57 in Judith H. Balfe and Margaret J. Wyszomirski, eds., *Art Ideology and Politics* (New York: Praeger, 1985).

15 See Iain Chambers, *Urban Rhythms* (New York: St. Martin's Press, 1985); John Clarke and Chas Critcher, *The Devil Makes Work* (Urbana: University of Illinois Press, 1985); Dick Hebdige, *Subculture* (London: Methuen, 1979).

16 *The Social History of Art*, vol. 4, pp. 99, 101.

17 (New York: Harper and Row, 1976).

18 *The Art-Makers of Nineteenth Century America* (New York: Atheneum, 1976).

19 See, for example, Dwight E. Robinson, "Fashions in Shaving and Trimming of the Beard," *American Journal of Sociology* 81 (1976), 1133–1145.

20 In discussing the dynamics of change for the visual arts, Judith Huggins Balfe notes, "Among the possible dissynchronics is the semi-inevitable 'generation gap', but there are other such 'gaps' as well, equally conditioned by specific historical events and particularly acute in periods of rapid social change and/or mobility." Quoted from her article, "Social Mobility and Modern Art," pp. 235–251 in *Research in Social Movements, Conflict and Change*, Vol. 4 (Greenwich CT: JAI Press, 1981), p. 236.

21 As Katherine Kuh notes, "As one looks over the last hundred years, the history of break-up becomes a key to the history of art." In *Break-up: The Core of Modern Art* (Greenwich CT: New York Graphic Society, 1965, p. 12); see also Harold Rosenberg, *The Anxious Object* (New York: Horizon Press, 1964); and the subversiveness in post-modernism is discussed by Hal Foster, *Recordings* (Port Townsen WA: Bay Press, 1985).

22 Richard A. Peterson and David G. Berger, "Cycles in Symbol Production," *American Sociological Review*, 40 (1975), 158–173.

23 For discussions about cyclical trends in elite art, see for example, Frederick Antal, *Classicism and Romanticism*; Manfredo Tafuri, *Theories and History of Architecture* (New York: Harper and Row, 1980). For an analysis of cycles in American popular culture see Foster Rhea Dulles, *America Learns to Play*.

24 *Social and Cultural Dynamics: Fluctuations of Forms of Art*, Vol. 1 (New York: American, 1937).

25 *The Long Revolution* (New York: Columbia University Press, 1961), pp. 52–53.

26 While the forces that generate the production of culture (particularly of commercial culture, such as films and television programs) are undoubtedly different from those assumed to govern market demand, there is no reason to suspect that they influence the forces underlying supply and demand that are considered here. In dynamic models generally, the possibility always exists that it is not temporal variation that is responsible for the observed patterns but rather different processes associated with various members of a heterogeneous population. (See Glenn R. Carroll, "Dynamic Analysis of Discrete Dependent Variables," *Quality and Quantity*, 17 (1983), 425–460.) Analyzed here are many types of cultural suppliers, which helps to disentangle time effects from those that might be introduced by heterogeneity. What would be worthwhile would be to distinguish types of communities, a task of some magnitude which is not possible within the scope of this project.

27 American Council for the Arts, *Americans and the Arts* (New York: ACA, 1981).

28 National Endowment for the Arts, *Artist Employment and Unemployment 1971–80*, Report #16 (Washington DC: GPO, 1982). There were some reclassifications, so this increase partly reflects the greater tendency of technical writers and designers who call themselves artists, but this results in a trivial increase compared with the actual growth in the numbers of artists. For an account of the dramatic increase in dancers and dance companies, see Leila Sussman, "Anatomy of the Dance Company Boom, 1958–1980," *Dance Research Journal* 16 (Fall 1984), 23–28.

29 Edward B. Keller, "The Public and the Arts," *The Annals of the American Academy of Political and Social Science* 471 (1984), 33–44.

30 Kenneth Goody, "Arts Funding," *The Annals of the American Academy of Political and Social Science* (1984), 144–157.

31 For particular examples see: P. B. Baltes, W. W. Cornelius, and J. R. Nesselroade, "Cohort Effects in Developmental Psychology," in J. R. Nesselroade and P. B. Baltes, eds., *Longitudinal Research in the Study of Behavior and Development* (New York: Academic Press, 1979); Marjorie Honig and Giora Hanoch, *Age, Cohort and Period Effects in the Labor Market of Older Persons*, Center for the Social Sciences, Working Paper 83 (New York: Columbia University, 1980); Matilda Riley and Edward E. Nelson, "Research Stability and Change in Social Systems," pp. 407–449 in Bernard Barber and Alex Inkeles, eds., *Stability and Social Change: A Volume in Honor of Talcott Parsons* (Boston: Little Brown, 1971); Norman B. Ryder, "Notes on the Concept of a Population," pp. 91–111 in Matilda White Riley, Marilyn Johnson, and Anne Foner, eds., *Aging and Society*, Vol. 3 (New York: Russell Sage, 1972).

32 Not all temporal comparisons are possible since some directories only appeared once in this decade. Most comparisons are not based exactly on 1970 and 1980 because the sources on cultural indicators are published at different times. The age distributions, however, are those for the 1970 and 1980 census years.

33 See Norval Glenn, "Cohort Analysts' Futile Quest," *American Sociological Review* 41 (1976), 900–905; "Age, Birth Cohorts, and Drinking," *Journal of Gerontology*, 36 (1981), 362–369.

34 See Michael T. Hannan, "Problems of Aggregation," pp. 473–508 in H. M. Blalock, ed., *Causal Models in the Social Sciences* (Chicago: Aldine, 1971).
35 P. V. Marsden, J. S. Reed, M. D. Kennedy, and K. M. Stinson, "American Regional Culture and Differences in Leisure Time Activities," *Social Forces*, 60 (1982), 1023–1049, p. 1037.
36 J. P. Robinson, T. Halford, and T. A. Triplett, *Public Participation in the Arts* (College Park: University of Maryland, 1985).
37 Significant changes in definitions and in the criteria for classification by the Bureau of the Census in 1977 for bands, variety entertainment, and dance halls (Appendix B, items U, V, W) preclude comparisons for the purpose of the trend analyses reported here. The change in the definition for commercial orchestras (item T) is not considered to be so major.
38 For the sake of parsimony the youngest and oldest strata are excluded from the tables. In all cases the relations between each of these strata and each cultural indicator is close to zero or negative. In the tables the youngest age group is between the ages of 20 to 24 and is a shorter interval than those reported for the other age groups. When the 15 to 24 year old category is employed instead (which is the same length interval as the other categories) the results are no different than those reported.
39 New types of music performed in live concerts by the 1980s include punk rock, new wave, rockabilly, and new African; 1980 concerts featuring folk, southern rock and blues were too few in number to include them in any analysis.
40 Cinema is one of the rare instances where the mean for 1980 is lower than that for 1970 (51.9 compared with 42.9). The likely reason is that many cinema establishments included more than one viewing theater in 1980. Unless this trend was more pronounced in SMSAs with unusual age distributions, it is unlikely that this biases the results.
41 The 1977 definition for commercial orchestras is not strictly comparable to that for 1972 since a nontrivial number that would have been classified as orchestras in 1972 are included under "other music and entertainment presentations" in 1977. For the purpose of the trend analysis the change is not so serious, whereas it precludes using commercial orchestras in the panel analysis reported in chapter 8. This decline, however, strengthens the assumption that the Census for Selected Services does not include many nonprofit establishments since nonprofit professional orchestras are extremely stable over time. From unpublished listings provided by the American Symphony Orchestra and their published listing of orchestras ("North American Orchestra Directory," *Symphony Magazine* 31 [Special issue, December 1981]), it is clear that nonprofit symphony orchestras virtually never disappear.
42 "The Invisible Avant-garde," pp. 179–192 in Thomas B. Hess and John Ashbery, eds., *Avant-garde Art* (London: Collier, 1968), pp. 182–183.
43 *Culture as History* (New York: Pantheon, 1973), pp. 176.

4 Co-occurrence, tipping in, and bridging

> We had not peas nor strawberries here till the 8th day of this month. On the same day I heard the first whip-poor-will whistle. Swallows and martins appeared here on the 21st of April. When did they appear with you and when had you peas, strawberries, and whip-poor-wills in Virginia? Take notice hereafter whether the whip-poor-wills always come with the strawberries and peas.
>
> Letter from Thomas Jefferson to Maria Jefferson (June 13, 1790)

For all the credit given Jefferson as statesman, architect, and inventor, he is rarely noted in the annals of empirical science. Believing that matrices of co-occurring events would yield an understanding of the laws that governed nature, Jefferson searched for instances of combination and of the interdependence of phenomena. He maintained diaries of astronomical events, of rainfall, and of the first appearance and subsequent co-occurrence of about forty types of vegetables, using these data to speculate about "natural laws," and, more pragmatically, to make decisions about ploughing, planting, and crop rotation.[1]

Co-occurrence is an interesting problem for this investigation since a greater than chance probability of co-occurrence of two or more types of cultural suppliers in a large city provides an indication of either (1) organizational interdependencies, or (2) that critical masses involving substantial numbers of people share a taste for at least two types of culture.

The conclusion in chapter 2 was that popular, commercial culture exhibits regional variation whereas elite culture exhibits little such variation. This does not necessarily mean, however, that elite cultural institutions are randomly distributed among and within metropolitan places. It would be surprising if they were, since it is generally understood that there are ties of interdependence between, for example, museums and galleries.[2] Besides, it is believed that a variety of cultural groups draw on the same labor force and use the same facilities.[3]

The first problem to be taken up in this chapter is the nature of the functional relationships between population size and the number of institutions of different kinds. This analysis helps to answer questions relating to critical mass and also provides some indication as to how the numbers of suppliers of different kinds are related to the numbers of people in an urban location.

Urban size

Urban geographers and economists describe the agglomeration advantages that similar industries have when they are located in close proximity and how these agglomeration advantages increase with urban scale.[4] For example, owing to their direct economic ties and their dependence on a pool of educated white-collar workers, banks, a stock exchange, and corporate headquarters often tend to be concentrated in the same place. Besides, since they co-ordinate their activities over a large region, it is advantageous for them to be located in very large places that provide the diverse resources they require for such co-ordination. (There is an exception. Agglomeration economies of manufacturing are achieved increasingly outside of large metropolitan areas because the high costs of urban operations, notably due to high rents, do not offset the locational advantages of large scale that hold for other sectors of the economy, including those of finance, retail, and service.)

We would expect that cultural establishments benefit especially from being located in close proximity to one another and also from being situated in very large cities. Just as it takes a large population to support a delicatessen that flies in baguettes daily from Paris, so establishments that provide personal shopping or escort services, or dry cleaners that specialize in cleaning and pressing linen, also require a large metropolis to support a museum or an opera company. The arts also benefit, presumably, from the great diversity of background, tastes, and experiences of people who live in America's largest cities. Moreover, a populous place attracts conferences, trade shows, and conventions, and therefore tourists and visitors, who have high expectations that the city will provide cultural events and entertainment. These considerations – rooted in our shared urban experiences – suggest that large places especially provide many cultural opportunities and disproportionately support more cultural institutions compared with small places. However, this conclusion is inconsistent with empirical patterns discovered by economic geographers that pertain to city size and the number of establishments of most kinds.

Studies by economic geographers indicate that there are relatively fewer establishments of a given kind in the most populous urban places compared with smaller places because each establishment exhibits external economies of scale with a sufficient population base. While this is counter-intuitive, the interpretation is that the larger the city, the more people can be served by each economic establishment.[5]

It is possible that this generalization does not apply to cultural establishments because in contrast with, say, retail and wholesale firms, they may initially require a very large population base and fail after that to serve a much larger one. To be specific, we expect a ceiling on the number of people that can be served; only so many performances can be given in a season and a hall or auditorium has only so many seats. For these reasons, the number of "customers" may remain about the same for a given cultural establishment as the city grows, and the number of cultural institutions may not vary so much with population size. A final consideration that bears on the functional relationship between urban size and number of cultural establishments is that although we know little about the relationship between demand and supply, there is some indication that cultural supply simply increases demand further,[6] which is probably not the case for the products supplied by wholesale plumbing outlets, hardware stores, shoe repair shops, or many suppliers of other commercial commodities.

In sum, an analysis of the functional relationships between the number of many kinds of cultural suppliers and the size of metropolitan places provides some indication of how much cultural suppliers are advantaged by large urban scale, which in turn has bearing on our understanding of whether or not they are influenced by agglomeration economies, critical mass, and, inferentially, public demand.

Estimates of the effects of demand

Ceteris paribus, population size refers to demand. Yet size may have quite different implications – and demand operate somewhat differently – for elite and for popular art. Large numbers of people are directly important for commercial cultural activities, such as attending the movies or listening to the radio, whereas large numbers of people are both directly and indirectly important for elite cultural activities. A very large population size may be required before there are sufficient numbers of people who share a taste for, say, hand bell concerts or bel canto music to affect the probabilities of supply.

For the purposes of comparison, table 4.1 is subdivided by elite art establishments, both popular and folk art establishments and events, and a mixed group that includes elite art as well as popular art indicators for which no clear distinctions are possible.[7] The last category encompasses performing

Table 4.1. *Relations with population size (unstandardized coefficients)*[a]

	Log size (1)	Log size (2a)	Log size squared[b] (2b)
Elite culture			
Art museums – E	.44**	.34*	.11*
Galleries – F	1.40**	1.16**	.26*
Theater companies – H	.82**	.65**	.18**
Dance companies – J	.84**	.60**	.26**
Opera companies – K	.60**	.55*	.06
Opera workshops – L	.21*	.21	.00
Chamber music groups – N	.77**	.49**	.31**
Ensembles – O	.93**	.64**	.31**
Symphonies – M	.33**	.16**	.48**
Popular culture			
Cinemas – R	.93**	.90**	.04
Commercial orchestras – T	.92**	.88**	.04
Bands – U	1.39**	1.64**	−.27**
Legitimate theater – S	1.08**	1.04**	.04
Popular concerts – X	1.00**	1.05**	−.06
Radio – Z	.50**	.43**	.08
Folk culture			
Craft fairs – P	.50**	.41**	.10
Music festivals – Q	.05	.02	.03
Combined			
Performing arts groups – C1	.74**	.68**	.06
Performing arts buildings – C2	.93	.65**	.09
Performing artists – A[c]	1.11**	1.05**	.06
Nonperforming artists – B[c]	1.30**	1.31**	.07

[a] All cultural indicators logged (Appendix C); sources reported in Appendix B.
[b] See Appendix D.
[c] Raw numbers (not per capita) logged.
 * $p < .05$
** $p < .01$

artists (dancers, actors, and musicians) and nonperforming artists (writers, painters and sculptors, and designers). For these data on artists' occupations from the 1970 census of population, it is virtually impossible to distinguish the sector of employment or the specific occupation of individuals (for example, whether a dancer is a belly dancer or a ballet dancer). Performing art groups are similarly diverse, and while the type of performing art (theater, dance, music) can be distinguished, as they are in chapters 5 and 6, the distinction between high culture and pure entertainment for these performing groups is difficult to make. Similarly, buildings that sponsor or house the performing arts cannot be distinguished on the elite versus popular dimension, and it is very likely that most facilities house and sponsor both forms.

All arts variables are logged according to the procedure summarized in Appendix C, and SMSA size is the natural log of its population size.

A simple regression of the natural log of the number of cultural establishments, events, or cultural workers on the natural log of population size provides an estimate of the functional relationship between the two. A positive slope (that is, the unstandardized coefficient) indicates that there are more suppliers (establishments, events, or cultural workers) in large places than in smaller ones. More specifically, the coefficient indicates for each percentage change in population size the percentage change in the numbers of a given supplier. When the coefficient is greater than one, the proportionate increase in establishments is greater than that in the population, whereas a coefficient of less than one indicates that the percentage increase in establishments is less than that in population size. Column 1 of table 4.1 provides the coefficients (slopes) for the double-logged model.

Coefficients are positive and significant at the .01 level, at least, with the exception of opera workshops and country music festivals. The former tend to be located in university towns, such as Syracuse or Providence, that offer singers a retreat from the largest metropolitan places where opera companies usually perform. Since country music festivals are primarily held in rural places, they are credited to an SMSA if they are given in the state to which the SMSA belongs (in whole or part). As reported in chapter 2, the SMSAs for which residents have the greatest proximity to country music festivals include Newport News, Huntington, and Corpus Christi, which are among the smallest SMSAs.

In the case of the elite art suppliers, the effects of population size are greatest for galleries, theater companies, and experimental ensembles, but only galleries increase at a faster rate than population size, with its coefficient exceeding 1. In contrast, the coefficients for the popular art indicators are greater than those for the elite art variables, with coefficients for bands, commercial theaters, and popular concerts exceeding 1, and those for commercial orchestras and cinemas nearly 1. For those cultural variables that are exceptionally good indicators of the general level of cultural activity – artists, performing arts buildings, and all performing arts groups combined – the results are somewhat ambiguous. In percentage terms both performing and nonperforming artists increase faster than population size, suggesting that the very largest places are especially attractive as places for artists to live and work (or seek work). However, although the slopes for both performing arts groups and buildings are strongly positive, they do not exceed 1 and have values that are more similar to those of the elite art suppliers than to those of the popular culture suppliers.

In sum, these estimates of the functional relation between urban scale and all cultural indicators suggest that elite art suppliers exhibit less elasticity with size than do those of popular culture. That is, as cities increase in size, popular art increases at a faster rate than does elite art.

The difficulty with the double-logged function is that it fails to identify differences in the variable marginal effects of size on the cultural variables. That is, it fails to detect any multiplier effect of size, for which there is evidence in the scatter diagrams, and which is of theoretical interest. In order to estimate such multiplier effects each cultural indicator would, by convention, be regressed on two estimates of size – the natural log of size and its square. However, because of extreme problems of multicollinearity between log size and its actual square, the squares of the residuals of log size are used as the second term (see Appendix D). Columns 2a and 2b of table 4.1 report the coefficients with two predictors in the equation – the log of population size and the quadratic (squared) term for size.

With the single exception of opera, both terms for the elite cultural variables are significant, but the linear effects (column 2a) are not so strong as the simple ones (column 1) since part of the simple effects is absorbed by the multiplicative term (column 2b), indicating that demand increases with increasing city size. Demand, therefore, has a multiplier effect on most forms of high culture; elite art suppliers increase very slowly as cities grow to become medium-size metropolises, but with a sufficiently large threshold – as medium-size metropolises become large metropolises – elite art suppliers increase very rapidly. Thus, for example, the people of New York City exert a greater demand for dance companies than their numbers alone would predict, Boston has more chamber music than it "deserves," and Chicago has "too many" theater companies.

In contrast, the effects of size on most popular cultural indicators are linear, and in no instance is the coefficient for the polynomial significant and positive. Thus, Pittsburgh and Miami have about the number of cinemas that one would predict on the basis of the count of their respective populations. The negative coefficient for bands indicates, in fact, that the marginal effects of size on band music in very large places are negative and not positive. The conclusion that a "taste" for band music declines with population size is illustrated by the contrast between Harrisburg and Lancaster. While Harrisburg's population is

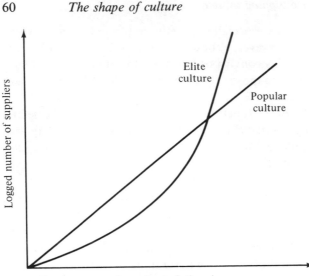

Elite
culture

Popular
culture

Logged number of suppliers

Logged population size

Figure 4.1. Graph of functional relations of suppliers with size: actual plots for art galleries and commercial theaters

about 90,000 greater than that of Lancaster's, Harrisburg supports only half the number of bands that Lancaster does. Performing and nonperforming artists as well as performing groups and facilities exhibit the same patterns as the indicators of popular culture, namely, a linear rather than a multiplicative relation with population size. Figure 4.1 provides a graphic summary of these contrasting results.

As already mentioned, economic geographers report that the percentage increase in economic establishments declines with increases in population size so that each economic establishment serves on the average a greater number of people. Thus, most establishments tend to exhibit internal economies with increasing scale. The results for cultural indicators suggest very different patterns. Elite culture establishments increase slowly with population size but given a particular (unspecified, but varying) threshold of population they increase much more rapidly. This is a critical mass effect. Thomas Schelling describes this phenomenon:

For our purpose we can think of critical mass as shorthand for critical number, critical density, critical ratio, or in special cases like body heat and the production of carbon dioxide, actual mass. What all of the critical-mass models involve is some activity that is self-sustaining once the measure of that activity passes a certain minimum level.[8]

At the micro-level there are two explanations as to why elite art benefits especially from a critical mass. It may be that once a place has a large population base and a few cultural institutions, many people have acquired an initial taste for culture, and then demand more. "Tipping in" is Schelling's term for this particular form of critical mass effect.[9] Alternatively, the explanation may lie not in the realm of demand but in the realm of supply. It is possible that once a place reaches a certain size and acquires, say, an orchestra, the chances are increased several fold that it will acquire chamber music groups, ensembles, and dance companies, owing to affinities of these different groups and organizations. "Stickiness" might be the apt term for such threshold effects. We return to this concept later in this chapter.

With the possible exception of radio, for which the coefficients in both equations in table 4.1 are very low,[10] and bands, which decline with proportionate increases in size, popular culture does not generally exhibit the scale economies described by economic geographers for commercial establishments. Nor does popular culture exhibit the multiplier effects observed for elite culture. Rather, such suppliers increase nearly uniformly with population size, suggesting that demand is relatively constant and these suppliers do not mutually benefit from one another's presence.

Supply affinities

We know a great deal about taste affinities from the work of Pierre Bourdieu and others.[11] As Paul DiMaggio observes, "distinctive sets of cultural preferences come in packages rather than one at a time."[12] However, other than case studies of established interorganizational ties between specific arts institutions,[13] we know very little about the degree to which there are relations among the suppliers of cultural institutions of different kinds. Does the supply of high culture institutions accompany that of popular or commercial institutions? Do providers of the same or similar kinds of culture tend to locate in the same city? In Jefferson's terms, what types of culture tend to co-occur, or, in other terms, exhibit "stickiness"?

One approach to examining this issue is to analyze the relations among the numbers of different cultural indicators at the level of the SMSA. But patterns of relations ought to be examined independently of population size since size is a virtual determinant of the quantities of any cultural supplier. Table 4.2 is a matrix of significant partial correlations among the logged cultural indicators, controlling for both the log of size and the quadratic term for size.[14]

The results indicate that the distribution of elite culture is highly idiosyncratic, that is, when metropolitan size is partialed out. Independent of size, the numbers of museums, opera companies, and symphonies are not strongly related to one another or to other forms of elite culture. In contrast, there is considerably more coherence among the types of popular culture. For

Table 4.2. *Significant partial correlations, controlling for log population size and log size squared*[a]

	1	2	3	4	5	6	7	8	9	10	11	12	13	14	15	16	17
1 Art museums																	
2 Galleries																	
3 Theater companies																	
4 Dance companies																	
5 Opera companies		.30															
6 Opera workshops																	
7 Chamber music groups			.25														
8 Ensembles	.31		.24				.30										
9 Symphonies		.32															
10 Cinemas				.34	.24				.24								
11 Commercial orchestras					.24					.40							
12 Bands										.39	.63						
13 Commercial theaters		.36	.23	.25				.24	.37	.39	.39	.55					
14 Popular concerts		.33							.25	.34							
15 Radio	.35							.30		.27			.24	.30			
16 Craft fairs			.37										.27				
17 Music festivals																	

[a] See table 4.1, notes *a*, *b*. All are significant at the .05 level, at least.

example, there is a dominant cluster that includes cinemas, bands, commercial orchestras, commercial theaters, and live popular concerts.[15]

Not only do the popular cultural items tend to adhere more readily than the elite cultural items, but they also provide "bridges" between both types of culture. For example, cinemas are not only related to bands, commercial orchestras, commercial theater, and popular concerts, they also are related to dance, opera, and symphony orchestras. Besides cinemas, commercial theaters and orchestras also perform this bridging function.

A factor analysis of the complete matrix from which table 4.2 is extracted provides essentially the same results that are revealed by visual inspection. Whereas each indicator of elite culture loads high on a unique dimension, many indicators of popular culture load high on the same dimension. It is also the case that commercial theaters, cinemas, and commercial orchestras load on more than one, which confirms the interpretation that they have bridging functions.[16]

In sum, there is considerably more coherence and structure exhibited within urban places by popular arts institutions than by institutions that support the elite arts. For example, the presence of many museums in a place has few implications for whether the place has many galleries, theaters, dance companies, or operas. On the other hand, cities that have many cinemas are likely to have virtually all other kinds of popular art institutions, and many commercial theaters accompany many cinemas, bands, and commercial orchestras. Thus, in terms of the sheer quantity of institutions and in-dependent of urban size, there is considerable "stickiness" among the varieties of popular culture within a city, while the varieties of elite art are nearly randomly distributed, with little evidence of coherence. This of course does not mean that at some more specific level – among artists, among professional arts administrators, between given complementary institutions, such as museums and galleries – configurations do not exist. Rather, it means that institutional development for the elite arts within a metropolitan area is relatively haphazard, without much shape to it.

We have already seen that there are stronger regional patterns for the popular arts than for the elite arts, and the finding reported here – that different types of elite culture are not meaningfully connected within cities whereas those of popular culture are – supports the notion that elite culture exhibits pervasiveness whereas popular culture exhibits structure and pattern. Yet this is revealed only when size is "partialled out" and we presume all cities are the same size, which they are not.[17]

Just how footloose?

The Jeffersonian problem that relates to the likelihood of co-occurrence disregards the quantitative character of the event itself. When ten blackbirds appear on the same day that the radishes all sprout, the significance of the event does not depend on the number of blackbirds or the number of radishes but rather on the simple occurrence, and the fact that it is explicable – in principle, at least. The underlying mechanism that triggers the event can be related to the weather, or perhaps the amount of sunstorm activity, or in general, a naturally developing phenomenon that reaches a certain threshold level.

The question last addressed centered on the quantities of cultural suppliers, independent of the effects of population size. The question asked now deals with the likelihood of the co-occurrence of pairs (and triads) of cultural suppliers and relates that co-occurrence to population size, as we have already seen that size plays an important role generally and for the elite arts it plays a special role in creating critical mass effects. If cultural affinities cannot be established for elite cultural suppliers when their numbers are considered, it is possible that there are affinities at the elementary level, as dyads or triads.

The initial decision was to select institutions that provide similar cultural products, since we want to take into account organizational interdependencies and common reliance on a pool of artists. The best candidate is music since there are more suppliers on which data are available than for any other cultural form. The nine types used are listed in table 4.3, along with the total number of SMSAs that have at least one, which represents an initial appearance. Although it is plausible from the array of frequencies that cities exhibit a rank distribution with respect to musical suppliers, this is not the case.[18]

Dyads

To examine departure from chance co-occurrence, an expected and an actual probability is computed for each dyad. Assuming statistical independence, the expected likelihood that two different cultural types are located in the same SMSA is the product of the proportions of metropolitan places that have at least one of each type. The actual proportion of places for which the two suppliers do in fact co-occur is produced by a very simple computer routine. A comparison of these two proportions to indicate whether co-occurrence is greater or lesser than chance expectations requires a z statistic,[19] and the z values are translated into cumulative normal probabilities reported in table

Table 4.3. *Music supply variables: numbers of SMSAs with at least one supplier and minimum population size for which observed*[a]

Population	Number of SMSAs	Minimum size
Opera company – K	37	307,500
Chamber music group – N	55	248,300
Contemporary ensemble – O	64	257,200
Opera workshop – L	68	252,400
Commercial orchestra – T	79	275,600
Band – U	96	275,600
Symphony orchestra – M	103	252,400
Popular concert – X	113	248,300
Music festival – Q	118	248,300

[a] For sources see Appendix B.

4.4. In interpreting these results I consider a cumulative probability of at least .975 (that is, a z score with a value of at least 1.96) to merit the conclusion of nonrandom co-occurrence.

The joint occurrence of operas and chamber music, opera and ensembles, operas and commercial orchestras, ensembles and chamber music, and finally, between commercial orchestras and bands is more likely than chance, suggesting that there are stronger ties between elite art suppliers than implied by the previous analysis, since three of the five strong ties involve elite, not popular, music. Still, with only five instances out of a possible thirty-five exhibiting affinities, it would be impossible to conclude that there are strong predilections for aggregation among musical establishments.

Triads

"Is there a set of rules for combining elementary relations into a larger and more complex system?" asks Lévi-Strauss.[20] The implication is that more than simple dyadic relations are required to reveal an underlying structure. Structural equivalence provides one important rule for revealing such a structure: when the elementary relations of two given actors to a third are identical, they occupy the same status set even when they themselves have no direct relation between them.[21] When structural equivalence organizes a social system comprised, say, of an automobile assembly plant, a tool and die

Table 4.4. *Probabilities of co-occurrence of dyads greater than chance expectations*

	1	2	3	4	5	6	7	8
1 Opera								
2 Chamber music	**.999**							
3 Ensemble	**.988**	**.999**						
4 Opera workshop	.685	.500	.655					
5 Commercial orchestra	**.997**	.945	.908	.312				
6 Band	.958	.829	.898	.305	**.999**			
7 Symphony	.896	.567	.572	.766	.567	.573		
8 Popular concert	.794	.707	.761	.500	.710	.788	.659	
9 Music festival	.500	.641	.364	.366	.500	.345	.421	.500

Note: Probabilities exceeding .975 are in bold face.

shop, and a ball bearings factory, the assembly plant and the ball bearings factory would exhibit structural equivalence if they have a common bond to the tool and die shop. Or, two families may be structurally equivalent because they share the same baby sitter. The analysis of triads for cultural suppliers does reveal instances of structural equivalence. Bands and symphony orchestras occupy the same structural position *vis-à-vis* an opera company.

Another organizing principle, however, accounts for more of the structured relations observed in these data, which might be called the rule of generative equivalence. In this situation one "actor" suffices to establish a dyadic relation between two other actors, although the first actor may not have direct relations with either of the other two.

Generative equivalence, in other words, describes the situation in which an actor precipitates a bond between a pair, and the members of the pair may not necessarily be linked with an actor whose presence facilitates the bond. The presence of an automobile assembly plant may generate the economic conditions that make it likely that a tool and die shop and a scrap metal industry in the area establish close relations though neither has economic or trading ties with the automobile assembly factory. (It is not necessary to posit an historical or causal link at all; indeed, the tool and die shop may have existed long before the assembly plant, but had no prior ties of economic exchange in the absence of the plant.)

Or, to give another example, the presence of a college in a community may facilitate the establishment of a close relation between a recently organized peace collective and a much older theological seminary, although neither the collective nor the seminary may have direct organizational ties with the

Table 4.5. *Probabilities of co-occurrence of difference from chance expectations, given the presence of an opera company*

	2	3	4	5	6	7	8
2 Chamber music							
3 Ensemble	**.999**						
4 Opera workshop	**.999**	**.996**					
5 Commercial orchestra	**.999**	**.999**	**.984**				
6 Band	**.999**	**.999**	.933	**.999**			
7 Symphony	**.999**	**.999**	.934	**.999**	**.996**		
8 Popular concert	**.999**	**.997**	.829	**.999**	**.989**	.967	
9 Music festival	**.999**	**.979**	.586	**.994**	.936	.861	.739

Note: Probabilities exceeding .975 are in bold face.

university. Some instances, though not all, are the result of an historical process: the construction of a large condominium may attract expensive boutiques, which in turn generates a demand for new restaurants, to say nothing of an increase in street traffic and higher rents for everyone. It could be said that the condominium created an environment conducive to new sets of economic and social relations.

Given the high threshold of population size required for an opera it is not surprising (though intuitively paradoxical) that opera has the most powerful effects and helps to establish bonds of structural and generative equivalence. Table 4.5 provides the probabilities of departure from chance co-occurrence of dyads given the presence of an opera company. A comparison of table 4.4 and table 4.5, to give one illustration, shows how the presence of an opera company greatly enhances the probabilities of co-occurrence of many other cultural suppliers and in that sense generates equivalences. Whereas the smallest metropolitan place that supports an opera company has a population of 307,500, the minimum threshold required for opera to generate other ties is 349,500.

Instead of summarizing in tables all of the reiterations of triads, the saturated graph for triadic connections provides the graphic representation of structure (figure 4.2). It is clear that opera exhibits the greatest binding strength, while chamber music, ensembles, and commercial orchestras exhibit somewhat less.[22] The listing in figure 4.2 gives the total number of triads in which each supplier is implicated. Ranked from high to low, the more elite the music the greater is its power to generate dyads or to be implicated in triads, although opera workshops and symphonies are notably out of sequence.

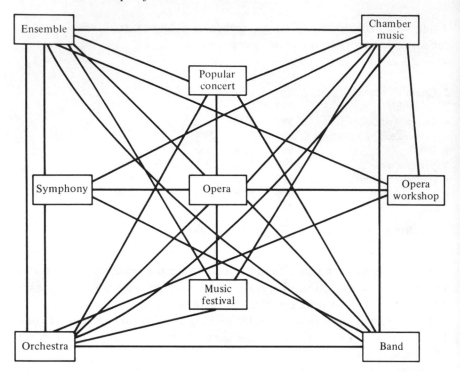

	Uncommonness rank	Number of triadic involvements	Triadic involvement rank
Opera company	1	21	1
Chamber music group	2	17	2.5
Contemporary ensemble	3	16	4
Opera workshop	4	4	9
Commercial orchestra	5	17	2.5
Band	6	12	5
Symphony orchestra	7	8	7
Popular concert	8	10	6
Music festival	9	5	8

Figure 4.2. Saturated graph

When "first appearance" considerations are taken into account (table 4.3 and the sequence of the actual list in figure 4.2), the rank ordering is even better explained since commercial orchestras fall approximately in the rank one would expect (although opera workshops do not). One would conclude that it is not so much the *nature* of the musical genre but rather its simple *uncommonness* that empowers suppliers of music to structure and to integrate the rest of the musical community.[23]

Discussion

Georg Simmel observed that there are major differences "according to whether the first step is the most difficult and decisive step and all later ones are of comparatively secondary importance, or whether the first step itself proves nothing, while only later and more outspoken steps realize the turn of events that was merely foreshadowed in the beginning."[24] Such differences are observed for high culture and popular culture, but there are different conclusions to be drawn depending on whether we consider the quantities of cultural suppliers or their initial appearance in a particular locale.

The numbers of all popular cultural indicators (let us call them "events," for convenience) increase proportionately with proportionate growth of the urban population; since all such "events" are relatively commonplace and increase in the same way, population size can be "removed" and their numbers will still be related to one another. This interconnectedness, it can be inferred, results from a uniform and constant aggregate demand for these varieties of popular culture "events." The first step – the city's acquisition of a commercial orchestra or a live popular concert – is not very consequential, but the final acquisition of a substantial number of orchestras or live concerts means that the city will have a large proportion of all popular culture "events."

Because elite art events depend on thresholds of population, any first step is a difficult one, and the rarest event – acquiring an opera company – is the most difficult of all. Lévi-Strauss describes how powerful are such institutions that are so rare that they are assigned a zero value. Paradoxically, rare (zero value) institutions acquire their power because they establish the necessary preconditions for the very existence of the social system to which they belong. "Their presence," he writes, "enables the social system to exist as a whole."[25] The appearance – whether early or late – of one opera company provides extensive integration for a wide range of institutions, making it virtually certain that there will be a structure for which there are direct connections between opera and three other musical establishments and twenty-one direct connections between the remaining eight other musical establishments.

If the most esoteric form of high culture, opera, provides cultural integration in a metropolitan place, it is not quite so successful as the commercial orchestra in spanning the gaps between high and popular culture. In terms of sheer quantity, and independent of size, commercial orchestras are related to a more diverse set of cultural indicators than any other single form. Because they are directly linked with opera and directly linked with bands, they have an unusual capacity to bridge main forms of elite and popular musical suppliers.

To return to the initial questions raised in this chapter, the results suggest, first, that at high population thresholds, interdependencies develop involving opera, chamber music, and ensembles; and that regardless of the size of the place, commercial orchestras help to establish links between the domains of elite and popular culture. Secondly, the collective demand for popular culture is a simple function of population size, whereas a critical mass must be reached before the demand for elite culture will be satisfied by suppliers. Then it will be more than satisfied. That is to say, the accumulation of demand for elite culture precedes the initial supply of it, but then supply accelerates at a faster rate than demand (population size). In contrast, the supply of popular culture develops about as fast as the numbers who demand it. Thirdly, and most paradoxically, the degree of the connectedness of the community of music suppliers is best explained by the first appearance of that rare event – the opera company – and the patterns of connectedness suggest that the community itself is better understood (though not perfectly) in terms of the relative rarity or prevalence of musical genre, rather than in terms of their intrinsic characteristics or how traditional or popular they are.

Notes

1 Harry S. Randall, *Life of Thomas Jefferson*, Vol. 1 (New York, 1858, p. 44).
2 Marcia Bystryn, "Art Galleries as Gatekeepers," *Social Research* 45 (1978); 390–408; Paul M. Hirsch, "Processing Fads and Fashions," *American Journal of Sociology* 77 (1972), 639–659; Diana Crane, *The Transformation of the Avant-Garde* (Chicago: University of Chicago Press, 1987); Raymonde Moulin, *The French Art Market*, trans. Arthur Goldhammer (New Brunswick NJ: Rutgers University Press, 1987).
3 Harold Horowitz, "Work and Earnings of Artists in the Media Fields," *Journal of Cultural Economics* 7 (1983), 69–90; Jeffrey W. Riemer and Nancy A. Brooks, *Framing the Artist* (Washington DC: University Press of America, 1982), p. 7; Robert R. Faulkner, *Music on Demand* (New Brunswick: Transaction Books, 1983).

4 R. J. Johnson, *The American Urban System* (New York: St. Martin's Press, 1982); Edgar M. Hoover, *The Location of Economic Activity* (New York: McGraw Hill, 1948), pp. 126–144.

5 Brian J. L. Berry, *Geography of Market Centers and Retail Distributions* (Englewood Cliffs NJ: Prentice Hall, 1967); Brian J. L. Berry and W. L. Garrison, "The Functional Bases of the Central Place Hierarchy," *Economy Geography* 34 (1958), 145–154; E. C. Conkling and M. Yeates, *Man's Economic Environment* (New York: McGraw-Hill, 1976).

6 John P. Robinson, Terry Hanford, and Timothy A. Triplet, "Public Participation in the Arts," (College Park: University of Maryland, 1985); National Research Center of the Arts, *Americans and the Arts* (New York: Louis Harris and Associates: October, 1984), p. 49.

7 A comparison over time would be superior to this cross-sectional analysis; however, metropolitan size does not increase so much over a ten-year period to permit as meaningful interpretations of these differences as differences among SMSAs at one point in time.

8 Thomas C. Schelling, *Micromotives and Macrobehavior* (New York: W. W. Norton, 1978), p. 95.

9 *Micromotives and Macrobehavior*, p. 101.

10 It is not unlikely that radio stations exhibit the same kinds of economies of scale that economic establishments do. By upgrading facilities a radio station can reach much larger numbers of people.

11 Pierre Bourdieu, *Distinction* (Cambridge MA: Harvard University Press, 1984); Alan R. Andreason, "Predictors of Attendance at the Performing Arts," *Journal of Consumer Research* 7 (1980), 112–120; K. Peter Etzkorn, "On the Sociology of Musical Practice of Social Groups," *International Social Science Journal* 34 (1982), 555–569.

12 Paul DiMaggio, "Classification in Art," *American Sociological Review* 52 (1987), 440–455.

13 See note 2.

14 Those indicators that confound commercial or popular culture with noncommercial and elite culture (buildings, performing groups, performing and nonperforming artists) are not included in table 4.2.

15 The magnitudes of the partial correlations are unaffected when New York City is excluded, except for theaters for which the partial is slightly, but not significantly, reduced.

16 Basing results on factor scores of .50 or higher, the first factor is largely defined by galleries (the factor loading is .91), the second by ensemble groups and chamber groups (.85 and .66, respectively), the third by dance companies (.78), and the final factor by cinemas (.64), commercial orchestras (.62), and commercial theaters (.51). Cinemas, commercial theaters, and commercial orchestras have loadings of at least .35 on several factors.

17 There are isolated affinities between particular types of elite cultural institutions reported in table 4.2, such as between art galleries and opera companies. These may be accounted for by the urban presence of facilities that house different types of

cultural events and groups. However, when the partial residual correlations between the logged number of performing arts centers and all logged cultural indicators are examined, the results do not support that conclusion. The only significant relation involving elite culture is that between the (logged) number of performing arts buildings and that of dance companies.

18 The earliest work on ranking is reported in Walter Christaller, *Die Centralen Orte in Sudendeutschland* (Jena: Gustav Fischer, 1933). The conception of market demand underlies the rank size rule, namely that activities or functions which have broad geographical markets but not uniform demand will be located in the largest places, whereas those that are in high demand everywhere will be located in virtually all places. In addition, it is assumed that nested relations develop among establishments that perform complementary activities. If these suppliers conform to the rank size rule, we would expect that an urban place with opera would have all other musical suppliers, that a place with chamber music (but without opera) would have all other musical suppliers that are more plentiful, and so forth. The Guttman scale analysis yields insignificant results, demonstrating that there is no evidence of sequential building from the most prevalent to the least prevalent supplier.

19 $z = (p_s - p_u)/((p_u q_u)/N)$ where p_s is the proportion of SMSAs with at least one cultural indicator of each of two types and p_u is the chance of co-occurrence given the marginal distributions.

20 See *The Raw and the Cooked*, Vol. 1. Trans. John and Doreen Weightman (New York: Harper Colophon, 1969), pp. 1–32.

21 Ronald S. Burt, *Toward a Structural Theory of Action* (New York: Academic Press, 1982), p. 40.

22 Further exploratory analyses demonstrate that when a dummy variable for each of the triads including either opera or chamber music is regressed on a variety of urban characteristics, the only significant predictors of these triads are the log of population size and the squared term for size. On the other hand, regressions of each triad that includes ensembles reveals that age of the central city is often significant (in six of sixteen regressions). Triads that include commercial orchestras are, in part, explained by region, with the likelihood of commercial orchestras involved in triads higher in the south and west than in the east or north central regions.

23 On a somewhat speculative note, the momentum underlying the process of generative equivalence may be established through elite competition. Opera, the queen of the cultural arts, with its patrons being the members of a top elite, may establish a patronage climate that encourages competition among elites in the second or third rank. They in turn may organize other sectors. A full test of this hypothesis would require a wider range of elite suppliers, including dance companies, museums, and symphony orchestras.

24 *The Sociology of Georg Simmel*, trans. Kurt H. Wolf (Glencoe IL: The Free Press, 1950), p. 140.

25 *Structural Anthropology*, trans. Claire Jacobson and Brook Grundfest Schoeff (New York: Anchor, 1967), p. 156.

5 Organizational assembly and disassembly

> Kyosai sent a picture of a crow to an exhibit, fixing the price at 100 yen. When people made remarks about the exorbitant price, he replied that the sum was but a small fraction of the price of his fifty years of study that had enabled him to dash off the picture in this manner.
> W. Anderson, 1899

In contrast with professional workers (for example, engineers, doctors, and veterinarians) and service workers (such as cooks, security personnel, and morticians), whose relative power and autonomy reside in the indispensability of their services, cultural workers provide services that are an accessory to the good life. For precisely this reason, cultural workers and cultural institutions are to an exceptional extent dependent on their clients and on others for their good will and support. Definitions of what constitute the criteria for work done by professionals – designing safe bridges or curing diseases – and those provided by service personnel – keeping city streets clean, catching criminals, and embalming the deceased – are relatively standardized and clear cut. While such tasks may not always be easy to carry out, there is public consensus that they have to be done and what the results should be. Moreover, the criteria for evaluation of professional and service tasks change slowly over time and are subject to legal and administrative scrutiny. Both within each profession and each service sector providers compete and co-operate with one another to perform a given task according to the same standards. Professionals and service workers experiment very little.

Services provided by cultural workers, in contrast, are not essential for meeting people's basic needs and they are also governed by quite vague criteria as there are varieties of taste publics, whose members are capricious besides. Aesthetic standards held by artists are also often at odds with one another and frequently out of sync with critical standards. It is paradoxical that cultural workers provide a non-essential service that is highly unstandardized yet they themselves value autonomy and independence so highly that they risk offending public conventions, and at the same time are totally dependent on the interest and support of the public.

73

Another source of uncertainty is that the conditions that prevail in cities are not all the same. In some places cultural activities are handsomely endowed, and in other places they are not. In some cities there is a proliferation of cultural workers and cultural institutions, whereas in others there is no such abundance of them and thus little competition among cultural producers. Given the paradoxical nature of cultural work and the varying uncertainties of urban environments, a main question raised here is how cultural institutions of different kinds are assembled under varying urban conditions.

Publics and patrons

Dependence on an amorphous public and a complex economic and political environment is relatively new in the history of the arts. Music, drama, dance, and the visual arts have traditionally had simple relations of dependence, whether these involved the church, the nobility, or a state bureaucracy. In the Middle Ages, prelates and abbots dictated aesthetic canons on the basis of ecclesiastical interpretations of the Holy Writ. Renaissance patrons tended to be interfering and authoritative in their supportive roles with artists, as suggested, for example, by Isabella d'Este's resolute command to Perugino, "You are not to add anything of your own."[1] Courtly and other patrons were usually knowledgeable and informed about style and technique. For instance, Henry VIII was an accomplished musician;[2] in the twelfth century, church notables played major roles in developing the iconographic programmes for the design and construction of cathedrals;[3] and throughout the times of imperial conquests colonial envoys and merchants played a decisive role in defining art conventions for various aesthetic revivals and in guiding curatorial decisions.[4]

As the performing and visual arts were slowly liberated from the authority exercised by the nobility and church during the seventeenth century, the new patronage systems that developed were more centralized and bureaucratic, as states played a greater role in dominating artistic activities. By 1664, Colbert had established the French Royal Academy that secured control over the visual arts and Jean Baptiste Lully, superintendent of music under Louis XIV, had created institutions that ensured absolute state power over music, theater, and opera.[5]

Patronage may not be the preferred form of support for the arts, but it has two advantages over the contemporary system. First, once impressed, patrons tended to be extremely reliable. The comparison between Holland and the rest of Europe is instructive; while most of Europe had stable patronage systems in the seventeenth century, the Dutch bourgeoisie constituted a disorganized market for artists' works, with the result that many painters, including some of great renown, lived and died as paupers.[6] Secondly, patronage was a relatively simple system with direct negotiations between performer or artist and patron and this was so even when the patron was a state bureaucracy. Dependence on patronage is markedly different from having to rely on ill-defined audiences, publics, and multiple funding agencies. The *bête noire* of contemporary dependence is tempered, of course, by some artistic freedom to choose among many possible niches of dependency.

American cultural enterprises and artists have never had such a reliable relationship with a monolithic patronage system and still depend for their support on publics – rather than on official institutions – to a far greater extent than do their European counterparts. Somewhat like patrons in the past, European funding agencies are highly involved in the arts they sponsor and work relatively closely with artists. It would be safe to say that the audiences on which American performing artists depend are collectively less knowledgeable about what they see and hear – and about what they purchase tickets to see and to hear – than arts agencies or patrons. The problems of depending on a paying public to keep, say, an orchestra in business, while simultaneously attempting to maintain musical standards and occasionally to experiment with a new composition, pose dilemmas that confront most musicians in America. Audiences have a relatively casual attitude towards the arts they enjoy in their leisure, and as a result they tend to be somewhat conservative in their tastes. Claudio Arrau comments on the difficulty that musicians, composers, and conductors have in attempting to experiment with contemporary music and at the same time not alienate a paying public:

Most listeners do have one blind spot – contemporary music . . . Modern music asks for a lot of effort from the listener, to open up, listen again and again until the meaning of the music becomes clearer. Twentieth-century compositions are simply not what commercial audiences have been trained to enjoy.[7]

And as director Andre Antoine notes, the general theater audience "apparently . . . has no idea of the labor that goes into a play it has just applauded."[8] Describing the viewers' reaction to a dance performance by experimentalists Sage Cowles and Molly Davies, Hanna writes, "Jarred expectations characterized the reaction to the concert. . . . The performance typified the avant garde: some strong enthusiasm and some strong disappointment, with more of the latter than the former."[9]

The triumph of art for the public[10] – which is to say, the development of mass audiences – makes artistic risk-taking a difficult affair, undermines the radical potentialities of art, and impairs standards of excellence. It is not that traditional patrons tended to support the vanguard or artists who threatened the status quo, but patrons and artists usually saw eye to eye on matters of style and conventions of taste. To paraphrase Marcuse, traditional canons will support what can and what ought to be whereas contemporary guidelines are vague and middling, strengthening the sweep of what is.[11]

In attempting to deal with the problems involving aesthetic autonomy and a collectivist or public ideology, most marxists pose difficult and confounding solutions. While emphasizing the political and ideological role of art – that art must serve universal human needs – public art often is debunked as banal and commonplace. Marx, after all, preferred classical Greek art even though there existed nineteenth-century genres of painting that provided far more sympathetic portrayals of proletarian life; Trotsky's favorite author was Dante; Luxemburg and Stalin shared conventional elitist preference for Renaissance painters; Adorno was contemptuous of the general public's acceptance of commercial residues evident in the compositions of Stravinsky, Hindemith, and Sibelius; and Lukács championed classical realism and opposed modern art and literature that was governed by consumer preferences.[12]

Thus, as Janet Wolff succinctly concludes, conceptions of aesthetic criteria have potent ideological significance even when they are not reducible to ideological or political values.[13] The point to be made here, however, is that there is a fundamental dilemma in the current situation: art is governed by its own aesthetic norms that relate in complex and ambiguous ways to social and political values, but at the same time, artists are inextricably locked into dependent relations with the public, corporations, foundations, and public agencies. Summing up the perennial dilemma this poses for artists, Egbert writes:

Therefore, while it is true that the greatness of the artist . . . can best be fostered or gravely hindered by the society in which the [artist] lives, the relation between artistic merit and society is a complex one . . . It becomes simple only when an artistic style is imposed upon artists for non-artistic ends, to the inevitable detriment of the arts because of the ultimately personal nature of artistic talent, imagination, and insight, and thus of great art itself.[14]

If artistic freedom and autonomy are perceived to be jeopardized by elusive public values, and experimentation demeaned by conservative elite devotees, then a third nemesis for contemporary art, especially in the United States, is bureaucracy and organization. The extent to which American performing and non-performing artists themselves are dependent on bureaucracies is probably no greater than it is in most countries since all contemporary artists need galleries, museums, theaters, orchestras, or some other organized institution. However, the extent to which arts organizations in the United States are dependent on a multitude of external funding and sponsoring agencies –

private foundations, municipal governments, state and county governments, corporations, the federal government, philanthropists and philanthropic organizations – is greater than it is in most industrialized countries. Compared with European cultural funding practices, U.S. subsidization is modest in scope and also highly unco-ordinated.[15] This in turn engenders complex patterns of dependence for art organizations.

Arts in the marketplace

There are profound philosophical differences between capitalist economic theory and marxist theory about the nature of the political economy of the arts, but there are some interesting similarities between Keynes and most marxists with respect to their concerns about centralized state or corporate control over artistic endeavors. According to marxist theory, culture is financed on the backs of workers, through the extraction of surplus labor. The growing production requirements of capitalism dictate increasing commercialization of culture – to guarantee a growing supply of consumers – and an increasing bureaucratization of the arts – to maintain control over cultural workers and what they produce. Braverman describes these two processes of commercialization (commodification) and incorporation:

Corporate institutions have transformed every means of entertainment and "sport" into a productive process for the enlargement of capital . . . So enterprising is capital that even where the effort is made by one or another section of the population to find a way to nature, sport or art through personal activity and amateur or "underground" innovation, these activities are rapidly incorporated into the market as far as it is possible.[16]

Keynes' position concerning the relationships between cultural activities, capitalist enterprises, and the state changed over time as did his views on the vulnerabilities of artistic enterprises. The main question for Keynes was how to maintain financial security for artistic endeavors while at the same time not imperilling artists' creative integrity. In "The End of Laissez-Faire," published in 1926, he contended that the acquisitiveness of commercial enterprises constituted a threat to culture, and since the market could not be entrusted with the support of the arts, the state should be. Anticipating the concept of merit goods, Keynes wrote:

The most important *Agenda* of the State relate not to those activities which private individuals are already fulfilling, but to those functions which fall outside the sphere of the individual, to those decisions which are made by *no one* if the State does not make them. The important thing for Government is not to do things which individuals are doing already, and to do them a little better or a little worse; but to do those things which at present are not done at all.[17]

But with wartime recovery, Keynes, witnessing the dramatic increase in interest in the arts, retracted his earlier statement, arguing instead that the arts should be self-supporting, and rely on the competitive marketplace and its ordinary capital investment and purchasing schemes.[18]

Some economists tend to agree with Keynes' earlier position that support for the arts in the form of federal and state subsidies is warranted on the basis of economic need.[19] Because in the absence of public support, arts institutions will raise ticket prices to levels that only the affluent can afford to pay,[20] subsidies insure a more democratic culture by keeping prices down, and they also promote more innovative productions owing to a more diverse constituency.

Isomorphism or debureaucratization

Thus, economists and political philosophers express concern and some ambivalence about the relation between art and the political, economic environment. In different ways Keynes and Braverman were alarmed about the prospects of pre-emptive control of artistic enterprises since dependence on larger institutions, they maintained, would bureaucratize cultural life and stifle artistic autonomy. More recently, DiMaggio spells out this argument in more neutral terms: arts organizations as well as other dependent organizations "internalize" the external bureaucratic environment by incorporating into their structures administrators, development specialists, market researchers, and managers. In other words, arts organizations become isomorphic with the bureaucracies in the complexly organized environments with which they deal.[21] It follows that the more munificent and culturally well endowed the environment, the more bureacratic and hierarchical the arts organization. This argument is consistent with contingency theory that suggests that in complex environments that are abundant in resources, the beneficiary organizations are likely to grow administratively and hierarchically. More specifically, contingency theory states that transactions with a complex environment increase the tendency of any organization to formalize and amplify its administrative functions.[22] Administrators are precisely the ones who span the boundaries between the organization and the external environment, routinize exchanges between the organization and its public, and help to preserve a safety zone between the organization and the myriad of other organizations.

As Zolberg suggests in the case of the contemporary American art museum, great reliance on funding and the efforts to disseminate culture to a large segment of the population have resulted in the growing importance and influence of professional administrators. The basic issue, she states, is the increasing intensity of demands for public service at the expense of interests to maintain the museum as a quiet sanctuary.[23]

Contrary to this view, Heydebrand argues that dense complexities in the political-economic environment do not foster the growth of local institutional bureaucracies but rather tend to encourage debureaucratization. Under such conditions, co-ordination is achieved through semiformal and informal alternatives to strict hierarchical control, by dismantling the various elements of bureaucracy, and by adopting a flexible division of labor. Dealing with clients (such as audiences and patrons) in affluent and complex environments leads to informal arrangements that are based on loose coupling and symbolic hierarchies of power.[24]

Although Heydebrand's argument is addressed abstractly to issues of public administration and the corporate state, the general premise is that once any organization is endowed with legitimacy, it can deal with the larger environment as if it were loosely embedded in that environment rather than maintaining an obsequious or contentious relation with it. This greatly reduces the need for a formal interface between the organization and its external context, allowing the organization to compete not for resources but rather to compete for clients, as Eisenstadt once suggested.[25] Disproportionate growth under these conditions will not take place at the managerial and administrative levels, but rather at the productive level, which is to say, as increases in the numbers of performers (and possibly, more performances and even better performances).

In sum, DiMaggio's theory of isomorphism[26] and contingency theories[27] suggest that complex and prosperous environments will augment cultural bureaucracy.[28] On the other hand, it is consistent with Heydebrand's and Eisenstadt's position that a complex and prosperous environment pre-empts the role of bureaucrats by endowing legitimacy on the arts organization, greatly curtailing the necessity of negotiating over scarce resources, and allowing the organization to compete over clients rather than over public resources.

Thus, one focus of this chapter is on the ways in which urban environments affect the bureaucratic character of arts organizations. The issues that must be addressed first, however, deal with the ways that the characteristics of these organizations and their memberships influence how bureaucratic they are. Artists, it will not be forgotten, profess abiding disdain for organizations and their routines.

Artists in bureaucracies

Bureaucracies, according to Max Weber, are the most efficient social instruments for attaining rational co-ordination of complex tasks and for maintaining authority over people as they carry out those tasks.[29] They are superior to all relatively informal alternatives – clans, extended families, collectives, and princely courts – in that they are reliable, stable, disciplined, and maintain a relatively high degree of precision through formalized procedures.

Though all artists, performing and nonperforming, must deal with bureaucracies in some manner or another, these relations are fraught with ambivalence and, often, hostility. Because bureaucratic work organizations place a high value on reliability, accountability, precision, and efficiency they are very often perceived by artists to be antithetical to innovation and creativity, as Ben Shawn so clearly illustrates in the following parable:

A traveler in thirteenth-century France met three men wheeling wheelbarrows. He asked in what work they were engaged and he received three answers: the first said, "I toil from sunup to sundown and all I receive for my pains is a few francs a day." The second said, "I am glad enough to wheel this wheelbarrow for I have been out of work for many months and I have a family to support." The third said, "I am building Chartres Cathedral." I always feel that the committees and the tribunals and the civic groups and their auxiliaries harbor no misgivings about the men who wheel their wheelbarrows for however many francs a day; the object of their suspicions seems, inevitably, to be the man who is building Chartres Cathedral.[30]

Social science research tends to support Shawn's contention that over-organized art worlds have difficulty sustaining creativity and excellence. Large, formal institutions impose routine, generate lines of rigid specialization, and increasingly cast artists into the role of wage laborer. For example, Couch argues that the large size of modern orchestras tends to lead to centralized control and the proliferation of rules that reduce the autonomy of individual musicians. He writes:

the musician has been transformed from amateur to free-lance businessman, to wage labor, and the orchestra from a small, relatively egalitarian, loosely structured group into a large, complex, highly pressured and highly disciplined organization quite akin to a factory.[31]

These conclusions are similar to those drawn by other students of culture.[32] Performing artists are especially concerned about the effects of rational enterprise and financial priorities both on artistic autonomy and on the cohesiveness of the artistic community. Composers such as Milton Babbit, and performers like Julius Levine, describe facets of this issue in interviews with the Rosenbergs.[33] Drama teacher Robert Corrigan suggests that increasingly formalized, large theater companies create alienating distances between the performer and audience.[34] Specialization in commercial art is, of course, even more extreme than in the nonprofit art sector, as Faulkner describes the problems of expediency, competition, and specialization among musicians in the film industry.[35] Summing up the problems for the musician in commercial work, Clive Davis, an executive for CBS Records Division writes, "Being in music is much like being in the shoe industry."[36]

Few workers are so beleaguered by their organized work environments as artists, but then few workers have such limited alternatives as do artists in finding the "right" work organization or, for that matter, any work at all.

Artists as professionals

When a professional is defined in terms of credentials, such as higher education and certification, the definition excludes the artist.[37] However, when profession is defined in more abstract terms, as Everett Hughes does, as a group that delivers esoteric services, and when the practice rests on some branch of knowledge which is acquired by virtue of long study or apprenticeship, an artist can be considered to be a professional.[38] Such mastery of esoteric knowledge and apprenticeship training, whether or not we consider them to constitute a justifiable claim for professional status for artists, help to temper the deleterious effects of bureaucratic constraints on artistic autonomy. Like doctors, veterinarians, and scientists in research labs, artists maintain a relatively high degree of self-discipline and high standards for their work. This must be the case in arts organizations since after all, performances by orchestras and theaters are evaluated on aesthetic grounds, not merely on their demonstrated efficiencies.

However, unlike conventionally defined professionals, artists' autonomy and discretion are often extended by being generalists rather than experts in a narrowly defined area. Many violinists learn to play the viola; Shakespearean actors try to get parts in contemporary plays; playwrights often act in plays or direct them; and, in general, the aim of any performer is to expand his or her repertoire. This is not the case in law, medicine, or probably in any other recognized profession.[39] There is impressionistic evidence that the less specific their skills, the more highly valued are performing artists in their organizations.[40]

Perhaps it is partly because such a high value is placed on the combination of versatility and originality that the orientations of artists play such a major role in shaping the structure of the work organization. For example, design philosophies in architecture firms account for variation in their organizational structures; film companies are organized differently depending on the relative emphasis placed on artistry or technique; the organization of museums is affected by the curators' conceptions of the proper mix between aesthetic and public missions.[41] While the examination of such fine differences in aesthetic conceptions among various performing arts organizations is not feasible in this study, it is possible to compare different types of performing arts organizations to determine whether or not the artistic product affects the character of the organizational structure.

The empirical problem: measurement and indicators

Ideally, to address the issues raised we require an indicator of both internal administrative co-ordination (the extent to which administrators exercise control over work and decisions inside the organization) and of external co-ordination (the emphasis on negotiations with funding agencies, clients, the providers of subcontracted services, and other arts organizations). The ratio of paid administrators to the total number of people who work in the performing arts organizations is a measure that both captures and confounds the extent of both types of co-ordination. Although it is impossible to directly ascertain the extent to which administrators in arts organizations spend more time on internal matters or on external ones, the results of the analysis help to disentangle the conditions of these separate preoccupations of administrators.

The *National Directory of Performing Arts and Civic Centers*[42] provides a fairly comprehensive listing of performing arts groups in the United States. About one-third (324) out of the 918 performing groups listed provided sufficient information on their staffing and other organizational characteristics to examine several hypotheses concerning why some performing arts organizations are more bureaucratic than others.[43] The measure of the relative size of the bureaucracy is the ratio of the paid administrative staff to the sum of all staff.[44]

All things being constant we would expect that the more affluent the organization, the greater the relative numbers of administrators in a performing arts organization. One of their tasks, after all, is to raise money and the more funds administrators raise the greater the need for even more administrators to manage and deploy resources – tasks that dancers, actors, and musicians would rather not do themselves. Similarly, the more dependent the arts organization is on a variety of funding sources, including private donors, corporations, state and federal agencies, the greater the need for managers, clerks, and personnel and fiscal officers. Both the size of the budget and the complexity of funding sources can be expected to increase the relative size (and probably the power) of the administration.[45] The annual operating budget, given in dollar amounts, is used in the analysis with natural log transformation to correct for its skewed distribution. The questionnaire employed to gather the information asked specifically whether the organizations received funds from government grants, private donations, or corporation donations. Because neither one of these has a distinctive consequence for the administrative ratio, a summed index is used, with a score of zero indicating no outside support and a score of 3 indicating support from all three sources.

The conventional view, that the larger the organization the more bureaucratic it is, has been shown in a long series of studies to be false. In an early investigation of over 3,000 organizations of 26 different types, including hospitals, universities, public employment agencies, and finance agencies, Peter Blau concludes the larger the organization the smaller the relative size of the bureaucratic component.[46] Size of the organization is measured here by the natural log of the total number of personnel.

As organizations age, they tend to grow at the top. That is, the longer an establishment is in business the more administrators it tends to have relative to its size.[47] The indicator of age used here is the number of years since the performing arts group was established. Another relatively unique factor that must be taken into account for these organizations is the length of the annual season. It was coded in months. It can be expected that artists are willing to invest their own time and energy into managing the administrative details if there are performances for only a few months out of the year but that they are less willing to do so when the company is in operation for a substantial part of the year.

Whether artists are professionals or not is a question that raises both conceptual and measurement problems. A tradition in the arts, both despised and cherished, is that the true artist suffers under the onus of mundane employment while engaging in the meaningful, creative work in the hours away from their jobs. Notable examples of "amateurs" include academics, such as Saul Bellow and William Kennedy, librarians, such as Luis Borges and Ivan Arguelles, or businessmen, such as Charles Ives. A substantial number of female literary and commercial writers write in their spare time in addition to keeping house, taking care of children, and working at a full-time or part-time job.[48] Stebbins convincingly argues that the practical difference between the "amateur" and the "professional" is not so much to be made on the grounds of qualifications or performance criteria, but rather on the basis of whether the activity provides the major source of income or not.[49] This distinction is consistent with a main condition of employment in the performing arts, namely whether or not artists are hired and paid under contractual arrangements, and it is the basis of the *Directory*'s definition of whether the organization is professional or not.

The working relations between administrators and professionals are different from those between administrators and nonprofessionals, and professional organizations are structured differently than nonprofessional ones. In general, professionals require less supervision and direction than amateurs, and professional organizations are, therefore, relatively decentralized.[50]

Yet, paradoxically, professional organizations tend to be more bureaucratic than nonprofessional ones, since professionals are unwilling, and are not paid, to carry out routine clerical work or to be involved in administrative and managerial tasks.[51]

With the exception of length of the season, the factors thus far considered – organizational affluence (budget), complexity of funding sources, organizational size, age, and degree of professionalization – are ones that can be used to describe any organization. The ways in which these factors influence bureaucratization are fairly well established in the sociological literature, and it is not expected that arts organizations will exhibit patterns that are much different than those observed for social service agencies, employment offices, or factories.

What is not clear, however, is how the nature of the cultural endeavor will affect the relative number of managers. In fact, there is very little systematic research on the problem of how the character of work affects the structure of the organization. A question to be explored is whether performing arts groups of different kinds tend to have disproportionately many or few administrators and, correlatively, disproportionately few or many cultural workers.

In considering this issue it is suggested that there are fundamental differences between groups that are involved in making music (whether it be a choral group or choir, symphony or chamber symphony, small ensemble or chamber music group) and other arts groups like theaters or dance companies. A company that performs music may not be a homogeneous group of performers but it does consist of people who have training in the same notational system, have a universal understanding of the scale (with few exceptions, it will be the major scale), and who in other ways share a common language. Co-ordination of the actual performance of any musical work, even an orchestral version of Strauss's *Salome*, requiring 113 instruments, is entrusted to a single conductor, who is a musician and who relies on the shared conventions of instrumentalists. While orchestras and most music groups do,

Table 5.1. *Regression of administrative ratio on organizational variables*

	A Without interaction terms			B With interaction terms	
	r	B	b	B	b
Budget (logged)	.21	.36	.085(.014)**	.38	.090(.014)**
Complex funding sources	.06	.05	.014(.016)	.02	.007(.016)
Size (logged)	−.35	−.53	−.107(.011)**	−.55	−.112(.018)**
Length of season	.02	−.00	−.000(.005)	.02	.003(.005)
Professional (1,0)	.04	−.04	−.027(.031)	−.35	−.208(.077)**
Age of company	.08	.12	.015(.006)*	.13	.002(.001)*
Music (1,0)	−.14	−.10	−.059(.030)*	.28	.164(.076)*
Music × size				−.44	−.062(.019)**
Professional × size				.39	.054(.020)**
Constant		3.32		3.34	
$\hat{R}^2$		.28		.32	

*p <.05
**p <.01
N = 324

of course, require managers, clerical workers, and other administrators, these administrators largely play support roles as they deal more with publics and with funding agencies than with the supervision of musicians and co-ordination of their work. On the other hand, theater groups require far more in the way of administrative direction and task organization, owing to the diversity of art occupations involved in theatrical productions. Dance companies, too, are expected to have relatively large bureaucracies since they have complex occupational configurations. Staging a dance requires costumes, lighting, often scenery, and frequently musical accompaniment, all of which require co-ordination. For the purposes of this analysis all performing groups are divided into music and non-music groups.[52]

Preliminary results

The initial results are reported in table 5.1, panel A. (The simple correlations of the independent variables are provided in the appendix to this chapter). As hypothesized, the regression results in panel A show that companies or groups with large budgets tend to have disproportionately many administrators. Presumably large budgets increase the need for and the ability to hire more managers to handle the funds, and it is also likely that large revenues are raised through the work of many administrators. In other words, big bureaucracies and big budgets go hand in hand, and with information on only one time period it is impossible to know which is temporally prior. Yet, contrary to expectations, the complexity of funding sources has no influence on the relative size of the administration. It is sheer prosperity, not a wide base of financial support, that accompanies a high administrative ratio.

Consistent with research on many other types of organization, larger arts organizations are found to have relatively fewer administrators than small ones, indicating that management functions – once bolstered with routinized procedures and operating rules – become increasingly streamlined with the growing size of the performing arts group. This means, of course, that the relative numbers of other personnel, including artists, increase with the size of the group. However, large size has two contradictory influences: it *directly* reduces the relative size of the bureaucratic component and it *indirectly* increases it because large performing arts organizations have larger budgets than small ones and size is positively related to the amount of the annual budget.[53] Hence, the negative influence of size on the magnitude of the bureaucratic component would be somewhat greater if it were not for the fact that large companies are relatively prosperous and prosperity increases the proportionate number of managers.

These findings concerning size replicate those observed for other kinds of organization. The reason, presumably, why size reduces the administrative ratio is because the larger the organization is, the more routinized and formalized are its procedures, reducing the need for supervision and co-ordination. As a result, growth results in a relatively larger "productive" component. On the other hand, an expanding budget means an increase in transactions with external agencies and in activities related to development. This does not entail a relative decline of the administrative component but rather its increase.

Other organizational characteristics of performing arts centers – complexity of funding sources, length of the season, and whether or not it is professional – have trivial or insignificant effects, although, as expected, older companies are more likely than younger ones to have larger administrative components. The fact that professionalization does not play a role in the explanation of bureaucratization is somewhat surprising, but this conclusion will later be qualified.

Perhaps the most interesting finding relates to the significance of the substantive nature of the performing arts. As conjectured, music groups do require fewer administrators relative to their size than do dance companies or theaters, presumably because musicians co-ordinate their own work through their common understanding of musical conventions. In contrast, the diverse occupational orientations and the more numerous, different occupational groups that are required for dance and theatrical performances tend to increase the relative numbers of administrators.

The influences summarized are independent of one another, which is to say, as an illustration, that regardless of the size of the music group – whether it is an orchestra or a small ensemble – it will have relatively few administrators compared with dance and theater companies. It might be expected that the variation in the sizes of music and of nonmusic groups and variation in the budgets of each of these two major types of performing arts groups will have different organizational consequences. All plausible comparisons (as interaction terms) were examined, but only two are significant: the comparison of music groups versus others with respect to organizational size and that of professional versus nonprofessional groups also with respect to organizational size. Table 5.1, panel B, indicates that the administrative ratio declines with size far more for music groups than for other groups. Aside from the fact that all music groups are more performer intensive than the others, the larger the music group the more performer intensive it is. That is, symphony orchestras, choirs, chamber orchestras, ensembles, and other music companies and groups have relatively fewer administrators than do dance and theater companies, but the largest music groups – opera companies and symphonies – are the most performer intensive of all.

Although the hypothesis that professional companies would have relatively more administrators than do nonprofessional companies is not supported, when size is taken into account there are substantial differences between the two. Large professional companies have relatively more administrators than large nonprofessional companies. That is, compared with amateur companies, the larger the professional company the greater is the proportion of administrators. There are probably many reasons why this is the case. First, professionals are paid to perform and they are presumably restricted by union conditions not to do other work, and the larger and the more visible the organization, the greater are such constraints. Secondly, even when successful, the large nonprofessional group may not have the financial resources to hire a large administrative staff, and, besides, amateurs may be interested in learning all facets of the craft, including day-to-day administrative tasks, even when they work in a large group. And finally, professional performers are undoubtedly more specialized than amateurs, which creates greater co-ordination problems the larger the group.[54]

To summarize, music groups of all kinds tend to be less bureaucratic than dance and theater companies, but this tendency is more pronounced the larger the music group. While musicians in very large symphony orchestras, according to Couch and others,[55] feel oppressed by their conditions, the source of that oppression cannot be explained by excessive bureaucratization, but rather must be understood in terms of other conditions in the large orchestra, such as the tendency to rely on a conventional repertory rather than to experiment with contemporary music, high demands for consistency, long seasons and tours that reduce the opportunities of playing in smaller groups and of teaching, low levels of mobility, or relatively conservative audiences. And, large companies that have nonprofessional status also tend to have relatively small bureaucracies, so that performers who themselves are paid little or nothing are obliged to handle the administrative work themselves.[56]

Organizational environments

Dependent as the arts organization is on its urban environment and on funding agencies, it is plausible, as I have already suggested, that the more affluent the environment the more bureaucratized is the arts organization. As already discussed, it is reasonable to suppose that organizational dependency on a complex environment fosters bureaucratic growth. Counterintuitive is Heydebrand's notion that complex environments tend to promote de-bureaucratization instead. The basic argument is that organizations become transformed through co-operation and absorption into the larger system, reducing the need for internal bureaucracy.

The arts, as we know, are becoming increasingly important in their urban settings as they are good for business and they enhance the image of the city. The case is made that arts organizations are now part of the primary sector of any urban economy; that is, they generate tourism and industry rather than siphon off resources.[57] Moreover, the scale is beginning to tip from the dependency of art activities in the direction of exploitation of art and culture for the purpose of tax benefits and corporate promotion. Corporate firms sometimes hire arts consultants who in turn provide the conduit of support for the cultural institution, reducing the need of the cultural institution to engage in sophisticated marketing practices and creating informal liaisons between an organization's donor and recipient. Large urban governments have art councils that carry out promotional campaigns for cultural establishments and provide support in other ways.

There are two measures of urban government affluence: revenues per capita,[58] and expenditures per capita.[59] The variation in urban cultural endowments is captured by the following factors: the total number of

Table 5.2. *Coefficients for urban context variables for six equations*[a]

	Administrative ratio		
	B	b (se)	$\hat{R}^2$
Expenditures per capita	−.20	−.199(.059)**	.36
Revenues per capita	−.22	−4.82(1.31)**	.36
No. of performing arts groups	−.16	−.010(.003)**	.35
NEA and foundation funds	−.20	−.383(.115)**	.36
No. of performing artists	−.13	−.247(.103)*	.34
Urban size (logged)	−.07	−.017(.013)	.34

[a] Each equation includes the variables listed in table 5.1, column 2.
*p < .05
**p < .01
 N = 324

performing arts groups,[60] the total number of performers,[61] and an estimate of overall funding for the SMSA's cultural institutions provided by the National Endowment for the Arts and by foundations.[62] Not only do these factors define the cultural wealth of a city, they also token a competitive environment in which a given organization must develop complex strategies for success and survival. Urban size is also employed as an indicator of the potential demand for the performing arts.[63]

Six separate analyses were carried out, each including all of the factors reported in table 5.1 and one of the indicators of the munificence of the urban or cultural environment. (In each regression a single context variable was stepped in after all the organizational variables were entered.) Since the basic results for the organizational variables are little altered, table 5.2 presents simply the independent influences (the coefficients from each of the six regressions) of each of the environmental conditions on the relative size of the bureaucracy of the performing arts organization.[64]

In general, the more abundant and, therefore, the more complex the environment is for the performing arts organization, the fewer administrators it has relative to its size. Thus, environmental complexity (with the exception of size, which is not significant, though its coefficient is also negative) fosters bureaucratic contraction. This means that arts organizations in complex and prosperous urban environments have relatively more artists and volunteers and relatively fewer administrators compared with those in other cities.

Although environmental conditions generally do not alter the effects of organizational characteristics on the administrative ratio (that is, the coefficients in table 5.1), there is one interesting exception. Disregarding features of the environment, large professional groups require a relatively large bureaucratic component and large nonprofessional groups require a relatively small one. However, when any indicator of environmental complexity or affluence is taken into account large professional groups no longer have a relatively large administration.[65] That the most established and largest performing arts organizations – which are very likely to be highly bureaucratized under normal circumstances – are no different from other performing arts organizations given a complex environment, offers additional support for the thesis of debureaucratization. That is, when a successful, large, and professional arts institution is embedded in a complex environment it tends to lose its distinctively bureaucratic character, and to acquire a structure that is similar to that of a smaller and less well established arts organization. Thus, in another way complex urban environments tend to obliterate distinctions among arts organizations.

Discussion

What promotes bureaucracy in nonprofit performing arts organizations? The answer to this question is similar in some, but not all, respects to conclusions drawn about other kinds of organizations. Three of the most important factors that contribute to a relatively large administrative staff are the age of the company, large financial resources, and small size. These findings are consistent with research on organizations of many different kinds. However, there are some important ways in which cultural organizations are different from most work organizations which, in turn, affect their structural configurations.

According to the most rigorous definition of professionals, which emphasizes long formal training and codified knowledge, artists are not professionals. Yet, according to the broader definition that emphasizes engagement in work that requires great commitment, a strong occupational identity, and the mastery of a set of techniques, then most people who devote much time to the arts, whether paid or not, have many of the attributes of professional workers. When we draw the line between companies that hire people under union contracts and those that depend on amateurs or freelancers, this seems to capture quite nicely the distinction that is traditionally made between the professional and the nonprofessional organization. It is quite reasonable to discover that large professional organizations have relatively many administrators, while in contrast, large, nonprofessional ones have relatively few. This is the case regardless of other internal conditions – such as the size of the budget – and largely reflects the greater demand for co-ordination that is entailed in any highly professionalized work setting. Similar findings are reported for other types of organizations that include this distinction. However, as will later again be mentioned, such differences between professional and nonprofessional arts groups are contingent on the urban context.

The type of performing art that the organization sponsors – music, dance, or theater – has considerable bearing on the extent to which performers need to be directed and their work co-ordinated. The larger the number of artistic roles, and, therefore, the less the extent to which there is a shared artistic culture, the greater the need for administrative co-ordination. This explains why dance and theater groups have relatively more administrators than do music groups. The results also indicate that the larger the music group, the less bureaucratic it is. Orchestras, to be specific, do not require many more administrators than does a chamber ensemble (which suggests that orchestra members – who seem to complain most about rules and formalization – are not all so badly off!) Of general interest, however, to students of organizations is the result that the character of work plays a major role in shaping the organizational structure, in making it more or less worker intensive, and in promoting particular types of co-ordination over others.

It is reasonable to expect that the more complex and prosperous the environment, the more bureaucratically complex the organization, especially when it is extremely dependent on external support. Transaction problems are acute in a complex environment; there is more competition among arts organizations when there is a glut of organizations and artists; members of the art-going public tend to be choosy when there are many cultural opportunities.

On the contrary, it is found that the better endowed the cultural environment and the more affluent the metropolitan place, the less bureaucratic are the performing arts organizations. What such environmental complexities and affluence apparently indicate is that culture has "arrived;" this reduces the pressure on the art organization to woo the city government for support, the people for legitimacy, and the government for funds. Having established a significant presence in a metropolitan place, cultural institutions are in a position to maintain casual working relations with government agencies, which in turn reduces the efforts they need to devote to formalized negotiations for funds and space, and to public relations activities.

Well-endowed environments also eradicate the organizational differences between professional and nonprofessional organizations. Without taking

Table 5.3. *Correlations among organizational variables and between organizational variables and context variables*[a]

	1	2	3	4	5	6	7
1 Complex funding sources							
2 Music	.08						
3 Length of season	.10	−.16					
4 Professional	.27	−.06	.00				
5 Age of company[a]	.16	.25	−.06	−.05			
6 Size (logged)	.28	.07	−.05	.10	.24		
7 Budget (logged)	.45	−.12	−.02	.32	.26	.39	
8 Expenditure per capita	.14	−.38	.24	.34	−.19	−.11	.09
9 Revenues per capita	.15	−.42	.27	.32	−.22	−.06	.08
10 No. of performing arts groups	.15	−.29	.21	.30	−.17	−.18	.04
11 NEA and foundations funds	.16	−.36	.22	.35	−.20	−.15	.08
12 No. of performing artists	.13	−.36	.20	.35	−.22	−.14	.04
13 Urban size (logged)	.07	−.27	.21	.28	−.20	−.14	.00
x̄	1.88	.45	9.09	.60	1951	3.62	3.42
s.d.	1.02	.50	2.63	.49	24	1.46	1.26

[a] Actual variable is year in which founded; signs in table reversed.

urban environment into account, large nonprofessional organizations have relatively small bureaucracies whereas professional organizations have large ones. When any indicator of urban affluence or cultural abundance is also considered this is no longer the case. Professional and nonprofessional groups of all sizes are structured more or less the same in complex and prosperous environments, suggesting that under such conditions there is considerable similarity between professionals and nonprofessionals, at least with respect to their daily work experiences.

Whether this signals deprofessionalization or the aggregation of distinctive niches occupied by nonprofessionals cannot be answered with these data, but the results do suggest that the consequences for institutional structure of whether performers are professional or not is less important when the environment is complex than when it is not. Bureaucratic structures not only decompose under conditions of environmental complexity, they also tend to become increasingly similar to one another.

Notes

1 Quoted from W. Braghirolli, *Giornale di erudizione artistica* II (1873) in Edgar Wind, *Art and Anarchy* (New York: Vintage, 1969), p. 91.
2 Marion Bauer and Ethel R. Peyser, *Music Through the Ages* (New York: G. P. Putnam's Sons, 1932), p. 77.
3 For example, Abbot Suger dictated in minute detail the redesigning and rebuilding of the abbey of St. Denis. This is a particularly celebrated (but not unique) instance of the important role clergy played in the design of church buildings because it was among the first Gothic buildings with construction of the west facade begun in 1137. See Otto von Simpson, *The Gothic Cathedral* (New York: Harper Torchback, 1964).
4 See John U. Nef, *Western Civilization Since the Renaissance* (New York: Harper Torchbooks, 1963 [1950]), pp. 250–272.
5 Elizabeth Gilmore Holt, ed., *The Triumph of Art for the Public* (Garden City NY: Anchor Books, 1979); Henry Vyverberg, *The Living Tradition* (New York: Harcourt Brace Jovanovich, 1978); Carl J. Friedrich, *The Age of the Baroque, 1610–1660* (New York: Harper Torchbooks, 1962 [1952]).
6 Nikolaus Pevsner, *Academies of Art* (Cambridge: Cambridge University Press, 1940, pp. 132–139).
7 Quoted in Deena Rosenberg and Bernard Rosenberg, *The Music Makers* (New York: Columbia University Press, 1979), pp. 223–224.
8 Quoted in Toby Cole and Helen Krich Chinoy, *Directors on Directing* (Indianapolis: Bobbs-Merrill, 1976), p. 98.
9 Judith Lynne Hanna, *The Performer–Audience Connection* (Austin: University of Texas Press, 1983), p. 144.
10 *The Triumph of Art for the Public* is the title of one of Holt's extraordinary collections of original documents, including the letters and essays of critics, artists, and collectors, that together provide a detailed historical account of the changing relations between artists and the public.
11 Herbert Marcuse, "Remarks on a Redefinition of Culture," pp. 218–235 in Gerald Holton, ed., *Science and Culture* (Boston: Beacon Press, 1967), p. 221.
12 See Donald Drew Egbert, *Socialism and American Art* (Princeton: Princeton University Press, 1967), pp. 49, 43; Theodor W. Adorno, *Philosophy of Modern Music*, trans. Anna G. Mitchell and Wesley V. Blomster (New York: Continuum, 1985); Georg Lukács, *Essays on Realism*, ed. Rodney Livingstone, trans. David Fernbach (Cambridge MA: MIT Press, 1981).
13 Janet Wolff, *Aesthetics and the Sociology of Art* (London: George Allen and Unwin, 1983).
14 Egbert, *Socialism and American Art*, pp. 128, 149.
15 J. Michael Montias finds that earned income in the early 1970s for a sample of nonprofit performing arts organizations was higher in the U.S. than in European countries. For instance, the proportion of income that is earned in the U.S. is 54 per cent compared with approximately 32 per cent for French organizations and about

20 per cent for Austrian, German and Dutch performing arts organizations. (Quoted in Paul DiMaggio, "The Nonprofit Instrument and the Influence of the Marketplace," pp. 57–99 in W. McNeil Lowry, ed., *The Arts and Public Policy in the United States* [Englewood Cliffs NJ: Prentice-Hall, 1984], p. 58.)

16 Harry Braverman, *Labor and Monopoly Capital* (New York: Monthly Review Press, 1974), p. 279.

17 *The Collected Writings of John Maynard Keynes*, Vol. 9, *Essays in Persuasion* (London: Macmillan, 1972), p. 291.

18 James Heilbrun, "Keynes and the Economics of the Arts," *Journal of Cultural Economics* 8 (December 1984), 37–50.

19 For example, William J. Baumol and William G. Bowen, *Performing Arts – The Economic Dilemma* (New York: The Twentieth Century Fund, 1966); Thomas Gale Moore, *The Economics of the American Theater* (Durham NC: Duke University Press, 1968); Dick Netzer, *The Subsidized Muse* (Cambridge: Cambridge University Press, 1978).

20 Paul DiMaggio, "The Nonprofit Instrument and the Influence of the Marketplace," pp. 54, 78.

21 DiMaggio, "State Expansion and Organizational Fields," pp. 147–162 in Richard H. Hall and Robert E. Quinn, eds., *Organizational Theory and Public Policy* (Beverly Hills CA: Sage, 1983). Also see Paul DiMaggio and Walter W. Powell, "The Iron Cage Revisited," *American Sociological Review* 48 (1983), 147–160.

22 Organizations that are dependent on complex or prosperous environments are found to be administratively more complex than organizations that are not. See, for example, Derek Pugh, David Hickson, and Robert Hinings, "The Context of Organizational Structures," *Administrative Science Quarterly* 14 (1969), 91–114; Michael A. DuBick, "The Organizational Structure of Newspapers in Relation to the Metropolitan Environments," *Administrative Science Quarterly* 23 (1978), 418–433; Howard E. Aldrich, *Organizations and Environments* (Englewood Cliffs NJ: Prentice-Hall, 1979), pp. 257–261; Pamela S. Tolbert, "Resource Dependence and Institutional Environments," *Administrative Science Quarterly* 30 (1985), 1–13. This assumption is restated as it applies directly to arts organizations: Joan Jeffri, *The Emerging Arts* (New York: Praeger, 1980).

23 Vera L. Zolberg, "American Art Museums," *Social Forces* 63 (1984), 377–392.

24 Wolf V. Heydebrand, "Technocratic Corporatism," pp. 93–114 in Richard H. Hall and Robert E. Quinn, eds., *Organizational Theory and Public Policy* (Beverly Hills, CA: Sage, 1983).

25 S. Eisenstadt, "Bureaucracy, Bureaucratization and Debureaucratization," *Administrative Science Quarterly* 4 (1959), 302–320.

26 DiMaggio, "State Expansion and Organizational Fields," 1983. See note 21.

27 See note 22. For a review, see Hans Pennings, "The Relevance of the Structural-Contingency Model for Organizational Effectiveness," *Administrative Science Quarterly* (1975), 393–410.

28 This was a main worry for Braverman and Keynes, as already noted, and for others as well. See especially Raymond Williams, *The Long Revolution* (New York: Columbia University Press, 1961), p. 339; Theodor Adorno, "Culture and

Administration," *Telos* 37 (1978), 97–111; Herbert Marcuse, *One Dimensional Man* (London: Abacus, 1964), p. 24.

29 H. H. Gerth and C. Wright Mills, trans., and eds., *From Max Weber* (New York: Oxford University Press, 1946), pp. 196–204; Max Weber, *The Theory of Social and Economic Organizations*, ed. A. M. Henderson and Talcott Parsons (Glencoe, IL: Free Press, 1947), pp. 329–336.

30 Shawn, *The Shape of Content*, p. 105.

31 Stephen B. Couch, "The Orchestra as Factory," in Arnold W. Foster and Judith R. Blau, eds., *Art and Society* (Albany: State University of New York Press, 1989).

32 See Edward Arian, *Bach, Beethoven and Bureaucracy* (University AL: University of Alabama Press, 1971); Judith Adler, *Artists in Offices* (New Brunswick NJ: Transaction, 1979); Vera L. Zolberg, "Changing Patterns of Patronage in the Arts," pp. 251–268 in Jack B. Kamerman and Rosanne Martorella, eds., *Performers and Performances* (South Hadley MA: Bergin and Garvey, 1983); Robert Faulkner, "Orchestra Interaction," *Sociological Quarterly* 14 (1973); 147–157; Paul DiMaggio and Kristin Stenberg, "Conformity and Diversity in the American Resident Stage," pp. 116–139 in Judith Balfe and Margaret Wyszomirski, eds., *Art, Ideology and Politics* (New York: Praeger, 1985); Rosanne Martorella, *The Sociology of the Opera* (South Hadley MA: J. F. Bergin, 1982); Steven C. Dubin, *Bureaucratizing the Muse* (Chicago: University of Chicago Press, 1987).

33 Rosenberg and Rosenberg, *The Music Makers*, pp. 39–60; 263–276.

34 Robert W. Corrigan, "Where the People Are," pp. 130–150 in James E. Miller Jr. and Paul D. Herring, eds., *The Arts and the Public* (Chicago: University of Chicago Press, 1967).

35 Robert R. Faulkner, *Music on Demand* (New Brunswick NJ: Transaction, 1983).

36 Quoted in John Ryan and Richard A. Peterson, "The Product Image," pp. 11–32 in James S. Ettema and D. Charles Whitney, eds., *Individuals in Mass Media Organizations* (Beverly Hills, CA: Sage, 1982), p. 28.

37 This is the least problematical definition of professional; for a concise summary see Eliot Freidson, *Professional Powers* (Chicago: University of Chicago Press, 1986).

38 Everett C. Hughes, "Professions," *Daedalus* 92 (1963), 655–668; see especially pp. 655, 656.

39 Professional monopoly over realms of work is typically guaranteed through specialization; see Magali Sarfatti Larson, *The Rise of Professionalism* (Berkeley CA: University of California Press, 1977).

40 For architects, at least, there is evidence that the greater the scope of their interests and expertise, the more influential they are in their firms and the happier they are with their jobs. See Judith R. Blau, *Architects and Firms* (Cambridge, MA: MIT Press, 1984), pp. 54–56.

41 For how the nature of the orientation of cultural workers and the art form influence organizational structure see Vera L. Zolberg, "Displayed Art and Performed Music," *The Sociological Quarterly* 21 (1980), 219–231; Dorothy A. Mariner, "Ideology and Rhetoric," *Pacific Sociological Review* 14 (1971), 197–214; Lewis Jacobs, *The Rise of the American Film* (New York: Teachers

College Press, 1968); Judith R. Blau and William McKinley, "Ideas, Complexity, and Innovation," *Administrative Science Quarterly* 24 (1979), 200–219.

42 Beatrice Handel, ed., 3rd edition (New York: Wiley, 1975). Facilities, presenting groups, buildings, and sponsors that are listed in the *Directory* are not included in this analysis of organized groups and companies.

43 Discussions with the editor and examination of these data in conjunction with the other data collected on the arts indicate that the *Directory* is exceptionally comprehensive. However, the relatively large number of groups for which information is missing poses a problem of representativeness. Fortunately, cases for which there are missing data on staffing do include information on the type of performing art they support, which makes it possible to evaluate the most likely source of bias. The proportion of cases in the usable sample that are music organizations is very close to the proportion of all performing arts organizations listed that are music organizations, specifically 45 per cent compared with 40 per cent for the entire directory.

44 The dependent variable is thus the fraction of paid administrative staff to the entire staff, including volunteers, unpaid staff, paid artists, and paid administrative staff. An alternative measure is the ratio of paid staff to the sum of paid staff and paid artists. The former offers the advantage that the measure exhibits greater variance; moreover, it captures the notion that managerial authority in arts organizations depends not only on the number of artists that are on the payroll of the performing arts organization but also on the larger numbers of dedicated workers, namely volunteers who carry out artistic and administrative work. All analyses in this chapter were replicated using the ratio of paid staff to total paid personnel and the results are reported in notes.

45 For a summary see Jeffrey Pfeffer, *Power in Organizations* (Marshfield MA: Pittman, 1981), pp. 102–103.

46 Peter M. Blau, "Interdependence and Hierarchy in Organizations," *Social Science Research* 1 (1972), 1–24. Also see E. Haas, R. H. Hall and N. J. Johnson, "The Size of the Supportive Component in Organizations," *Social Forces* 42 (1963), 9–17. W. Richard Scott, however, points out that this relationship between size and the administrative component may be different for organizations of different kinds. See "Organization Structure," *Annual Review of Sociology* 1 (1975), 1–20.

47 For a summary see William H. Starbuck, "Organizational Growth and Development," pp. 451–533 in James G. March, ed., *Handbook of Organizations* (Chicago: Rand McNally, 1965).

48 Muriel G. Cantor, "Women Who Write Fiction," in Roana Rush and Donna Allen, eds., *Communication at the Crossroads* (Norwood NJ: Ablex, 1987).

49 Robert A. Stebbins, *Amateurs* (Beverly Hills, CA: Sage, 1979).

50 See Larson, *The Rise of Professionalism*, pp. 190–199; Freidson, *Professional Powers*, pp. 158–166; Jerald Hage and Michael Aiken, "Relationship of Centralization to Other Structural Properties," *Administrative Science Quarterly* 12 (1967), 72–91.

51 Richard H. Hall, *Organizations*, 3rd ed. (Englewood Cliffs NJ: Prentice-Hall, 1982), p. 142.

52 Music includes the following types of groups: chamber, symphonic, choral, other vocal, and opera. Non-music mainly includes dance and theater companies and some others, such as pantomime troupes. Analyses of variance indicate that a finer subdivision than music versus other is not warranted.

53 When the simple correlation is decomposed, the direct effect is −.53, as reported in table 5.1, and an estimate of the indirect effect via budget is .13.

54 The three-way interaction term that includes professional status, music versus other, and size is not significant.

55 Couch, *The Orchestra as Factory*; Arian, *Bach, Beethoven and Bureaucracy*; Kate H. Mueller, *Twenty-seven Major Symphony Orchestras* (Bloomington: Indiana University Press, 1973).

56 When the ratio of paid administrators to total paid staff is employed as the dependent variable, the results are virtually identical to those presented in tables 5.1 and 5.2. For the full results that parallel the equation presented in table 5.1, panel B, the regression coefficients (betas) are: annual budget (logged), .21; complexity of funding sources, −.02; length of season (months), .02; age of company, .18; professional status, −.27; log of size (total number of paid staff), −.64; music company (1) versus other (0), .20. The value of the coefficient for the product term involving music company times log of total number of paid staff is −.44 and that for the product term involving professional status times log of total number of paid staff is .33. Other regressions were carried out in which the log of the different staff components was substituted for the size measure. For example, when the log of total volunteers, the log of unpaid staff, and the log of art staff are regressed on the ratio of administrators to paid staff, the most pronounced negative effect is the log of paid artists (−.68). The log of unpaid artists and the log of volunteer staff have trivial coefficients (.01 and −.10, respectively), indicating that the relative size of the managerial component is most responsive to the total size of the paid, professional staff.

57 "Increasingly," writes Lindsey Cruson in the *New York Times* (March 27, 1986) "cities are frankly trying to cash in on a fact of life that New York has always known: the arts can also be an important economic prop." The economic value of the arts in local and national economics are discussed in William S. Hendon, Nancy K. Grant, and Douglas V. Shaw, *The Economics of Cultural Industries*, Vol. I, *Proceedings of the Third International Conference on Cultural Economics and Planning* (Akron OH: University of Akron, 1984), and Research Division, National Endowment for the Arts, *The Arts in the GNP* (Washington DC: NEA, 1982).

58 U.S. Bureau of the Census, *Census of Governments*, Vol. 4, *Compendium of Government Finances* (Washington, DC: GPO, 1967).

59 *Compendium of Government Finances*.

60 Coded from Handel, *National Directory of Performing Arts and Civic Centres*. Includes all performing groups (including those with missing information on staffing) but excludes buildings, facilities, and sponsors.

61 Includes dancers, musicians, and actors (1970 Public Use Sample).

62 Sum of NEA funding for urban performing arts for 1971 and 1972 (including funds

for theater, orchestra, opera, jazz, music, dance, and opera) and total urban foundation grants for 1970 and 1971. A breakdown of foundation grants by type of organization was not done since the information in the directory provided is not sufficiently detailed. Intervening years between 1972 and 1976 were not coded from NEA reports but the correlations for the time periods for which data are coded indicate that funding at the metropolitan level is extremely stable. For example, the correlations for 1971–72 and 1976–77 levels for theater, dance, and music funding are respectively .98, .98, and .91.

63 Log of metropolitan size (1970 Public Use Sample).

64 The results for all variables reported in table 5.1 are practically identical in the regressions that include one context variable. There is one exception: the beta for the product term involving professional status and log of size becomes insignificant when any context variable is in the equation (the beta ranges from .15 to .25, but is never significant at the .05 level). These regressions are also replicated using the ratio of paid administrators to total paid staff; the results are virtually identical to those reported in table 5.1. There is always some concern about heteroskedasticity in such an analysis due to the aggregation of the context variable. The standardized residuals of the dependent variable were examined for correlated errors; the conclusion is that the assumptions of least squares are not being violated in this analysis.

65 While most coefficients are stable in the context analysis, the one for the interaction term (size × professional status) usually becomes insignificant. It is reduced from .39 (table 5.2) to values ranging from .18 (with revenues per capita) to .28 (with funds in the equation). The only exception is in the equation with the log of urban size. Because population size is not significantly related to the administrative component, the coefficient for the interaction term is reduced only somewhat (from .39 to .30) but remains significant at the .05 level.

6 Increasing returns on diminishing artists*

Keeping the arts going in the twentieth century is a desperate enterprise
Harold Rosenberg (1957)

At what price to artists is organizational rationality? And, we can also ask, to what extent does any cost-conscious arts organization depend on full-time, professional artists and to what extent does it rely on amateurs and volunteers? The problem posed in this chapter deals with the work-force composition of performing arts organizations of different kinds and of different sizes. The issue arises from an understanding that in the contemporary performing arts there are many fundamental contradictions. One of them is between the imperatives for cost efficiencies and the incalculable values of creativity and quality, and another is between the commitment of artists to critical standards and the reality that members of the audience are really not all that fussy. While unraveling such Gordian knots is not the intention here, an acknowledgement of the complexities of cultural production provides the context for examining the consequences of organizational imperatives for the employment opportunities of trained performers.

These contradictions emerged with the breakdown of the patronage system, and the increasing dependence on disorganized congeries of publics, audiences, and financial contributors. At the same time, the elaboration of romantic ideals entailed the condemnation of public taste and the rejection of bourgeois life styles. To be sure, performing artists broke with patrons and were entangled in the chaos of the marketplace earlier than painters. *Commedia dell'arte* and opera entered the public realm in the sixteenth century; ballet moved out of courtly ballrooms into theaters at the end of the seventeenth century. And drama, which always had close connections with the church and secular festivals, was performed by professional (full-time) acting troupes as early as the sixteenth century in England and Spain. In 1781 Mozart broke off ties with Hieronymus, Archbishop of Salzburg, to set off on a public tour. His

* Written in collaboration with Joseph E. Schwartz.

99

main complaint, according to some accounts, is that his patron insisted that he eat with the servants.[1] Yet as late as 1819 Schubert occupied a post with Count Esterhazy, and Brahms' sinecure in the court of Lippe Detmold lasted until 1857.[2] Even if courtly conditions did improve for musicians between Mozart's time and 1857, the power of courts and princes eventually declined, and performers were dumped on to the open market.

Still, there is hardly a linear historical development for either the performing or the nonperforming arts. In their account of the artist's relation to society, Ernst Kris and Otto Kurz observe:

In each phase of this historical development new social types appear alongside the old, without ever displacing them. Diversity . . . appears among the artists of the nineteenth century whose world embraced the feted darling of his prince and country just as much as the clouch-hatted Bohemian living out his conception of genius on the social periphery, in Schwabing, Montmartre, or Greenwich Village.[3]

Clearly, there is no clear division between dependence on patrons and dependence on the public, relative uniformity in training and social background from great diversity. The declining consensus of what the artistic role ought to be has complex ramifications for the performing artist who not only must deal with an audience and critics but who also must co-operate with other performers.

Dilemmas posed by the contemporary situation for performing artists are complex and numerous: the dangers of reverting to mere entertainment in efforts to be successful;[4] the tensions between a community of performers and organizational imperatives of rationalization;[5] increasing specialization within the performing arts;[6] and the need to emphasize company stability over other objectives (such as experimentation) to attract outside funding.[7] What is at the forefront of our concerns, however, is the great diversity among artists with respect to their training and qualifications, which exists in large part because of the absence of a credentialing system. From the perspective of the arts institutions, this makes it impossible to control the terms and conditions of entrance by performers,[8] but it also means variation in the costs of performers' wages. From the trained performer's perspective this means that competition for openings is not governed by considerations of experience and formal qualifications. This constitutes a main difference between professionalism in other occupations and professionalism in the arts. It also constitutes a main difference between profit-making organizations that rely heavily on qualifications when they hire people to carry out work and nonprofit organizations that will ignore qualifications to obtain donated time of committed workers.

Having enthusiastic amateur colleagues may not be an unmixed blessing for professional artists. While many students of culture have emphasized the perils of dependency by artists on bureaucratic organizations, patrons, and conservative audiences, a direct threat to their employment possibilities, as it turns out, is posed by the seemingly benign and often keenly enthusiastic amateur artist.

Organizational efficiencies

"Any process of production," Kenneth E. Boulding writes, "is much like a recipe in a cookbook: take this and that and the other thing, cook in a slow oven for five hours, pour off the juice, and serve in ramekins."[9] Boulding adds that the process of cooking has qualitative elements, such as the grade of the beef, whether butter or margarine is used, and whether fresh or dried herbs are available. However, the most manageable and reliable elements involved in the process are quantitative in nature, such as the number of pounds of beef for the number of people to be served, the number of teaspoons of herbs, the ratio of butter to flour.

In this way, Boulding introduces the topic of production and cost functions in his classic economics textbook.[10] Production and cost functions are but members of a larger family of functions that deal with economic efficiencies, such as the net revenue per unit of output, the number of workers per acre of land, the relation between demand and price. Boulding anticipates in his discussions the work of sociologists who deal with efficiencies achieved through varying organizational arrangements. For example, Peter Blau reports that as organizational scale increases, the proportionate numbers of administrators decline, realizing savings in overheads.[11]

Efficiencies are also achieved in organizations when there are cost-free resources. This is not all that common, however, because for most kinds of organizations resources cost something, either as overhead – rent, utilities – or as input – wages, raw materials, technology. The nonprofit organization is, however, the exception, as advocacy groups, churches, schools, universities, and arts organizations all rely on donations of various kinds.[12] We shall examine one such cost-free resource, namely donated labor, and we will also discover that they entail some costs; as is often said, there are no free lunches. Before turning to the economies and diseconomies of gratuitous labor in performing arts organizations, it is useful to review the more general issues dealing with their financial situations.

The cost disease

In their classic study published in 1966, *Performing Arts: The Economic Dilemma*, William J. Baumol and William G. Bowen described the "cost disease" that afflicts the American performing arts.[13] More than most sectors of the economy, the performing arts are highly labor intensive, and typically do not achieve productivity increases as great as those in less labor-intensive sectors. Productivity increases in the arts are limited by the size of the hall and the number of live performances that can be given. And with an upper limit on productivity, wage increases can only be paid by raising the price of tickets and subscriptions, which Baumol and Bowen concluded would be difficult owing to inelasticities of demand.

Even more pessimistic accounts followed the Baumol and Bowen study. Moore, for example, reported in 1968 that not only were wages increasing at a faster rate than productivity, but so were other variable costs, including those for production and advertising.[14] Pooling data for 1960 to 1975 to supplement those used by Baumol and Bowen for 1929 to 1963, Netzer concludes that for each percentage increase in disposable personal income, consumer expenditures for the live performing arts rose only by .81 per cent, suggesting that demand is somewhat elastic but does not rise enough to compensate for the increases in production costs and wages.[15] Drawing more broadly on people's preferences given their knowledge of ticket prices, Withers reports that consumers will find low cost substitutes for theater, opera, symphonies, and dance, and he concludes that the price elasticity of demand for the performing arts is relatively small.[16]

On the other hand, people's willingness (or not) to pay more depends on the character (quality, prestige, or size) of the performing arts group. For example, one study reports that for any major orchestra a 10 per cent increase in ticket price generates more than $18,000 in increased revenues whereas for the relatively small metropolitan orchestra, a 10 per cent increase in ticket price will result in revenue declines of about $4000.[17] At the same time, the costs for orchestras of different sizes and of varying quality are not that different,[18] which suggests that the larger and more established a symphony orchestra the less vulnerable it is to Bowen and Baumol's "cost disease."

It is important to keep in mind that there are inherent differences among the types of performing arts that have important economic implications. Some performing arts, notably nonprofit theaters, have been able to maintain relatively stable costs;[19] very expensive musical art forms, such as the opera, must compete with less expensive genres, such as chamber music,[20] some have a tighter cap on productivity than others;[21] and some performing arts, notably dance, have benefited far more than others from increased public interest.[22] There is also some evidence that cost efficiencies are sacrificed by arts organizations engaged in the most innovative work.[23]

Organizational configurations

With the exception of those who study the wages of people who work in performing arts organizations, economists have been little concerned with the internal arrangements of these organizations and the mix of occupational groups. For the most part, economists have focused attention on the wages of artists, not their relative numbers. For example, Shoesmith reports, contrary to Baumol and Bowen's prediction, that the ratio of artistic personnel costs to expenditures for United States orchestras declined slowly from 1937 to 1979.[24] One reason for this decline may be that artists' wages have simply not increased. There is, in fact, some support for this inference. The National Endowment for the Arts concludes that the median earnings of all performing artists combined did not increase at all between 1970 and 1976, remaining at about $3,700 per year (in contrast with professionals for which the median salary increased from $8,800 to $11,300).[25] These figures may be somewhat misleading, however, because they are based on the earnings of all performers, whether they work part-time, full-time, or are unemployed much of the year.

Another reason for this decline in the ratio of artists' costs to total expenditures may be that the relative size of the artistic component in performing arts organizations is declining over time.[26] There are reasons to assume that this is likely. During the 1970s the increased reliance on public funding required an emphasis on long-term planning and aggressive administrative approaches to secure subsidies. In anticipation of the growing diseconomies predicted by Baumol and Bowen, Netzer, and others, performing arts organizations launched programs that would attract cost-free resources, such as volunteer auxiliaries, intern programs, and donated spaces.[27]

Committed workers

For reasons of the sheer pleasure and excitement of being involved in theatrical, musical, and dance worlds, performing arts centers and organizations attract unusually large numbers of committed workers – amateurs, hobbyists, as well as philanthropists. As culture became something of a social movement in the 1970s, there was a heightened level of volunteerism as well.[28]

The economic value of the committed volunteer is clear enough. There are other reasons why volunteers are tolerated and even highly valued in cultural activities. In the absence of standards for credentialing and given the preferences of some talented individuals not to risk professional careers in the performing arts but rather to enter other fields, many amateur performers may be nearly on a par with professionals.

As Stebbins points out, amateurs who are not constrained by tight rehearsal schedules and by conservative public taste may be more attuned to standards of excellence than many professionals. The amateur musician, he writes, "is likely to be able to spot the professional's mistakes, spiritless solos, late entries, and other artistic flaws."[29] Professional artists often start their careers as dedicated amateurs, and while very often professionals see amateurs as immature interlopers, they also consider them to be valued colleagues whether they engage in adjunct roles in the professional company (when union rules permit), or they perform together in nonprofessional settings. On their side, amateurs view marginal participation as maintaining involvement in the art without the economic burdens faced by professionals.[30] Besides amateur artists there is a second category of unpaid staff, namely volunteers, who carry out auxiliary administrative tasks, such as working in the box office, ushering, stuffing envelopes, or assisting in various backstage activities.

Staff ratios

The *National Directory of Performing Arts and Civic Centers*[31] provides information on the numbers of staff in four categories for 306 performing arts groups: paid artists, paid administrators, unpaid artists, and volunteers who presumably have no artistic background. Whereas the concern in chapter 5 was the conditions under which the administrative staff component tends to be relatively small or large, taking into account organizational features as well as those of the urban environment, the interest here centers on the relative sizes of each of these various groups, and most especially of paid performing artists.

Initially, analysis of variance was carried out to detect whether the proportions of personnel in the four categories vary systematically with type of performing arts organization, and music groups. This analysis yielded significant differences for the comparison of all music groups combined and all nonmusic groups combined. As the results in chapter 5 indicate, the inherent qualities of different genres of culture have important implications for the structural arrangements of their organizational settings.[32]

The main difficulty with the information provided in the directory is that there is no indication of the average time commitment for volunteers and unpaid artists (or an indication of full-time equivalents). It is assumed, however, that for different size groups and for performing arts groups of

Table 6.1. *Proportions of workers in performing arts organizations: total, music and nonmusic*

	Total	Music	Nonmusic
Paid staff	.12	.08	.16
Paid artists	.44	.45	.44
Unpaid artists	.20	.23	.18
Volunteers	.23	.23	.22
N	306	138	168

different types, the average time commitment of volunteers and unpaid artists is roughly equivalent.

Table 6.1 reports the proportions of staff in each of the four categories for all groups combined, for music groups, and for nonmusic groups (comprising theater and dance companies). For all groups there are on the average nearly four times the proportion of paid artists to paid administrators and nearly equal proportions of volunteers and unpaid artists.

The major differences between the music groups and the nonmusic groups is the higher proportion of paid staff in nonmusic groups (.16 compared with .08) and the slightly higher proportion of unpaid artists in the music groups (.23 compared with .18). The greater need for administrative co-ordination and supervision in dance and theater companies compared with musical groups has already been discussed in chapter 5. Very briefly, the greater diversity of occupational groups in any dance or theater company compared with any musical group is likely to increase the need for people who perform administrative tasks and co-ordinate the activities of specialists. Why music groups rely more than others on unpaid artists is a bit more difficult to explain. However, given the evidence that there are more amateur musicians than amateur dancers or thespians,[33] it is plausible that music groups are most likely to use the volunteer services of skilled musicians in quasi-professional tasks, such as transposing music, copying scores, or page turning.

Scale economies[34]

As already noted, the ratio of administrators declines with the size of the organization. The concern here is a more precise estimate of the relation of each component of the staff with organizational size and with each other. To the extent that arts organizations attract amateurs and volunteers they

Table 6.2. *Regression of proportions of cultural workers on (1) log size and (2) log size and log size squared (unstandardized coefficients, with standard errors in parentheses)*

	(1)		(2)		
	Log size	Constant	Log size	Log size squared	Constant
All groups N = 306					
Paid staff	−.025(.007)**	.219	−.024(.007)**	−.001(.004)	.218
Paid artists	−.087(.014)**	.773	−.092(.015)**	.007(.008)	.779
Unpaid artists	.053(.013)**	.004	.069(.014)**	−.021(.008)**	−.012
Volunteers	.059(.011)**	.004	.047(.012)**	.015(.007)*	.016
Music N = 138					
Paid staff	−.025(.008)**	.182	−.026(.008)**	.002(.004)	.182
Paid artists	−.086(.022)**	.790	−.086(.023)**	−.001(.012)	.791
Unpaid artists	.040(.022)	.074	.054(.022)**	−.032(.012)**	.086
Volunteers	.071(.018)**	−.047	.057(.018)**	.031(.010)**	−.059
Nonmusic N = 168					
Paid staff	−.021(.010)*	.232	−.015(.012)	−.005(.006)	.223
Paid artists	−.089(.017)**	.767	−.105(.020)**	.016(.011)	.793
Unpaid artists	.060(.016)**	−.039	.074(.018)**	−.013(.010)	−.061
Volunteers	.050(.014)**	.040	.047(.017)**	.003(.009)	.044

**p < .01
*p < .05

achieve savings, and it is expected, as is conventionally the case, that the larger the organization the more successful it is in exploiting such opportunities. To examine this further, each staff component (expressed as a proportion of the total) is regressed on, first, the log of size, and second, both the log of size and size squared.[35] The results (based on 24 regressions) are reported in table 6.2.

For all performing arts organizations combined, the percentage of paid staff and the percentage of paid artists both decline with increases in the size of the organization, and the slope of decline for paid artists is considerably more than that for paid administrators. In the second equation, the squared term is insignificant, indicating that the relation between total size and the relative size of each of these staffing components is approximately linear. On the other hand, the proportion of both volunteers and unpaid artists increases with increasing size. The results of the second equation demonstrate that the rate of

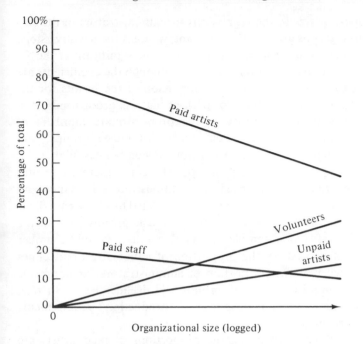

Figure 6.1. Graph of proportions of cultural workers

increase increases with size for volunteers and decreases with size for unpaid artists.

The large organization, in short, reaps overmuch advantage. First, it attracts disproportionately many volunteers and amateur artists (although there are some diminishing returns with size of increases in unpaid artists). Secondly, with declines in the proportions of paid personnel, including both paid artists and paid administrators, the large organization actually saves on labor costs. These increasing economic returns on diminishing numbers (relative to total numbers) of paid personnel – particularly of paid artists – are presented in simple terms in figure 6.1, where the proportions of artists, paid staff, unpaid artists, and volunteers are plotted against the total logged size of the performing arts groups.

Comparison of music and nonmusic groups

Music groups have a smaller proportion of paid staff on the average compared with nonmusic groups (.08 compared with .16), and this proportion declines for music groups more with increasing size than it does for nonmusic groups.

The negative slopes for size in the regressions for administrators in the two equations for music groups are highly significant, whereas the negative slope for size in the first equation for nonmusic groups is just significant at the .05 level and not significant in the second equation. Although the coefficients are not that different from one another, the comparison of the results for the administrative ratio for the two types of performing arts groups indicates, first, that there is greater variability in the proportionate numbers of administrators in nonmusic groups compared with music groups, and secondly that the intercept for the proportionate numbers is higher for nonmusic groups compared with music groups. Therefore, there are greater and more variable organizational needs for administrators in dance and theater companies and these needs are not so much related to scale as are those of music groups. At different levels of scale for music groups (say, in the comparison of a woodwind ensemble, a chamber music group, chamber orchestra, and a full orchestra), the proportion of administrators declines quite consistently, whereas the proportion of administrators for nonmusic groups is relatively high in very small groups and declines less with size, varying, one can assume, more in response to "production" requirements than simply with organizational scale.

In contrast to paid administrators, the proportions of paid artists are virtually the same on the average in both music and nonmusic groups and these proportions both decline the larger the size of the group.[36] Although the average proportion of unpaid artists in the music groups is somewhat higher than that for other groups (.23 compared with .18), the rate at which that proportion increases with increases in size is slightly less for the music group than it is for the nonmusic group, although the differences between the slopes are not statistically significant. When logged size alone is considered in the equation for music groups, the coefficient is positive but it is not quite significant, whereas it is positive and significant for nonmusic groups. When size is decomposed, however, into linear and nonlinear components, the contrast is more complex. For music groups, the estimate of the linear effect of size is positive whereas the multiplicative effect is negative, indicating that the initial differences in size produce an increasing proportion of amateur musicians but further growth produces declines in this proportion.[37] To give a specific example, for a music organization of around five people, it becomes "saturated" with amateurs when there are approximately ten amateurs. What this means, roughly, is that chamber orchestras attract disproportionately more amateur musicians than do the smaller chamber music groups, but there are ceiling effects so that orchestras and large choruses rely less (given their sizes) on amateur musicians than chamber orchestras do.

The likelihood of lay people donating volunteer services to music groups or to nonmusic groups varies somewhat as well. The slope of increase with size of volunteers for music groups is greater than it is for nonmusic groups, although not significantly so (equation 1), and there are significant multiplicative effects of size for music groups but not for nonmusic groups (equation 2).[38]

In very broad terms, it can be concluded that the larger the performing arts group, the smaller the proportion of bona fide artists and of paid professional administrators. The labor of committed workers increases in importance with the size of the organization. Yet the effects are not linear. The proportion of volunteers increases with organizational size at an increasing rate in the case of music groups, whereas that proportion increases at a fairly constant rate in the case of theater and dance companies. On the other hand, the proportion of amateur artists increases directly with size in the case of theater and dance companies, while that proportion increases to approach a saturation point in the case of music companies and then declines with further increases in size.

In strict economic terms, nothing can be precisely concluded about the savings achieved in salaries through substitution effects owing to our lack of knowledge about the number of hours volunteers and unpaid artists contribute to a performing arts organization. For the same reason we do not know if there are actual administrative or other overhead costs incurred when the ranks of volunteers increase. However, these two issues can be addressed in organizational terms. A useful indicator of both substitution effects and overhead costs is derived from a generalized model for estimating how segregated or integrated different types of cultural workers are in an organization. Two proportions are under consideration:

$$\frac{x\text{'s}}{(\text{unlogged})\ \text{size} - \#\ y\text{'s}} \quad \text{and} \quad \frac{\#\ y\text{'s}}{(\text{unlogged})\ \text{size} - \#\bar{x}\text{'s}}$$

where $x =$ one type of cultural worker, and
$y =$ another type of cultural worker

When the correlation between these two proportions is positive there are nonsubstitutabilities between the x's and the y's. That is, they are complementary. If the x's and the y's in question are administrators and volunteers, it is suspected that it is because volunteers entail costs of supervision, and thereby increase the need for administrators. When the correlation between these two proportions is negative, there are substitutabilities between the x's and the y's, and if the x's and the y's in question are artists and amateur artists, it is suspected that artists are in direct competition with amateurs.

For a base line comparison, the correlation involving paid artists and paid administrators is high and positive (r = .88), indicating both the high administrative costs entailed in co-ordinating artists and the obvious non-substitutability of administrators and artists. Volunteers who carry out auxiliary administrative tasks could, on the one hand, increase the needs for administrative co-ordination and overhead, or, on the other hand, take on some of the work of paid administrators and thereby reduce administrative costs. The correlation between the appropriate ratios is a mere − .06, indicating that volunteers neither "bump" paid staff nor do they add to overhead costs. In contrast, the correlation between the appropriate ratios involving amateur artists and paid artists is significantly negative (− .39). The substitution effect that can be inferred from this relation indicates that paid artists are more vulnerable to being replaced by amateurs than staff are by volunteers, and, as the slopes in figure 6.1 show, these substitution effects are greater the larger the size of the organization.

Thus, artists decline in relative numbers with increasing size of any performing arts organization, and, paradoxically, a reason for this decline is the replacement of artists by amateurs. This conclusion has to be qualified, of course, by the important consideration that the values of actual trade-offs in terms of individuals' time and quality of productions are not known. Nevertheless, these results do suggest that dedicated amateurs may well reduce costs, and they do so by replacing paid artists.

Summary

Dedicated workers are a hidden asset for performing arts groups. Volunteers and unpaid artists combined are roughly equal in numbers to all paid artists in the average group. Their proportion increases with the size of the organization, becoming greater than that of either paid staff or paid artists, indicating their greater importance in very large, established groups than in others.

Paradoxically, while the conventional view is that the large groups are the most professional, these results suggest that large groups benefit far more from amateur contributions than do the small ones. And while amateurism and volunteerism are conventionally considered the core of popular support for the arts at the grassroots level, they actually constitute the core of popular support for the largest, and presumably most established, arts groups. There is some indication that the effects of such popular support are to create substitution economies that involve artists, not administrators.

The larger the group, the less it depends on professionals and the more it depends on the donated time of volunteer lay people and amateur artists. One could conclude that one source of fragility of the smallest companies relates to their being unattractive to committed workers, who prefer, apparently, to work for large companies; a second source is the high costs that result from having to pay salaries to artists and administrators. On the other hand, one could also conclude that a source of strength of the smallest companies is their reliance on the professional artist, whose interest in experimental and avant-garde works is especially great.

Notes

1 Marion Bauer and Ethel R. Peyser, *Music through the Ages* (New York: G. P. Putnam's Sons, 1932), p. 187.
2 *Music through the Ages*, p. 309.
3 *Legend, Myth, and Magic in the Image of the Artist* (New Haven: Yale University Press, 1979, pp. 6–7).
4 John Pick, "More Means Better? Economics Lessons from Popular Entertainment," pp. 6–13 in William S. Hendon, Douglas V. Shaw, and Nancy K. Grant, eds., *Economics of Cultural Industries*, Vol. 1, *Proceedings of the Third International Conference on Cultural Economics and Planning* (Akron: University of Akron, 1984).
5 Howard S. Becker, *Art Worlds* (Berkeley: University of California Press, 1982), p. 81.
6 See Deena Rosenberg and Bernard Rosenberg, *The Music Makers* (New York: Columbia University Press, 1979), pp. 23–25; Joseph Bensman, "The Phenomenology and Sociology of the Performing Arts," pp. 1–38 in Jack B. Kamerman and Rosanne Martorella, eds, *Performers and Performances* (Hadley, MA: Bergin and Garvey, 1983).
7 Joan Jeffri, *The Emerging Arts* (New York: Praeger, 1980).
8 Eliot Freidson, "Les professions artistiques comme defi à l'analyse sociologique," *Revue Française de Sociologie* 26 (1986), 431–443.
9 Kenneth E. Boulding, *Economic Analysis*, 3rd ed. (New York: Harper and Brothers, 1955), p. 585.
10 Boulding's recent work in cultural analysis must also be recognized. He contrasts economics, "the ordinary business of life" with art, "the extraordinary business of life." See "The Arts Applied to Economics," pp. 1–8 in Virginia Lee Owen and William S. Hendon, eds., *Managerial Economies for the Arts*, Vol. 3, *Proceedings of the Third International Conference on Cultural Economics and Planning* (Akron: University of Akron, 1984), p. 1.
11 "Interdependence and Hierarchy in Organizations," *Social Science Research* 1 (1972), 1–24.
12 See Walter W. Powell, ed., *The Nonprofit Sector* (New Haven: Yale University Press, 1987).
13 (New York: The Twentieth Century Fund, 1966); see also Ford Foundation, *The Finances of the Performing Arts*, Vol. 1 (New York: Ford Foundation, 1974), p. 7.
14 Thomas Gale Moore, *The Economics of the American Theater* (Durham NC: Duke

University, 1968). There is some indication that production costs have declined; see Robert J. Anderson and Sonia P. Maltezou, "The Economic Condition of the Live Professional Theater in America," pp. 63–66 in *Research in the Arts: Proceedings of the Policy Related Studies of the National Endowment for the Arts* (Washington DC: NEA, 1977); Theatre Communication Group, *Theater Facts* (New York: TCG, 1985).

15 Dick Netzer, *The Subsidized Muse. A Twentieth Century Fund Study* (Cambridge: Cambridge University Press, 1978), pp. 28–30.

16 Glenn A. Withers, "Unbalanced Growth and the Demand for Performing Arts: An Econometric Analysis," *Southern Economic Journal* 46 (1980), 735–742.

17 Mark D. Lange and William A. Luksetich, "Demand Elasticities for Symphony Orchestras," *Journal of Cultural Economics* 8 (1984), 29–48.

18 Mark Lange, James Bullard, and William Luksetich, "Cost Functions for Symphony Orchestras," *Journal of Cultural Economics* 9 (1982), 71–85.

19 National Endowment for the Arts, *Conditions and Needs of the American Professional Theater* (Washington DC: NEA, 1981), p. 19.

20 Jeffri, *The Emerging Arts.*

21 Netzer, *The Subsidized Muse.*

22 Hilda Baumol and William J. Baumol, eds., *Inflation and the Performing Arts* (New York: New York University Press, 1984); Patricia A. McFate, ed., *Paying for Culture. The Annals of the American Academy of Political and Social Science*, 471 (1984), special issue.

23 Architecture firms that are oriented to production realize economics of scale and are able to reduce per unit costs as they deal with uniform projects and standardized commissions. In contrast, design oriented firms are not cost efficient and lack routine procedures and the internal organization to realize economies of scale. See Judith R. Blau and William McKinley, "Ideas, Complexity, and Innovation," *Administrative Affairs Quarterly* 24 (1979), 200–219.

24 Eddie Shoesmith, "Long-term Trends in Performing Arts Expenditures," *Journal of Cultural Economics* 8 (1984), 51–72.

25 National Endowment for the Arts, *Artists Compared by Age, Sex, and Earnings in 1970 and 1976* (Washington, DC: NEA, 1980), p. 23.

26 At least one economist, James H. Gapinski, reports some evidence suggesting this may be the case. See his article, "The Production of Culture," *Review of Economics and Statistics* 62 (1980), 578–586.

27 Paul J. DiMaggio, "The Nonprofit Instrument and the Influences of the Marketplace on Policies in the Arts," pp. 57–99 in W. McNeil Lowry, ed., *The Arts and Public Policy in the United States* (Englewood Cliffs NJ: Prentice Hall, 1984); Rosanne Martorella, "Rationality in the Artistic Management of Performing Arts Organizations," pp. 95–108 in Jack B. Kamerman and Rosanne Martorella, eds., *Performers and Performances* (South Hadley MA: Bergin and Avery, 1983); Thomas J. C. Raymond and Stephen A. Greyer, "The Business of Managing the Arts," *Harvard Business Review* 56 (1978), 23–31; Kenneth Goody, "Arts Funding: Growth and Change between 1963 and 1983," *The Annals of the American Academy of Political and Social Science* 471 (1984), 114–157; Samuel Schwarz and Mary G. Peters, "Growth of the Nonprofit Arts and Cultural Organizations in the

Decade of the 1970's," pp. 23–33 in William S. Hendon, Nancy K. Grant and Douglas V. Shaw, eds., *The Economics of Cultural Industries* (Akron OH: University of Akron, 1984).

28 Paul DiMaggio, ed., *Nonprofit Enterprise in the Arts* (New York: Oxford University Press, 1986).

29 Robert A. Stebbins, *Amateurs* (Beverly Hills CA: Sage, 1979).

30 Mary K. Garty, "A Case Study in Cultural Stratification," unpublished paper, 1983.

31 Beatrice Handel, ed., *National Directory of Performing Arts and Civic Centers*, 3rd ed. (New York: Wiley, 1975).

32 Also see Vera L. Zolberg, "Displayed Art and Performed Music," *Sociological Quarterly* 21 (1980), 291–331.

33 National Research Center of the Arts, *Americans and the Arts* (New York: Louis Harris and Associates, October 1984).

34 The analysis reported in this section earlier appeared in J. R. Blau, Laurie Newman, and Joseph E. Schwartz, "Internal Economies of Scale in Performing Arts Organizations," *Journal of Cultural Economics* 10 (1986), 63–76.

35 See Appendix D for the equation for size squared. Each coefficient reported in table 6.2, column 1 is obtained from a single regression equation as are the two corresponding coefficients in column 2. The differences in the unstandardized coefficients for the administrative ratio and the proportion of paid staff in table 5.1 and table 6.2 are due to the fact that the equation in the first table includes other variables besides the proportion of administrators (paid staff).

36 An analysis of covariance that includes two interaction terms of the music/nonmusic dichotomy with log size and with log size squared yields insignificant differences between the two types of organization with respect to the effect of size on the proportion of paid artists.

37 The differences, however, between the coefficients of log size and log size squared for unpaid artists for the two groups are insignificant.

38 This difference, estimated by the coefficient of the product term for log size squared and the dummy variable, is significant at the .02 level.

7 A little more on the hobby horse

Achilles: My pleasure. I can tell you a pair of koans which go together. Only . . . Well, there is one problem. Although both are widely told koans, my master has cautioned me that only one of them is genuine. And what is more, he does not know which one is genuine, and which one is a fraud.

Tortoise: Crazy! Why don't you tell them both to me and we can speculate to our hearts' content!

Douglas R. Hofstadter, *Gödel, Escher, Bach*

Two opposing camps in cultural studies define the terms of the debate, or the "hobby horse" of art studies, according to E. H. Gombrich.[1] At one extreme, art is defined in terms of something else, such as a set of conventions, a commodity, or an institution. The underlying assumption is that art is completely dependent on some aspect of its external context or is created by it. The task of the student of culture is to explain it in terms of that other aspect. It is this approach that motivates the series of inquiries in this book. The alternative position is that art transcends other conditions and possesses its own obscure yet intrinsically meaningful character. The task of the student of culture is to interpret it, not to explain it, which is to say, to decipher the full rich meaning of particular works, ignoring the social, economic, historical, and intellectual context. Gombrich's *Meditations on a Hobby Horse*[2] does not resolve this debate, but discloses the contradictions between their different sets of assumptions.

Taking Gombrich's major works as a whole, my understanding of his position is that the two opposing traditions cannot be reconciled but that they both have merit. In his Mellon lectures[3] of 1956 he discusses the meaning and the language of expression that underlie artistic styles, suggesting that art has a logic all of its own since each new tradition solves certain problems while creating new ones. In *Meditations on a Hobby Horse*, Gombrich presents a far reaching discussion that ranges over topics on style, the psychology of creativity, as well as the social factors that facilitate the expression of style and

114

the ideas of representational art. In *Norm and Form*, Gombrich focuses more on explanation and less on interpretation.[4] Here he discusses patronage, connoisseurship, and social influences on art.

Thus, walking and crossing the line between aesthetics and social history, Gombrich provides a rich and complex perspective on art and culture. His works contrast markedly with the general partisanship of the field of cultural studies, the sides of which might be termed the art-as-art position and the art-as-something-else position.[5]

The art-as-art position is that cultural products can be legitimately interpreted only within their own domain and that the economic, social, political, or intellectual context is irrelevant. This is the tradition of Schiller, Schelling, Hegel, Schopenhauer, and Santayana. In the terms of scholastic philosophy, art expresses a priori universals (*universalia ante rem*) and the analysis of any work of art – whether it be drama, painting, or musical composition – requires formal analysis of these universals, which are defined variously as abstract emotions (Schopenhauer), meaning (Panofsky), inner perfection (Schelling), tension and contrast (Ross), or process (Hegel). For some marxist scholars, as well, art remains sufficiently detached from any social or economic order to give it the potential for radical critique, and yet at the same time retains, as Marcuse states it, "transhistorical, universal truths."[6]

At the other extreme, the art-as-something-else position stresses that art is governed by forces external to it, and they are of the same character of those that influence, say, economic development, juvenile delinquency, or career choices. These forces can be material, social, or cultural (normative). Howard Becker, for example, explains how the conventions that develop in art communities composed of artists, critics, and publics shape standards about what art is and how it is to be evaluated.[7] Arthur Danto, not a sociologist but a philosopher, agrees: "It is the role of artistic theories these days, as always, to make the art world and art possible."[8] According to this approach (the "institutional school"), what turns a pitch fork into art is placing it in a museum, just as what turned Michelangelo's sculpture into art involved a labeling process by the wealthy and powerful commissioners of the sixteenth century.[9]

Interpretation and explanation are essentially different as they rest on different foundations of understanding. To posit and then to disclose the meaning of a work of art leads to a synthetic understanding and an appreciation of significance at multiple levels – cognitive, affective, sensual, aesthetic. For example, Panofsky's interpretation of iconographic symbols relates form and meaning, universal and particular, and in this way, creates for his readers an increased appreciation that is simultaneously intellectual and emotional.

Explanations, on the other hand, posit a causal or reciprocal nexus and focus attention on the nexus itself without doing very much justice to the complexity and totality of meaning. To wit, if I want an explanation of what type of schooling enhances artistic creativity or a better understanding of the difference between students who take up commercial art and those who take their chances as studio artists, I would read works by Jacob Getzels; but if I want to enrich my understanding of an artist's paintings I would read Meyer Schapiro.

This investigation is centrally motivated by an interest in explaining cultural phenomena, but the focus of this chapter is on different qualitative aspects of culture, such as innovation and style, and these topics evoke some attempt at deciphering meaning as well. It is easy to become entrapped in this endeavor, either by failing to maintain the analytical distinction between art and its social context (the fallacy of reflectionism[10]), by placing so much emphasis on the present circumstances of art that its historically relevant meanings are ignored, or by attributing to individuals what is observed at a higher analytical level (the ecological fallacy).

The three topics examined in this chapter – theatrical innovation, the character of museums' collections, and styles of popular music – are modest in scope, but they provide an opportunity of linking explanation and interpretation in order to make inferences about the meaning of cultural products. For that purpose it must be assumed that codes of meaning are both possessed by art and appropriated by groups. The empirical evidence used to test that assumption is provided by an association between the supply of an art product and an aggregate that is sufficiently large and for which there is a priori evidence to suppose that its members constitute an identifiable group that would reasonably constitute the base of demand for that art product.[11]

American residential theater

The history of American residential theater is nicely summarized by Emanuel Levy as a series of successive social movements.[12] The first residential, noncommercial theater movement lasted between 1910 and 1929 and was based on the repertory principle. Unlike later movements, this first was a national one and not confined to New York City. It encompassed theaters sponsored by municipalities, communities, settlement houses, and was both a rural and an urban phenomena. The main dilemma that faced the theaters in this early movement – as in all subsequent ones – was to sustain high standards for innovation and quality and at the same time attract sufficient financial support. Increasingly, however, theaters turned to commercial backers and lost their innovative orientations. The second movement of the 1930s was greatly imbued with a socialist and working class orientation, and many were founded and supported by leftist political parties. The reasons for the demise of this movement, Levy reports, are more complex than those for the demise of the first. Some of the theaters lost federal support owing to their leftist orientations, but another reason is that the quality of commercial theater was improving and there was a growing social conscience that was reflected in many plays sponsored by commercial theater.

The Off-Broadway theaters that started in the late 1940s were launched in opposition to Broadway's commercial priorities, yet nevertheless, by the early 1960s plays from Off-Broadway were produced with the possibility of moving them uptown to become commercially successful, spawning the Off-Off Broadway movement, newly committed to risk-taking and to austerity. While Off-Off Broadway and Off-Broadway still today constitute the major centers for theatrical innovation, since the late 1960s there has developed throughout the United States an increasing number of experimental theaters that offer serious competition to New York City's claim to dominance. Thus, a study of theater in the mid-1970s is a study of national theater companies, not just of companies located in Manhattan.

The best source of information on resident theaters is the Theater Communications Group whose membership includes most large and established resident groups. DiMaggio and Stenberg estimate that the Theater Communications Group's annual *Theater Profiles* includes information on only about 30 per cent of all resident companies but these account for virtually all the resident companies that are not ephemeral and that have established reputations.[13]

The research on theater innovation carried out by DiMaggio and Stenberg is based on data obtained from *Theater Profiles* for the seasons from 1971–72 through 1980–81.[14] They find that the most innovative companies are those that are short-lived, and although the longest surviving theaters become more conformist over time, the increasing conformity of older theaters is due to growth and dependence on earned income, not aging *per se*. The analysis presented here is different from DiMaggio and Stenberg's in several respects. Theirs is a longitudinal study whereas the interest here is in investigating the significance of differences in the urban contexts for theater innovation and thus the data were collected for only a single two-year period. Moreover, my concern with the dilemmas that theaters face in attempting to reach broad audiences with innovative plays suggested that this analysis incorporate indicators of productivity and popularity. Finally, the measure of innovation is different from the one that DiMaggio and Stenberg employ.

The index of innovation used by DiMaggio and Stenberg actually measures the degree to which a theater has a distinctive repertory or not, and it does so in a precise and unambiguous way. It is the Herfindahl index, which is a measure frequently used in industrial economics. In their study an index value is the mean number of times that each play a theater produced was also produced by other theaters. A score of 1 on the index means that no other theater produced any of the plays in that theater's repertoire. A score of 8 means that each play in a theater's repertoire was produced on the average by seven other theaters.

The measure of innovation used here is very "soft" and questionable by conventional criteria governing reliability, but it takes into account information available from a variety of secondary sources, including descriptions of a theater's approach and philosophy, nature of awards the company has won, staging, whether premieres are launched or not, and the literary merits of the plays produced.[15] A poet who was engaged in graduate study in a creative writing program was employed for the purpose of coding the degree of innovation exhibited by each theater on the basis of its repertory for the 1977–78 season.[16]

The coding scheme is based on a four-point scale, from 4, very innovative or experimental, to 1, very conventional. To illustrate, a theater such as Playwrights Horizons, which almost exclusively produces contemporary plays, many of them premieres, was coded 4, while a theater whose core program consists of comedies, musicals, and operettas, was considered relatively conventional and coded 1. A theater that offers a broad program of comedy, classics, contemporary and new works was usually coded 2. A theater that primarily supports contemporary plays or regional premieres with a smattering of classics and musicals usually received a score of 3. Some theaters, on the other hand, whose repertory was based on the classics but that had established high standards for production or that used abstract and unconventional theatrical techniques were coded 4. For the theaters coded from *Theater Profiles* for the 1977–78 season, the correlation between the Herfindahl index and the qualitative index employed here (with the sign of the correlation reversed) is .60.

Productivity, popularity, and innovation

By all accounts, innovation is difficult to sustain without financial resources and a dedicated following, but such resources and following can undermine innovation. The finding reported by DiMaggio and Stenberg that theater conformity is fostered by dependence on earned income and growth (increases in operating expenses over a ten year period) tends to support this conclusion. In this analysis, a direct measure of a theater's "following" – audience size – is taken into account, as well as financial resources (budget, or total operating expenses). Age of the theater is also included in the analysis, although the results for age are identical to those observed by DiMaggio and Stenberg in the longitudinal analysis, specifically, that its effects are mediated by other factors and age has no direct influence on innovation. While they emphasize the negative effect that dependence on earned income has on innovation, it is fruitful to examine the other side of the coin, namely dependence on subsidies or unearned income. Another factor considered is productivity since it is possible that launching many new productions during a season inevitably entails a heavy toll on actors, directors, and auxiliary staff and may preclude risk-taking.

In sum, the measure of innovation used is a four-point scale that captures the extent to which a theater is experimental or not; productivity is the number of different productions staged during the two seasons divided by the length of the two seasons considered; and popularity is the average monthly atten-dance. In the analyses of popularity, productivity, and innovation the effects of the theater's age, budget or operating expenses, and dependence on subsidies (the ratio of unearned to total earnings) are examined; the effects of popularity and productivity on innovation are also analyzed. The correlations among the measures of popularity, productivity, and innovation are not very high, but there is a slight tendency for very productive companies to have larger audiences ($r=.17$) and for productive companies to be less innovative than others ($r=-.15$). Contrary to what might be expected, there is virtually no association between popularity and innovation ($-.02$). (The correlations among the independent variables are given in table 7.4).

Though the relationship between productivity and popularity is very low, the results summarized in table 7.1 suggest that age, subsidies, and budget have parallel influences on both. Age of the theater has no direct effect either on productivity or on popularity because older companies have larger budgets, and a high level of resources increases both productivity and popularity. The proportion of the budget that is unearned or the extent of subsidization is negatively related to both productivity and to popularity, but in each case subsidization has no direct net effect. The reason is that theaters with larger operating expenses also depend relatively more on income earned through subscriptions and ticket sales and relatively little on subsidies. Thus, the most important factor affecting the launching of many productions during

Table 7.1. *Analysis of theater popularity and theater productivity*

	Popularity			Productivity		
	r	B	b (s.e.)	r	B	b (s.e.)
Age of company[a]	.11	.01	.050(.284)	.14	.05	.034(.056)
Subsidies	−.20	−.03	−4.721(13.98)	−.24	−.13	−4.159(2.765)
Budget[b]	.49	.48	.016(.003)**	.36	.30	.019(.006)**
	Constant = 2.15			Constant = 17.05		
	$\hat{R}^2$ = .22			$\hat{R}^2$ = .13		
	N = 133			N = 133		

[a] Coded as year; signs reversed.
[b] Coded in 1,000s.
**$p < .01$

a season and of attracting a large audience is a large operating budget. Of course, there is circularity here that eludes this analysis, since it is plausible that being able to sustain a high attendance and launch a large number of new plays increases the number of ticket buyers and, therefore, the size of the budget. While many features of theaters that must be important for productivity (such as cast size) and for popularity (such as critical reviews) cannot be ascertained, the most important features relating to the economic conditions of theaters are measured. The conclusions are that compared with theaters with small budgets, those that have large budgets are more productive or have larger audiences or both. On the other hand, neither productivity nor popularity is related to the extent to which theaters rely on subsidies.

As already noted, there is a slight negative correlation between innovation and productivity and no relationship between innovation and popularity. Table 7.2 also shows that innovative theaters have somewhat lower budgets ($r = -.16$) and, consistent with the findings reported by DiMaggio and Stenberg, are not primarily supported through earned income but rather through subsidies and donations ($r = .36$). In the regression analysis (panel 1), however, all but the effects of subsidization are trivial. Contrary to prevailing belief, a theater with a lavish budget, a large public following, and even a tight production schedule is not more likely to have conventional theatrical performances or be less innovative than other theaters. What does matter for innovation is subsidization; theaters that receive outright financial support

Table 7.2. *Analysis of theater innovation*

	(1)			(2)		(3)	
	r	B	b (s.e.)	B	b (s.e.)	B	b (s.e.)
Age of company[a]	−.08	−.04	−.003(.006)	−.04	−.003(.006)	−.05	−.004(.006)
Subsidies	.36	.35	1.266(.323)**	.27	.999(.328)**	.29	1.050(.318)**
Budget[b]	−.16	−.05	−.386(.765)	−.06	−.419(.745)	−.07	−.513(.722)
Productivity	−.15	−.06	−.006(.010)	−.07	−.008(.010)	−.06	−.006(.010)
Popularity	−.02	.10	.002(.002)	.09	.002(.002)	.07	.001(.002)
NYC (1, 0)	.32	†		.24	.415(.147)**	.10	.171(.162)
Median earnings	.34	†			†	.28	.040(.013)**
Constant		2.49			2.49		.226
$\hat{R}^2$		.11			.16		.21
N = 133							

[a] Coded as year; signs reversed.
[b] Coded in 1,000s.
† Not in equation.
**p < .01

are more likely than others to launch experimental plays or plays by contemporary playwrights. As will be further noted below, this finding raises serious questions about the validity of claims made by Banfield and others that the arts should not be supported by public funds.[17]

The history of American resident theater and our own observations about the geographical distribution of innovative theaters suggests that location in New York City ought to be taken into account. Out of the 133 theaters included in this analysis, 28 of those evaluated as most experimental are located in New York. New York theaters, I find, are not particularly more productive nor even have larger audiences compared with theaters located elsewhere,[18] but they do tend to be more innovative. Location is entered in the regression analysis as a dummy variable (1 = NYC; 0 = outside NYC) in panel 2 of table 7.2. The results show that location in New York is associated with innovation, supporting the contention that New York indeed does constitute the center of the theatrical avant-garde, as its theaters are more likely than those located elsewhere to launch a controversial production, stage a premiere, or experiment with multi-media theatrical presentations. This confirms the obvious, but it also does raise a question as to *why* New York City theaters are highly innovative.

While cultural tradition or history might suffice in describing New York City's distinctiveness, this interpretation fails to explain why it is that New York City has been successful in maintaining such a strong theatrical tradition, and also fails to account for the variation among other metropolitan places. The strategy becomes one of identifying a factor that helps to account for why New York City is particularly distinctive. The factor that was discovered is population affluence, specifically, median earnings. Once this factor is controlled, New York City location is no longer related to the likelihood of innovation. Because New York City is not simply a proxy for affluence[19] (the correlation between the dummy variable and median earnings is .49), the results indicate that affluence in general increases the likelihood of theater innovation, wherever the theater is located.

Thus, while it is true that New York theaters have sustained a tradition of the avant-garde, they do so apparently by virtue of a climate of prosperity and affluence.[20] The conclusion is that cultural traditions of innovation are not independent of social conditions, and, apparently, social conditions account for such traditions. What is unique about New York City's cultural traditions and its intense level of theatrical innovation is due primarily to its relative affluence.

The results that indicate that theatrical innovation is primarily supported in prosperous urban places at first appear to lend support to Banfield's argument that the arts depend on the rich, not the wider public, and the inference that he draws from that, namely that the arts should therefore not be publicly supported.[21] A more careful assessment of the full set of findings demonstrates that they do not support this inference, and, indeed, that they imply quite the opposite. Rich cities, not rich people, foster innovation since the relationship between median earnings and the level of private support is negligible ($r = -.07$).[22] This means that Banfield's assessment of private income is correct, but for the wrong reasons. Cities that have high overall affluence do provide an environment that is congenial to artistic innovation, but affluence does not translate into high levels of private support for the arts. What does directly contribute to innovation, however, is public funding. High levels of such external sources of support, and not patrons, ease the constraints on experimentation.

These are the practical implications of this empirical study of innovation in residential theater. But what can be learned that has bearing on the perennial debate in cultural studies – the hobby horse of investigations of art and culture? Measuring quality, artistic innovation, or creative experimentation is fraught with hazards, and, in any case, many critics question the validity of the enterprise altogether. The Herfindahl index measures in a clear and reliable way the singularity or the uniqueness of a theater's repertory. In this research the measure of innovation was based on the qualitative attributes of theater repertories and individual plays. Yet as "soft" as the measure is, the analysis replicates the findings of the research by DiMaggio and Stenberg, suggesting that a given qualitative dimension of cultural production possesses sufficient robustness of meaning to lend itself to different metrics.

This study of theaters also indicates that what is taken to be a "significant reason" may be mere description, which is to say, not an explanation. New York City is the pre-eminent center for many artistic activities and possesses a rich cultural tradition that makes it particularly attractive to artists and to cultural entrepreneurs. Nevertheless, there are, I had assumed, underlying economic, social, or political reasons to account for the cultural patterns of any particular locale; that is, to account for its traditions aside from their contents. The empirical identification of the relevant underlying factor was in this case admittedly crude, involving the initial examination of a great variety of possible factors. But the persisting influence of economic conditions in this entire investigation is so consistent, as well as being plausible in the framework of cultural studies, that the finding that it is the prosperity of a place that promotes innovative theater is theoretically and substantively significant. The more general point is that the objective is not merely to describe a particular historical place but to find a set of prevailing conditions that accounts for its distinctiveness.

Everybody's linden tree

Art critic Barry Schwartz employs a metaphor from Chekov's play to describe the American public art museum; it is the "cherry orchard" of the American middle class.[23] Fearing the plundering and the desecration of the orchard, Lyubov confronts the rabble: "Cut down? My dear fellow, forgive me, but you don't know what you are talking about. If there is one thing interesting – remarkable indeed – in the whole province, it's just our cherry orchard." The cherry orchard of Chekov's play was the valued property of the aristocracy.

Cultural historians document the extent to which museums have been an important symbol of the American middle class; owing to their greater institutional permanence compared with dance companies, symphony orchestras, and even opera companies, museums are especially meaningful as an expression of enduring cultural respectability both for social classes and for cities. Museum construction, policies, and staffing have to a greater extent than any other cultural institution been interwoven in economic, social, and political currents.[24] The political significance of the American museum is already manifest in its early origins. Tammany was the first sponsor of a museum, and it was in Manhattan's City Hall that a "museum" room was set aside in 1790 for the display of wax figures, curiosities, and collectables. The bawdy theatricality of the public museum was fully institutionalized by P. T. Barnum whose "dime museums" provided the public with opportunities to see European relics, flea circuses, American Indians, and live entertainment. But such museums constitute only one strand of the museum tradition in America, one that ostensibly disappeared as an institutional form but nevertheless is still considered to be a component of the contemporary museum. As Meyer notes, these "dime" museums helped to prepare the way for an "American hybrid."[25]

While dime museums provided entertainment in the early nineteenth century for the broad public, wealthy and established New England families were giving their support to small galleries, historical museums, and college collections. These elite institutions represent the second strand of the tradition that would become the hybrid of the twentieth century.

The two most significant events in the history of the American museum occurred in the same year, 1870, the year in which the Boston Museum of Fine Arts and the Metropolitan Museum were established. Although the Boston Museum was backed by old wealth, the founders of the Metropolitan were largely self-made businessmen whose wealth came from banking and railroads. Still, the differences between the sources of wealth and the social origins of philanthropists became increasingly insignificant as old rich and new rich discovered they could co-operate to yield themselves dividends in pleasure, prestige, and public service.[26] Members of the American middle class were duly impressed and became the main benefactors and defenders of the American public museum. In turn, museums were for a time able to balance, with more or less success, their dual roles as popular institutions and scholarly repositories.

Yet by mid-century this hybrid version became increasingly unstable, as taxpayers – no longer perceiving themselves to be the main beneficiaries – exerted pressures on museum board members and curators for change and reform, including improved accountability, more community exhibits, better representation of works by minorities and women, and more contemporary art. At the same time, professional administrators, who were assuming powerful posts above curatorial positions, were sufficiently concerned with the financial solvency of museums that they adopted new policies to reinforce public demands. At the expense of the old elitist traditions, and against the wishes of many scholars, museums placed greater emphasis on the public mission than on the traditional conception, as evidenced in more contemporary art exhibits, blockbuster shows, commercial joint ventures, community and traveling exhibits, larger bookstores, and, of course, a vastly expanded gift shop for the sale of curiosities and copies of relics. The live performance may be a chamber music concert and not a trained flea show, but the entertainment functions of the earliest American museum are still preserved.

The difference between a traditional and a public emphasis is largely an analytical one, but an initial question is whether or not collections can be empirically distinguished along these or similar lines. If there is a meaningful difference between them, it is important to analyze the ways in which they are fostered by different organizational and urban characteristics. The observation by Meyer that the American museum is a hybrid of two disparate traditions, accompanied by our understanding that the museum has served at different times in history the interests of contending groups and also reflects salient features of social and economic currents, all suggest that the content of a museum's collections are determined, at least in part, by their organizational and urban contexts.

The sources of the information on collections are the 1975 and 1985 editions of the *Official Directory of the American Association of Museums*.[27] Although the criterion used for including a museum was that it have a substantial art collection, some art museums are very specialized – for instance, they exhibit primarily drawings – whereas others have diverse collections. We would suppose that museums with very diverse collections are more oriented to the public than those that are very specialized. Collections for both 1975 and 1985 are classified by the *Directory* into the following categories: painting, folk art, sculpture, graphics, photography, prints, drawings, textiles, numismatics, musical instruments, decorative arts, living arts, video, and history.

For the purpose of identifying underlying dimensions that can account for distinct groupings of types of collections, a factor analysis was carried out, using the 1975 data on the collections for the 417 museums. Altogether five factors were identified, but the first three are statistically the most important, accounting for 41 per cent of the total variance, and of these the first two are substantively most important.[28] The first factor is defined by the following types of collections: paintings, sculpture, and graphics.[29] This is quite consistent with the descriptions by Meyer and others as constituting the basis of the traditional collection, rooted in silk-stocking and haute couture connoisseurship and strengthened by the tradition of curatorial pre-eminence in defining what a museum ought to be. The convergence of historical scholarship on museums with the empirical results suggests that this factor represents traditional collections.

The second most important factor is defined largely by the following collections: folk art, textiles, decorative arts, costumes, and history.[30] Each of these collection categories has a substantial loading on this factor (at least .50), but two of the three types that define traditional collections, namely paintings and sculpture, also have moderate loadings on this factor (.20 and .22, respectively), suggesting an eclectic pattern but one that is largely defined by public interest in an all-around and comprehensive museum – one that accommodates all tastes and interests. This factor appears to define the public museum.

The third factor accounts for collections that have a relatively narrow base of appeal; the collection types with high loadings are prints and drawings.[31] Because the mean number of prints and drawings collections is much smaller than either traditional or public collections,[32] and because the primary focus is on the difference between the two types that manifestly reflect the two historical antecedents of the contemporary museum, little further discussion is required, except to briefly indicate here that collections of prints and drawings are rooted in organizational contexts that are quite similar to those of traditional collections.

The most relevant organizational characteristics that influence a museum's mission relate to its stature, and the professional and aesthetic orientations of its staff.[33] While information is, unfortunately, not available on the orientations or goals of the staff, there are three measures that reflect how highly professionalized a museum is, which undoubtedly is related to staff members' conceptions as well as its stature. The first is accreditation, which indicates that a museum has met minimum standards with respect to acquisition decisions, care of its works, and exhibition policies. The second is whether or not a museum has a research department or research activities. It is a rough indication of its emphasis on scholarship and related activities, such as authentication and restoration, and keeping accurate records of its works of art. Finally, membership in the American Association of Museums, the primary professional and advocacy organization, is an indicator of a museum's integration in a cosmopolitan network of museums.

Also to be taken into account in any attempt to compare public with traditional museums is the age of the museum, for it is plausible that newer museums are more likely to have adopted current practices of collecting and exhibiting works of art. It is also plausible that museums located in the central city of metropolitan places are more likely to emphasize public over traditional collections.

As implied, each museum is described on each of two major dimensions. That is, it is assigned two total scores, each of which is based on the number of collections that define the factor. The range of scores for the dimension 'traditional' is between 0 and 3, and that for the dimension 'public' is between 0 and 5.[34]

Table 7.3. *Analysis of types of museum collections, 1975*

	Traditional			Public		
	r	B	b (s.e.)	r	B	b (s.e.)
Age of museum[a]	.22	.19	.005(.001)**	.23	.19	.007(.002)**
Central city (1.0)	.12	.07	.166(.120)	.13	.07	.187(.128)
AAM membership (1.0)	.19	.13	.316(.126)**	.25	.16	.436(.135)**
Research (1.0)	.14	.07	.167(.112)	.23	.14	.363(.120)**
Accredited (1.0)	.17	.08	.221(.141)	.24	.12	.375(.151)**
Constant		12.69			13.48	
$\hat{R}^2$	.10			.16		
N=417						

[a] Coded as year; signs reversed.
**$p < .01$

Though, surprisingly, differences between a traditional and a public emphasis cannot be traced to differences in age or location, as table 7.3 shows, they differ on the professionalism variables: museums that have a notable public orientation are more likely to be accredited and also to have research departments, although they are not more likely than museums with a traditional orientation to be members of the American Association of Museums (AAM). Though we have no way of knowing from this result whether museums that have collections geared to a diverse public also have relatively more professional administrators than curators in top positions, these findings are not counter to that supposition. However, the general point is that the museum that supports a public mission, compared with one that maintains a purist, traditional one, is relatively more professional as indicated by its research activities and its accreditation status.

Even though public oriented museums in 1975 had higher levels of professionalism than traditional museums, the gap between them had widened by 1985 as professionalism became increasingly more important for public museums but not for traditional ones. For the traditional museums for 1975, the three professionalism variables together account for an increment in the R^2 of .042 after age and location are entered into the regression; by 1985, this increment is very little more, specifically, .058. On the other hand, in identical equations for public museums, the increment of R^2 for 1975 is .092 and in 1985 increases to .134.[35]

The traditional collection based on the timeworn principles of defining the art museum as the repository of old masters and the art treasures of the past that, by convention, are limited to a few genres of the visual arts – paintings, sculpture, and graphics – has been lauded as the hallmark of the exemplary museum. Nevertheless, its exclusionary conception of art accompanies a reluctance to keep up with contemporary museum trends towards increasing professionalization. The broad-based public collection, on the other hand, in 1975 was already more likely than the traditional collection to be developed in the context of a professionalized museum environment.[36]

Further clarification of the significance of the link between professionalism and types of collections can be attained by examining the variation in the urban environments of different types of museums. It was discovered that museums with large public collections have no distinctive urban environments that could be identified. Public collections are not more likely to be found in small metropolitan places than large ones; they are not more likely to be in wealthy than poor places, nor in cities that have prosperous rather than impoverished governments; nor do historical characteristics of cities, including the early presence of wealthy families, help to account for the prevalence of such collections. Extensive exploration yielded no special feature of the urban context that could help to account for the extent to which a museum supported a public collection or not. The same absence of urban influences was found for collections largely made up of prints and drawings. To be sure, there are small scale influences that cannot be captured by metropolitan-level factors that one suspects play a role in the development of museums with these collections. Such influences may be highly idiosyncratic and, therefore, not detectable in a large scale comparative study (such as the importance of an individual patron in some cities and corporate patrons in others), or they may involve unusual historical conditions that cannot be captured systematically with crude indicators.

On the other hand, the extent of traditional collections is positively related to a group of variables that tap various aspects of cultural homogeneity – percentage of native stock ($r = .14$), ethnic homogeneity ($r = .14$), language homogeneity ($r = .13$), and nativity homogeneity ($r = .15$).[37] Traditional collections are also more prevalent in small places than in large ones (the simple correlation between log of population size and traditional collections is $-.14$). When substantial numbers of the community are native born or of nonforeign extraction and have strong identification with a single cultural heritage, it is plausible that the community resists the expansion of a museum's activities into nontraditional and relatively experimental areas.[38]

It can be suggested that a predominantly homogeneous population is a source of cultural conservatism. While the effects of per cent native stock and other indicators of homogeneity are not very pronounced, perhaps it is surprising that they could be detected at all, given the greater role played by factors that are more proximate to the decision-making processes that shape the collection policies of museums. Of course, it is impossible to know who pays the admission fees to see the exhibits of the traditional collection, but these results suggest that long established Americans – WASPs – are most likely to foster a social climate that is congenial for museums that are primarily devoted to paintings, sculpture, and graphics and that resist broadening their collections along less conventional lines. Thus, cities that have relatively small proportions of people with foreign origins and also cities with little ethnic and language diversity exhibit forms of cultural conservatism that affect the character of major cultural institutions.

When Barry Schwartz referred to the American museum as a cherry orchard, he argued that the middle classes were defending an antiquated aesthetic conception against the demands of the working classes, minorities, and against the interests of a pluralistic city. To the extent that this analysis captures the analytical differences between public collections and traditional collections, the finding that the traditional collection tends to survive primarily in more provincial enclaves suggests that it will slowly be replaced by public collections, and a comparison between 1975 and 1985 indicates that this is possibly the case.[39] The much stronger professional base of the public museum compared with the traditional museum undoubtedly increases the museum's capability of dealing with diverse constituencies and of changing along more democratic lines. As Stanislavski said of The Cherry Orchard:

It hides in itself and in all of its flowering whiteness the great poetry of the dying life of the aristocracy. The Cherry Orchard grows for the sake of beauty, for the eyes of spoiled aesthetics. It is a pity to destroy it, but it is necessary to do so, for the economics of life demand it.[40]

To complete the analogy, it might be suggested that it is the vitality of the small-leaf linden tree to which the public museum might be compared. Although less manifestly beautiful than the cherry, it is far more adaptable, long having roughed it in an urban environment. Unlike the cherry, the linden trees of urban America are not the exclusive domain of any provincial group or neighborhood.

Tracing the historical roots of these two disparate traditions that have shaped the contemporary museums has been one task of cultural historians. In accounting for current patterns, historians rely on archival records for a few museums, which are taken as major instances for the rest. Instead I use information on virtually all museums for the 125 largest places in the United

States, which leads to conclusions that downplay the significance of the most prestigious museums but which capture the full range of variation among them. The details of the historical record are almost entirely ignored. Nevertheless, there is a high degree of complementarity in the conclusions drawn from this analysis and from historical research. For example, the analytical components of the American hybrid museum that Meyer discusses are also identified in this investigation, and the results support Burt's observation that the interests of professional administrators converge with those of the public.[41] Moreover, these results suggest the declining significance of the narrowly focused high art museums, as large, heterogeneous urban places inevitably fosters the social diversity that makes cultural orthodoxy anachronistic.

Codes of meaning and music

If there is a link between interpretation and explanation it is to be discovered through the analysis of codes, for they sustain the meanings inherent in cultural products and at the same time are rooted in the intentions and values of groups who appropriate and create those products. To empirically identify a connection between a group and an indication of prevalent culture (without studying individuals), it is necessary to identify a group of people who share the same identity that is manifestly asserted in cultural codes and that are reasonably linked to art products. For example, it has already been suggested that the traditional museum is a symbolic expression of exclusivity and group solidarity for homogeneous communities, many of whose members are white and native born. Culture functions as a language of social rhetoric.

Scholarship on popular culture has been guided by a mixture of normative considerations concerning its aesthetic merits and more neutral concerns with the functions it plays in society. In mass culture theory, popular music is considered to be monotonously straightforward, while "serious" music is complex and demanding. The undifferentiated masses, it is assumed, generate demands for simple music that does not tax the imagination or intelligence.[42] Paradoxically, the conclusions of the conservative wing of mass culture theory are not very dissimilar from inferences drawn by marxist theorists. For example, Gramsci argues that the dominance of a group in political and economic spheres is achieved through the promulgation of an ideology that involves the manipulation of the media and the dissemination of uniform entertainment, "bread and circuses" that co-opt and pacify the masses. Such entertainment and cultural products offer escape from reality – rather than involvement in it – and legitimize the existing status quo by images through which subordinate classes begin to make sense of their existence.[43]

Cultural pluralist theory focuses instead on the great diversity of groups in terms of their different social and economic life styles, and it stresses that this diversity is important for popular culture. Gans, for example, conceives of social groups as a plurality of taste cultures, which need not necessarily be organized, but members of which are similar in their social and economic situations.[44] This approach is not markedly different from that of English social scientists, notably Stuart Hall and other scholars affiliated with the Centre for Contemporary Cultural Studies, who incorporate semiotic and ethnographic analysis into a marxist framework.[45] For example, Hebdige studies the personalization of popular music into styles by working class youths as part of an expression of opposition to mainstream society.[46] The active use of popular culture as a subtle technique of sabotage is investigated by Modleski, who demonstrates how the narrative content of Harlequin romances, gothic novels, and soap operas may appear to be merely escapist, but actually challenges traditional values, behavior, and attitudes.[47] In more general terms, Gottdiener employs a semiotic approach to interpret sub-cultural codes of meaning, indicating that the link between the users and producers of culture is mediated by "raw" cultural objects that are trans-functionalized by producers from exchange values to arbitrary signs as commodity objects, which are, in turn, personalized by users or audiences. This personalization attenuates the primary function of commodity objects and also their use value, and in this sense culture is actively created by consumers.[48] Notwithstanding the differences in the approach and assumptions of cultural pluralist theory and those of this diverse group of marxist ethnographers and semiotic theorists, the conclusion is that there are social forces rooted in the demand for culture that generate diversities of cultural products, not uniformities.

To a great extent confidence in the results of the ecological analysis depends on their replicating robust findings of studies of individuals, and consistent findings at both levels might suggest the individuals' preferences are translated into more powerful collective preferences.

At the individual level there are established differences with respect to preferences for musical styles. For example, women are especially interested in popular music, and Denisoff points out that since women are perceived by the recording industry to be the primary purchasers of cultural and leisure products generally, the producers and distributors of popular recordings package their products with the tastes of women in mind.[49] While British studies have focused on music as a marker of class lines and on the importance of music for the cultural heritage of the working classes, Gans observes that in the United States some types of music, such as rock, country, and folk, which were initially enjoyed by the rural or urban working classes, are increasingly popular with the middle classes.[50] Several studies report ethnic or racial differences that relate to individual preferences for music; for example, the largest following for rhythm and blues, Motown and soul is found among urban blacks.[51]

Urban popular music*

This analysis is based on information on more than 1800 live concerts performed in 1975 and reported in *Rolling Stone Magazine*.[52] The concerts were classified by the following categories: R&B/soul, pop/soft rock, progressive rock, hard rock/metal rock, generic rock, folk music, country music, and southern rock. (Too few listings for jazz, blues, and reggae precluded using these concerts for analysis.[53])

With SMSA as the unit of analysis, the numbers of concerts in each of the categories are the dependent variables. Recognizing that sheer quantities of cultural supply items are always affected by the size of the metropolitan place, both the log of population size and a squared term for population size are entered in the equation.[54] Included in each of the regression analyses are those factors that are identified in the literature on individual preference as being relevant: the percentage of women, the percentage of blue collar workers, and the racial composition of the SMSA. The percentage of single people is also included on the supposition that they have life styles and leisure preferences that constitute demand factors for popular concerts. Because youthfulness would appear to be a major predictor of popular concerts, the percentage of teenagers and of young adults is also examined.

The assumption that aggregates must be of a sufficient size to constitute markets that affect the supply of cultural products is difficult to test precisely with population characteristics. Therefore, the conclusions discussed here (as well as the others in this chapter), are based solely on results that are statistically significant at the .01 level, somewhat more stringent than the conventional .05 level. Because this is a macro-level investigation the analysis of popular music yields far more substantial results than do those for theaters and museums. In these regressions, with SMSA as the unit of analysis, most values for $\hat{R}^2$ are above .40 (with the exceptions being in the analyses for southern rock and country music, for which the $\hat{R}^2$ values are .19 and .29, respectively).

A major conclusion is that women constitute a primary source of market demand for music of all kinds. There are strong relationships between the

---

* For assistance with this section I thank William E. Hall.

percentage of the population that is female and concerts of the following types: pop/soft rock, generic rock, folk music, hard rock/heavy metal, and progressive rock.[55] Although many have emphasized that women are interested in popular culture because it provides role models for fantasies involving dating and courtship, I cast the explanation somewhat differently. Inequalities persist for women in their opportunities for leisure just as much as in their opportunities for work. Their interests are channeled into "appropriately passive" leisure activities, namely those that are nonaggressive and home-based, and this makes popular music an appropriate feminine interest, like cooking or swimming. Men's interests, on the other hand, are channeled into leisure forms that are aggressive, competitive, and physically demanding. Families and schools work in tandem to legitimize such inequalities in leisure, and this reinforces the notion that popular music is a feminine interest (along with aerobic dancing, swimming, jogging, and tennis).

The percentage of the population that works in blue collar jobs is negatively related to the number of folk concerts,[56] which indicates that the demand for folk music is not largely defined by those whom folk musicians sing about – the poor, for example – but rather is defined in the cafes of university communities, in the clubs of sophisticated neighborhoods, and, generally, is popular with liberal, well-educated white collar and professional workers.

The greater the relative number of blacks in a metropolitan place, the more R&B/soul and hard rock/heavy metal concerts are there.[57] The codes of R&B and soul that refer to specifically black traditions and experiences have always helped to explain why blacks as individuals prefer these forms of music, which indicates how individual preferences can be inferred from conclusions about aggregate demand.[58] Why blacks (along with women) constitute a market for heavy metal/hard rock is not easy to explain except that of all the forms of music that had sufficiently numerous concerts to include in these comparisons, heavy metal/hard rock was in 1975 newer than the others and had the most pizzazz, and urban blacks have been in the vanguard of the development of popular music, including forms that developed after 1975, such as rap.[59]

Young people are undoubtedly primary consumers of popular music,[60] yet there is no evidence on the metropolitan level that age plays a very significant role,[61] indicating that young audiences do not thus exert an influence over the supply of a cultural commodity. However, consistent with the findings on individuals' preferences, the metropolitan-level data show that in places with a relatively large number of white collar workers there are many folk music concerts, and in places with a relatively large black population there are many R&B/soul and hard rock/heavy metal concerts. The two types of concert that are not easily accounted for by gender, occupational grouping, or race (nor by the percentage of single people, teenagers, or young adults, or population size) are southern rock and country music. The negligible effects of size on both might suggest their marginality in large urban places.[62] (There are fewer concerts of each of these types than of any others, specifically, a total of 79 country concerts and 97 southern rock concerts.)

These results are generally consistent with studies of individual preferences for popular musical genres, but what do they tell us that we cannot learn from studies of individuals? Not trivial perhaps is the explicit assumption made here that when findings based on studies of individuals and those based on studies of aggregates (defined as real groups) converge, there need be less concern about the fallacies of ecological interpretation. These data reveal nothing about who attends concerts and who does not, and they fail to identify which individuals prefer certain types of music over others. Nevertheless, they do reveal which groups make a significant difference for the kind of concerts that are performed in metropolitan places, and because of the general consistency of the results with many studies of individuals, it is possible to conjecture that the influence exerted by groups in large collectivities is based on stable conceptions of a group's identity, cultural values, and its members' shared social situation. (This conjecture is quite different from positing that a global or average attribute of an urban place – such as the average income of its members or the degree of educational inequalities in the population – influences its cultural resources.)

Of course it is possible that the members of the groups that are identified as exerting a demand on musical styles are not themselves the primary constituents. It is quite possible that the R&B and soul concerts, for example, that are in heavy demand in cities with a large per cent blacks, are widely enjoyed by whites, Hispanics, Asians and others, as a climate of sophistication and appreciation develops when there are disproportionate numbers of blacks. Identifying the audience was not so much the question, however, as identifying the critical mass that makes music popular in a city.

Though this remains a problem of explanation, there is meaning that must be posited at both ends of the argument, specifically, that there are meanings that are incorporated into cultural products to which groups lay claim and that individuals adopt. While this does not overcome the problems of extrapolating ecological correlations from a large unit – the metropolis – to groups that compose it, the meanings of cultural products and those of groups can be analytically synchronized.

Discussion

Cultural products are appropriated by groups because they express members' deep-seated values and their identities, and help to articulate group distinctiveness. Sometimes the cultural products that a group appropriates help to legitimize the group in terms of its origins and distinctive past; they symbolize traditional values that define the boundaries and integrity of that group. Main constituencies for museums with old masterworks and conventional collections are old-established Americans of native origins. Visual arts that have unquestionable authenticity and are historically and aesthetically "correct" provide composite meanings that are in accord with time-honored orthodox values. This is consistent with what we know to be the sources of social, political, and economic conservatism.

While fundamentally basic groups defined by social class, ethnicity, age, or any other such primitive criterion are constitutive markets for art products, it is difficult to conceive that a locale can operate in quite the same way, at least in contemporary times. American society has very high rates of geographical mobility (and individuals carry their cultural interests with them wherever they go); there is a great dispersion of resources for artists and for art producers, and, besides, there is keen competition among places for cultural distinction. New York City's reputation for theatrical innovation suggests, however, that New York possesses a special and very distinctive cultural tradition that other places do not. The results of the analysis indicates that this is the case, but the underlying reason is more fundamental than the explanation that attributes a unique cultural climate to New York. Specifically, relatively affluent cities, including New York, are more likely to have experimental and renowned theater companies compared with less affluent cities. In this way, idiosyncratic cultural values offer a less potent explanation than does the economic well-being of a place.

The attempt was made in the study of popular music to locate generative values in groups that are consistent with the meanings encoded in cultural products. Women and blacks constitute the major markets for popular music of different kinds. Because an interest in music, unlike other activities and interests, is legitimate within the constraints of sexism, the very specific symbolic codes of particular genre are less important for women than is music itself. It was concluded that women constitute a major market for music because it provides an acceptable form of leisure activity. The music styles that were the newest in the mid-1970s, heavy metal and hard rock, appeal to urban blacks, perhaps because black performers played a major role in the creation of new musical genres throughout the 1970s. However, another interpretation was offered that helps to account for why both blacks and women exert a high demand for live concerts. Inequalities of opportunity in many spheres may well channel both blacks' and women's interests in music. That blacks constitute the primary market for R&B and soul is a confirmation of the assumptions that a group that is large enough to constitute a critical mass will appropriate cultural forms that are consistent with its members' identities and values.

A question raised in this chapter is: what is the significance of culture that exists apparently without structural moorings? For example, public museum collections have no distinctive social or economic base, nor are there identifiable aggregates of sufficient size that provide for their support. Of course, local institutions undoubtedly play major roles in the creation and the maintenance of public museums and account for metropolitan variation in the numbers of such museums. Not everyone attends museums but the decisions of those who do influence the chances of survival and growth of museums, as the empty corridors in the Huntington Hartford museum in the early 1970s indicate.

How the preferences of museum-goers influence the prevalence of museums (or of any other form of institutionalized culture), however, is not the question that is being asked here. A failure to identify major social and economic conditions or cultural currents that can account for variation in a given cultural institution leads to two, admittedly speculative, conclusions. One is that the cultural institution and its products integrate diverse sectors and groups of the population and serve to maintain meaningful values with general, and therefore not distinctive, significance. The other is that if cultural products are detached from all social and economic conditions, they have trivial meaning. Whichever inference is drawn there is only one paradoxical conclusion that can be drawn: culture – whether widely shared or generally ignored – is not monopolized by any single group or stratum.

Table 7.4. *Correlations among independent variables for analysis of theaters*

	1	2	3	4	5
1 Age of company[a]	—				
2 Subsidies	−.08	—			
3 Budget[b]	.26	−.36	—		
4 NYC (1, 0)	.01	.28	−.05	—	
5 Median earnings	.06	.07	.07	.49	—
x̄	1966	.47	639	.29	56.3
s.d.	10.5	.22	1102	.46	5.5

[a] Signs reversed. Coded as date founded.
[b] Coded in thousands.

Table 7.5. *Correlations among independent variables for analysis of museum collections*

	1	2	3	4	5
1 Age of museum[a]	—				
2 Central city (1, 0)	−.14	—			
3 AAM membership (1, 0)	.03	−.07	—		
4 Research (1, 0)	.04	.10	.28	—	
5 Accredited (1, 0)	.16	.10	.33	.29	—
x̄	1933	.72	.70	.44	.21
s.d.	36.2	.45	.46	.50	.41

[a] Signs reversed. Coded as date founded.

Notes

1 E. H. Gombrich, *Meditations on a Hobby Horse* (London: Phaidon, 1963).
2 Gombrich, *Meditations on a Hobby Horse.*
3 E. H. Gombrich, *Art and Illusion* (Princeton: Princeton University Press, 1969 [1960]).
4 E. H. Gombrich, *Norm and Form* (London: Phaidon, 1966).
5 This is parallel to the distinction made by M. H. Abrams between art-as-such and the institutional approach in "Art-as-Such," *Bulletin of the American Academy of Arts and Sciences* 38 (1985), 8–23.
6 Herbert Marcuse, *The Aesthetic Dimension* (Boston: Beacon Press, 1978), p. 29.
7 Howard Becker, *Art Worlds* (Berkeley: University of California Press, 1982).
8 Arthur Danto, "The Artworld," *Journal of Philosophy* 61 (1964), 571–584.
9 A related approach is that it is neither merit nor aesthetic qualities that establishes a painter's reputation but rather luck, connection, and the eccentric whims of buyers or patrons. A study of the artistic career of Jackson Pollock suggests that his rise to pre-eminence occurred in spite of mixed critical reviews and was largely due to a promotional campaign on the part of an influential group of friends. See Michael Mulkay and Elizabeth Chaplin, "Aesthetics and the Artistic Career," *Sociological Quarterly* 23 (1982), 117–138.
10 Wendy Griswold, *Renaissance Revivals* (Chicago: University of Chicago Press, 1986), pp. 9–10.
11 Because the assumption of critical mass is required to detect group demand – not simply social influences – a relatively stringent level of statistical significance is advisable. This chapter reports only findings significant at the .01 level.
12 Emanuel Levy, "Youth, Generations and Artistic Change," *Youth and Society* 12 (1980), 145–172. Primary sources include: Thomas Gale Moore, *The Economics of the American Theater* (Durham NC: Duke University Press, 1968); Stephen Langley, *Theater Management in America*, rev. ed., (New York: Drama Book Specialists, 1974); Jack Poggi, *Theater in America* (Ithaca: Cornell University Press, 1968); G. B. Wilson, *Three Hundred Years of American Drama and Theater* (Englewood Cliffs NJ: Prentice-Hall, 1973); Mary Garty, "A Case Study in Cultural Stratification," unpublished paper, Pittsburgh, 1983.
13 Paul DiMaggio and Kristen Stenberg "Conformity and Diversity in American Resident Theaters," pp. 116–139 in Judith H. Balfe and Margaret Jane Wyszomirski, eds., *Art, Ideology and Politics* (New York: Praeger, 1985).
14 DiMaggio and Stenberg, "Conformity and Diversity in American Resident Theaters."
15 These sources included: John Willis, *Theater World*, Vol. 33 (New York: Crown, 1978); Catherine Hughes, ed., *American Theater Annual*, 1978–79 (Detroit: Gale, 1980); Donald W. Fowle, ed., *Notable Names in American Theater*, rev. ed., (Clifton NJ: James T. White, 1976). The primary source used was *Theater Profiles* (New York: Theater Communications Group, 1977–78).
16 Donald Nitchie's research contributions are gratefully acknowledged.
17 Edward C. Banfield, *The Democratic Muse: A Twentieth Century Fund Book* (New York: Basic Books, 1984).

18 The correlation between the New York City dummy variable and popularity is
    $-.01$ and between it and productivity is $-.02$.
19 Because about one-third of the theaters are located in New York, any contextual
    variable that is highly related to urban size is also highly related to innovation.
    Correlates of the dichotomy (New York City versus other) include the percentage
    that work downtown, age of central city, and number of firms. All of these
    variables (and others that are a close function of scale) have correlations of at least
    .85 with the New York City dummy variable.
20 Since Paul DiMaggio was kind enough to supply the index values for the theaters
    on which I have information, the identical analyses were carried out with the
    Herfindahl index. The results reported in table 7.2, panel 3 are confirmed in the
    replication, except that productivity exerts a somewhat stronger positive influence
    on conformity than it does a negative influence on the innovation scale. (The beta is
    .019, but is significant at only the .02 level.)
21 Banfield, *The Democratic Muse*.
22 Nor is urban affluence related to theater productivity $(r = .00)$ or popularity
    $(r = .09)$.
23 Barry Schwartz, "Museums: Art for Who's Sake?" *Ramparts* (May 1961), 39–49.
24 This brief discussion of the social history of museums draws particularly on the
    following sources: Vera L. Zolberg, "Conflicting Visions in American Art
    Museums," *Theory and Society* 10 (1981), 103–125; Herbert and Marjorie Katz,
    Museums USA (Garden City NY: Doubleday, 1965); Karl E. Meyer, *The Art
    Museum. A Twentieth Century Fund Report* (New York: William Morrow, 1979);
    Nathaniel Burt, *Palaces for People* (Boston: Little, Brown, 1977).
25 Meyer, *The Art Museum*, p. 23.
26 Joseph E. Choate, one of the founders of the Metropolitan, appeals for supporters
    in explicitly self-interested terms: "Think of it, ye millionaires of many markets –
    what glory may yet be yours if you only listen to our advice, to convert pork into
    porcelain, grain and produce into priceless pottery, the rude ores of commerce into
    sculptured marble, and railroad shares and mining stocks – things which perish
    without the using, and which in the next financial panic shall surely shrivel like
    parched scrolls – into the glorified canvas of the world's masters, that shall adorn
    these walls for centuries." Quoted from Meyer, *The Art Museum*, p. 27.
27 *Official Museum Directory*, (Washington DC: American Association of Museums,
    1975, 1985). A total of 429 are listed in the 1975 directory and there is missing
    information for only 17. Of 558 listings in 1985, only 5 have incomplete
    information. Unfortunately, museums do not report sponsorship in sufficient
    detail to use this information.
28 Principal component analysis with varimax rotation was the procedure used. The
    first factor accounts for 19 per cent of the common variance, the second for 12 per
    cent, and the third for 10 per cent.
29 The factor loadings are: paintings (.75), sculpture (.79), and graphics (.76).
30 The highest factor loadings are: folk art (.59), textiles (.58), decorative arts (.60),
    costumes (.52), and history (.62).
31 The factor loadings are: prints (.82) and drawings (.79).
32 The mean size of prints and drawings collections is .39 compared with the size of

traditional collections of 1.57 and of public collections, 1.21.

33 See Zolberg, "Conflicting Visions in American Art Museums."

34 See note 32. The difference between the numbers of public and traditional collections that museums have is not significant. If proportions of all collections that are public or traditional are used as dependent variables, the results are consistent with those reported.

35 For traditional collections in 1975 the $\hat{R}^2$ for the equation with age and location is .056 and after the professionalization variables are added is .098. Comparable figures for 1985 are .058 and .116, respectively. For public collections in 1975 the $\hat{R}^2$ for the equation with age and location is .065, which is increased to .157. Comparable figures for 1985 are .046 and .180, respectively. There is some evidence that the greater influence of the professionalization variables for 1985 public collections is not due so much to the increased professionalization of existing museums but rather the higher levels of professionalization of newly created museums, a disproportionate many of which had public collections. There is an increase of more than 100 museums during this period, from 429 to 558.

36 Additional empirical support for this contrast is provided by the results for museums with collections based chiefly on prints and drawings (that is, defined by the third factor of the factor analysis solution). The results are virtually identical to those reported for traditional museums reported in table 7.3. Beyond the variance accounted for by age and location, the professionalism variables account for little increase in the $\hat{R}^2$ (.043 in 1975 and .049 in 1985). Thus, both types of museums with collections based on traditional conceptions are least likely to have developed in a context of high professional standards.

37 Homogeneity is computed by the following equation:

$$(\Sigma_{xi}^2/(\Sigma_{xi})^2)$$

See Jack P. Gibbs and Walter J. Martin, "Urbanization, Technology and the Division of Labor," *American Sociological Review* 27 (1962), 667–677. The index for ethnicity is based on fifteen categories; language on two; nativity on twelve.

38 These variables are too highly related to one another to include more than one of them in a regression equation, although whichever is added as a context variable the results are about the same. For example, when per cent native is added to the regression analysis for traditional collections in table 7.3 its beta is .14, which is significant beyond the .01 level. When both the log of population and per cent native are in the equation, log size is not significant but per cent native is. (The correlation between the two is high, however, − .69, raising some questions about statistical independence.)

39 New museums are more likely to have public collections than traditional ones. In 1975 public collections were not more likely to be supported by younger museums compared with traditional collections, but they are in 1985, when the correlation between age of museum and extent of public collections is .19 and that between museums age and extent of traditional collections is .24.

40 Quoted in Schwartz, "Art for Who's Sake?" p. 49.

41 Burt, *Palaces for People.*

42 See Ernest van den Haag, "Of Happiness and Despair We Have No Measure," pp. 504–536 in Bernard Rosenberg and David Manning White, eds., *Mass Culture*

(Glencoe IL: Free Press, 1957); Edward Shils, "Mass Society and its Culture," pp. 206–229 in Phillip Davison, Rolf Meyersohn, and Edward Shils, eds., *Literary Taste, Culture, and Mass Communication*, Vol. 1 (Teaneck NJ: Somerset House, 1978).

43 A. Gramsci, *Selections from the Prison Notebooks* (London: Lawrence and Wishart, 1971).

44 Herbert J. Gans, *Popular Culture and High Culture* (New York: Basic Books, 1974).

45 See Stuart Hall, Dorothy Hobson, Andrew Lowe and Paul Willis, eds., *Culture, Media, Language* (London: Hutchinson, 1970); John Clarke, Chas Critcher and Richard Johnson, *Working Class Culture* (London: Hutchinson, 1979).

46 Dick Hebdige, *Subculture* (London: Methuen, 1979).

47 Tania Modleski, *Loving With a Vengeance* (Hamden CT: Anchor, 1982).

48 M. Gottdiener, "Hegemony and Mass Culture," *American Journal of Sociology* 90 (1985), 797–1001.

49 R. Serge Denisoff, *Solid Gold* (New Brunswick NJ: Transaction, 1975), p. 475. Also see George Melly, *Revolt into Style* (Harmondsworth: Penguin, 1970).

50 Herbert J. Gans, "American Popular Culture and High Culture in a Changing Class Structure," pp. 40–57 in J. H. Balfe and M. J. Wyszomirski, eds., *Art, Ideology and Politics* (New York: Praeger, 1985).

51 Partia K. Maultsby, "Soul Music," *Journal of Popular Culture* 17 (1983), 51–60; J. Kamin, 'Parallels in the Social Reactions to Jazz and Rock," *Journal of Jazz Studies* 2 (1974), 95–125.

52 A more detailed summary of this analysis appears in William E. Hall and Judith R. Blau, "The Taste for Popular Music," *Popular Music and Society* 11 (1987), 31–50. We had the help of a consultant who works in the industry in developing the categories for classifying each of the more than 1800 concerts listed in the 1975 issues of *Rolling Stone Magazine* (San Francisco: Straight Arrow Publications). It is possible that these listings are biased in favor of the most popular groups which may result in under-reporting for styles of music that are not widely popular. However, because the lists are generated by local agents and owners of facilities, there is no reason that this under-reporting would lead to serious bias by urban place or region.

53 To briefly clarify: R&B/soul includes Motown and funk; pop/soft rock is generally top 40 music; progressive rock is a fusion category and incorporates classical, jazz, contemporary music, and Indian music with rock; hard rock/heavy metal is updated nonmelodic, and dramatically noisy rock; generic is mainstream rock and roll incorporating music of the 1950s and 1960s garage bands; folk expresses a social consciousness and is tied to traditional music; country encompasses country and western, western swing, rockabilly, honky tonk, and bluegrass; southern rock is a blend of country and rock.

54 The square of the deviations from the mean of the logarithm of population size is used to detect the multiplicative effects of size.

55 The unstandardized coefficients (with standard errors in parentheses) are: pop/soft, 21.955 (5.059); generic, 17.043 (4.963); folk, 14.994 (4.249); hard rock/heavy metal, 24.134 (5.656); progressive rock, 15.394 (5.103).

56 The unstandardized coefficient is -2.650 (s.e. $=.792$).

57 The unstandardized coefficient for hard rock/heavy metal is 1.320 (s.e. $=.443$); the coefficient for R&B/soul is $.920$ (s.e. $=.340$).

58 While Denisoff (*Solid Gold*) suggests that R&B and soul have been diluted in the process of commercialization, others argue that far from being diluted, they have been incorporated into the mainstream in unadulterated forms and have served as a vehicle of social change by providing opportunities for black artists, and by providing historical and social reference points for blacks. See Maultsby, "Soul Music."

59 Heavy metal is usually associated with young white males and is considered to have racial overtones, which raises some question about the interpretation of black demand. It may very well be the case that a high percentage of blacks in an SMSA fosters white demand for heavy metal. On the other hand, black performers have incorporated heavy metal sounds into their own music, which lends some support to the original interpretation.

60 Denisoff, *Solid Gold*, p. 427.

61 Age categories are already in each regression. The product terms that include age with all other variables were examined and no significant interaction effects were discovered.

62 Log size is significant at the $.01$ level for all but southern rock and country music. The squared term is only significant at the $.01$ level for folk music.

8 Masses and classes

The universality of a work of art is only subjectively valid. It entails that, in principle, the meaning and value of the work of art are somehow accessible to any potential consumer of aesthetic values. It does not entail the unity of many things, but rather the unity of many minds.
Georg Simmel (1882)

Early sumptuary laws passed in Europe from the fourteenth to the seventeenth centuries protected the rights of the privileged classes to wear luxury clothing, furs, and jewels as emblems of their status and symbols of their superiority over peasants and tradesmen. The specificity of dress codes is summarized by Chandra Mukerji:

These sumptuary laws outlined the types of cloth and style of dress appropriate for each social station; they also proscribed overdressing, and restricted the use of important fabrics and decorations to the highest levels of the aristocracy.[1]

In the same way, craft works – what we would now call art works – expressed the purity of class interests throughout the Medieval period.[2] Until the Renaissance, Johan Huizinga observes, art had no intrinsic worth as such; it was a means by which the taste for luxury could be satisfied and was used to impress upon others the importance of one's own social station.[3] And just as the elite depended on the products of cultural workers for symbols of status, so cultural workers depended on the elite for they alone had sufficient resources and leisure to provide support and patronage. Yet, as the intrinsic worth of art was discovered, so too, presumably, was the complexity of its social worth enhanced. Into the Renaissance and beyond, competition among the different segments comprising society's established upper stratum – the aristocracy, the haute bourgeoisie, the clergy, and the *nouveaux riches* – further stimulated the growth of the traditional arts while being benefited by it. A differentiated elite, whose various groups competed for prominence on the basis of hereditary distinction, claims of learnedness, and discerning taste, was a primary mechanism of cultural development.[4]

Yet the upper class that emerged in the later part of the nineteenth century had a more singular – and therefore more fragile – claim to dominance than its historical predecessors. Entitlement claims for privileged status rested almost entirely on wealth – on the ownership and control of the means of production – and this was particularly the case in the United States. An important factor helping capitalists to justify a tenuous claim that they were a genuine elite – not merely rich – was their support of high culture, which served to draw class boundaries between themselves and the masses. Various historical studies document the critical role that support for the arts has had for securing social recognition and for legitimizing the claim for privileged status.[5]

The immediate relation between high status and valued cultural products that is repeatedly uncovered by historical scholarship also suggests that it is sustained through the functions patronage serves for the monied or social elite who support art, as well as the art and the artists that are thus supported. This functional relation that is imputed to the class–culture nexus has been further refined by Pierre Bourdieu in his book *Distinction*.[6] Valued cultural goods and resources operate as cultural capital as they are a basis for social selection and reproduction, while in turn cultural goods and resources acquire value when they are beyond the "realm of necessity," which they are for the working classes.

Empirical findings on audiences support this interpretation, even when researchers express concern about the persistence of class and educational differences between those who attend elite art events, such as the theater, opera, and ballet, and those who do not. For example, summarizing temporal trends in the composition of performing arts audiences, DiMaggio and Useem conclude:

Moreover, cultural democratization (if defined as increasing representation of nonelites among visitors to museums and performing arts events) does not seem to be occurring, despite arguments to the contrary, outreach efforts of some arts administrators and a degree of pressure from those responsible for public funding of the arts. The absence of discernible democratization suggests that there may be formidable barriers to any effort to open up the arts.[7]

Thus, there is considerable evidence in the literature on high culture to support the following conclusions: first, that the elite arts play a significant role in defining and maintaining class boundaries; secondly, that perpetuation of class inequalities relies on the display of cultural symbols and aesthetic preferences; and thirdly, that the survival of elite art depends on a rich upper stratum, and thus on social inequalities.

In the literature on popular culture there is much less agreement about the significance of class differences. Some leftist theorists of mass culture consider popular culture a vulgarized version of high culture created by the ruling class as a means to dominate and exploit the masses. The passive acceptance of inferior art products – kitsch – is explained by the frustrating conditions of alienating work from which mass culture provides an escape. This sort of art, as Rojeck puts it, creates "the illusion of freedom and self-determination which is the necessary counterbalance to the real subordination of workers in the labor process."[8] In even more explicit terms Gramsci maintains that the cultural arena of capitalist society is a major source of social control since culture is the institutionalized ideological basis of class hegemony.[9] In short, high culture fortifies class standing while popular culture is produced by capitalists to divert the attention of the working class from their often meaningless lives.

Paradoxically, a main difference between Gramsci's position and the conservative one that can be traced from de Tocqueville and Matthew Arnold to the writings of the mass culturalists is largely a philosophical and moral one. Both make the distinction between popular and elite art and both perceive this distinction to be a function of class differences, for good or for bad. According to mass culture theory, high culture is essential for maintaining deserving distinctions and saving society from anarchist tendencies, and because it exhibits intellectual and expressive qualities it is capable of preserving ideal values that contrast with the banality and cheap thrills provided by mass culture.[10]

Others view popular culture in a different light, that is, as an authentic expression of group life that, even when mass produced, has meaning for large audiences and many consumers. Some social scientists suggest that the working class achieves its own identity, either by developing its own distinctive cultural styles or by parodying or filtering mainstream culture.[11] Others state that ethnic and localized cultural traditions – for instance, the celebration of weddings, funerals and holidays; regular meetings in neighborhood saloons; attending sporting events; and other shared leisure activities – reaffirm class and subgroup identities and mitigate the burden of an oppressive economic system.[12]

Much cultural theory, therefore, tends to emphasize the role played by elite and popular culture in defining class distinctions and, likewise, the relevance of such class distinctions for maintaining culture. Elite art is the province of a privileged minority who can truly appreciate it, or, alternatively, can use it to fortify status and power. In contrast, popular culture, whether interpreted as created by the ruling class to manipulate exploited masses and consumed by the masses as an escape from a humdrum life, or as produced by the masses as an oppositional and alternative lifestyle, is also generally considered to be associated with class inequalities.

The functionalist premise

Two propositions are joined by the functionalist premise, namely, that aesthetic choices make and reinforce status differences and that these status differences are important for distinguishing types of art. This assumption – that status differences account for art preferences and that public expressions of these preferences account for status differences – can be questioned on the grounds that it is teleological and circular. (Trees may provide shade but shade is not the reason for trees, nor trees for shade.) Besides, many of the claims about the functional relation between art and status differences are based on observations made on the individual level – about consumers or about audience members – that lead to misleading conclusions about class differences and art in an entire society.

Moreover, there are definitional problems. As Howard Becker astutely observes, there is a filtering and labeling process that affects how a cultural commodity is priced and institutionally situated, which in turn has consequences for which people and groups are likely to enjoy it.[13] Purchasing a Porsche, a house in Malibu, and a Picasso may be the mark of discerning taste, but discerning taste is here indistinguishable from what wealth buys. In the same sense, the evaluations made by art historians and the selection process of history itself inform our conventional labels for elite and popular culture.

Scholarship on the class–culture nexus has tended to ignore important features of large complex societies that have a bearing on the relationship between the class structure and the nature of its cultural products. In cultural marketplaces, hordes of suppliers compete for great numbers of buyers. The buyers themselves are different in many ways, not only with respect to social class, but also in terms of ethnicity, gender, age, lifestyle, family status, and residence. The conditions of modern society mean expanding opportunities for leisure, for the observation of other people's cultural activities, and for "shopping around" in different cultural worlds.[14] These are similar to the conditions that Norbert Elias observed led to the easy adoption throughout all social strata of practices governing good manners.[15]

Simmel, who delighted in paradoxes, noted that singular art becomes universal when it has the same meaning for very many consumers.[16] One implication of this is that art can signify class differences so long as there are clear understandings of class membership, but fails to when class configurations are sufficiently complex. That is, cultural values stick to the contours of strata and groups in highly stratified societies, whereas they wash over the intricate complexities in more egalitarian societies.

A test of the inequality hypothesis

This chapter examines how the characteristics of places in 1970 and subsequent changes in those characteristics influence the expansion of cultural supply over a ten year period. While such an analysis does not provide evidence of people's consumption patterns and preferences, it does help to resolve the conflicting views about the relationship at the societal level between social and economic inequalities and culture. For, as we have seen, some of these views are based on extrapolations from studies of individuals and others imply questionable functional relationships. Since stratification has been the prime focus of interest in historical and social science scholarship on art, attention chiefly centers here on overall class characteristics (such as median levels of income and education) and on indications of class inequalities (in these same respects). Another focus has been on the presumed decline of differentiation along horizontal lines or the homogenization that accompanies universal education, urbanization, and industrialization. The mass culturalists contend that such leveling impairs high culture,[17] whereas marxist theorists argue that whatever initial differences exist among the masses of workers, a dominant capitalist class can largely eradicate them by means of an intensively standardized, homogeneous, and commercialized culture.[18] For this reason, various forms of horizontal differentiation are examined, including differentiation with respect to occupation, sectors of employment, and language.

One broad indication of the supply of culture is the relative number of artists who live in metropolitan places. Artists, like all workers, are responsive to employment opportunities. They work in labor markets that are composed of congeries of commercial establishments, nonprofit cultural organizations, universities, entrepreneurs, and individual buyers. Income for contemporary artists comes from multiple sources, including free-lance work, commissions, employment in their art field, employment in non-art fields, welfare, and – particularly for musicians – street work. Artists are also interested in inexpensive housing. It is important to keep in mind that the unemployment rate for actors or dancers is rarely less than 20 per cent and the median earnings reported for all performing artists during this ten year period were around $5,000. We might suspect that the superior locations for artists combine abundant opportunities for well paying jobs with a housing market that provides "cheap digs."

For purposes of comparison, architects are also examined. Because architecture is classified by the Census as being an artistic occupation and because architects' occupational ideology centers on creativity and aesthetics, we might expect certain similarities between the social conditions that attract and promote the growth of both artists and architects. On the other hand, architects are much more closely tied over long periods of time to established firms, and architects may, therefore, exhibit patterns more similar to institutional suppliers of culture than artists who are relatively footloose in large and unarticulated labor markets.

The third broad indication of culture are institutions that supply various forms of it. While it is the case that high culture institutions benefit from the support of wealthy benefactors and popular culture establishments depend on the investments of capitalists, no high culture institution can survive on its endowment just as no popular culture establishment can stay in business on merely the initial investment money. All cultural institutions require a large potential market comprised of consumers, art lovers, devotees. Such basic differences as these between artists, architects, and institutions of culture provide the context for the analysis of change reported here.

Methodology of change analysis

The difficulties of inferring causality and of obtaining unbiased estimates of regression coefficients on the basis of cross-sectional analysis are well known.[19] Panel analysis reduces the difficulties of identifying the sources of nonspurious causality because it makes it possible to examine the level of the dependent variable at Time 2 as a function of lagged (Time 1) conditions, as well as the level of the dependent variable at Time 1. It is also possible to examine how changes in conditions between Time 1 and Time 2 influence changes in the dependent variable. How stable the cultural factor is over time is estimated by the coefficient of its level at Time 1 in the two-wave panel analysis. The generalized model for change is expressed in formal terms by the following equation, with V and Z representing two exogenous variables, and the subscripts to Time 1 and Time 2:

$$Y_2 = a + bY_1 + bV_1 + bZ_2 + b(V_2 - V_1) + b(Z_2 - Z_1) + U$$

In the initial analysis, all Time 1 variables and all difference scores (Time 2 − Time 1) were included in each equation. In the interest of parsimony, any 1970 independent variable or change score that was not significant was excluded in the final equation; and, in those cases in which a 1970 independent variable and its change score are multicollinear, the 1970 independent variable alone was included in the regression equation.

In any model of change it is imperative that the units of analysis remain constant; in fact, however, the geographical boundaries of SMSAs were revised by the Bureau of the Census during this ten year interval. The solution was to reconstitute 1980 SMSAs according to 1970 boundaries after extracting 1980 data from the census summary tapes by counties. Thus, 1980 independent variables are based on aggregated counts for SMSAs defined by 1970 boundaries. To ensure similar comparability for 1970 and 1980 cultural indicators, information that was coded from directories and magazines included city location or place which then could be translated by Census FIPS codes into SMSA location by 1970 boundaries.[20]

An initial problem posed by the sources for the independent variables is that the 1970 data had been obtained from the Public Use Sample and as they are based on individual level data, most provide ratio level measures (e.g., median income), whereas the 1980 variables were obtained from the 100 per cent census of population that provides data classified into broad categories. For the purpose of computing measures that would be comparable for the two time periods, the 1970 individual data were initially regrouped to correspond to 1980 categories.[21] For example, instead of using the actual 1970 data on years of schooling for the purpose of computing education mean, median, and a measure of inequality, these data were first regrouped into five categories that correspond to the 1980 education categories. An examination of the means, standard deviations, and the correlations based on the original 1970 variables and those on the recalculated 1970 variables yielded remarkably high consistency, indicating that the consequences due to the loss of precision are not great.[22]

The most extreme problem involving the conversion of 1970 measures to ones that are comparable to 1980 measures involved data on detailed occupations. In the 1970 census there are over 400 detailed occupations, whereas the 1980 summary tape only provides information on twelve major occupational groups. Originally each detailed occupation was assigned a prestige score (SES), based on Duncan's socio-economic index. It measures social class broadly defined as it is based on occupational prestige, education and income.[23] It is therefore considered to be a good indicator of life style, cultural tastes, and the opportunities and inclinations for leisure. The 1970 SMSA aggregate measures were computed on the basis of individuals' SES scores, including a measure of inequality, namely, the Gini coefficient, which indicates the extent to which there is a large average difference in a given dimension between all possible pairs relative to the average value of that dimension in the population.[24]

For the purpose of computing a 1970 index of SES inequality that would be comparable to an index computed on 1980 major occupations, the 1970 detailed occupations were regrouped taking into account the Bureau of the Census' reclassification of particular ones.[25] Fortunately, these scores based on major categories are remarkably similar to those based on detailed ones.[26]

While the Gini coefficient is used as a measure of inequality when a ranked difference is involved, the Gibbs–Martin index of diversity is used to measure the degree of differentiation when categorical differences are not ranked.[27] A high value on the index means that persons are relatively evenly distributed among a set of categories and a low value means that persons are highly concentrated in one or a few categories.

Though measurement error in the dependent variables under consideration is probably not as great as it is in investigations of self-reported behavior or of attitudes, any measurement error poses particular problems in a change analysis. An obvious difficulty is that there is some variation in the actual year for which information on the cultural indicators is available, but generally, institutional data are coded from directories published in the early 1970s and early 1980s, as indicated in Appendix B, and the data on artists and architects are from the 1970 and 1980 census of population.

Decisions about which directories and other listings to use for the institutional analysis were made after consulting the editors and staff members of the associations who compiled the listings. In the few instances where it was possible, multiple sources were compared and sometimes information from more than one was coded.[28] Obviously, it was not feasible to code multiple sources for every cultural indicator (nor even possible since it is rare that a given cultural institution is covered by more than one directory), but every attempt was made to select what was considered to be the more reliable source when two were known to exist. Unfortunately, directories generally fail to provide sufficient information to take into account the sizes or attendance figures for institutions and events.

One concern, as already discussed, has to do with the consistency of the information from the Census on Selected Services,[29] but this source is the most comprehensive for commercial cultural establishments and throughout the analysis these indicators exhibited a high degree of external validity. Another concern is the apparent decline in the number of live popular concerts. This was discussed with the calendar editor of *Rolling Stone Magazine*, who told me that the editorial policy (and staff) have not changed since 1975, the first year for which data are coded. It may be that concerts have declined in numbers while increasing in size as large stadiums and arenas are now being used.

In the study of institutional change all cultural supply variables for which comparable information is available for the early and late period are analyzed.[30] The dependent variables are logarithmically transformed. There is one exception. Because the number of craft fairs is extremely skewed in the earlier period (71 SMSAs did not have a craft fair) and moderately skewed in the later period (the number was down to 46), the dependent variables for 1980 and 1970 are dichotomies – whether or not an SMSA had at least one craft fair.[31] The dependent variables based on counts of individuals in art occupations and in architecture pose few problems. To obtain these occupational data, information was extracted from the 5 per cent and 15 per cent county group files from the 1970 and 1980 censuses.[32]

The central theoretical problem is the significance of class inequalities for the supply of culture and of cultural workers. However, it is recognized that other factors relating to a city's urban features (for example, density, percentage who work downtown), or a city's administrative structure (for example, size of the urban government), or its economic structure (for example, median firm size), or a city's financial health (for example, urban revenues) may also play a role in explaining the prevalence of culture in a place. Preliminary regressions were carried out that incorporated all known influences on urban culture based on inspections of matrices of correlations. Virtually all correlates of art, other than those relating to social class composition and urban diversity, are spurious owing to the effects of population size.[33]

In all regressions, regional effects were examined as a set of k-1 (or 3) regions because, as the purely descriptive analysis demonstrates, there exists regional variation for most popular arts, and it is possible that regional differences would be revealed for elite art indicators under other controls. In most cases, regional effects are due to the socio-economic characteristics of regions, and in two cases where they are not, the single region that is responsible for regional effects is entered into the equation.

It is of interest to ascertain the effects of sector specific federal funding on cultural institutions. Because the National Endowment for the Arts (NEA) provides information on fairly broad categories of funding, caution dictates that funding be examined only in those instances for which there is a fairly good match. These instances are art museums, dance companies, and nonprofit theater.[34] Except for museums, for which funding information was coded for only 1971–72, funding data were coded for the following years: 1971–72, 1976–77, and 1982–83. The extremely high correlations among these variables at three time points for both dance and theater warranted pooling them to create a relatively robust measure.[35] Both the logged funding variable and the squared funding variable were examined in the institutional regressions; usually both are positive in an equation, but both are not significant in which case the squared log term rather than the logged term is included.

There are two additional, but related, problems. New York City is an outlier on many dependent variables including population size. When the dependent variable is logarithmically transformed and size is logged, New York is still an outlier but in most cases is not far from the regression line. In the cross-sectional analysis of suppliers (not shown) the squared logged term for size fully explains any remaining influence that New York City has. In the panel equations, the squared term for log size is rarely significant and New York City's removal has no effect on the regression solution.

Restating the issues

Given that culture purportedly helps to maintain class differences, and class differences in turn reinforce evaluative and categorical definitions of culture, we would expect that culture would be responsive to social and economic inequalities. Scholarship on art and cultural history and empirical research on audiences imply that class inequalities and cultural development are closely interlocked. Yet initial research involving the residential patterns of artists and the prevalence of art institutions led to contradictory conclusions concerning the relationships between the social class composition of urban places and these indicators of cultural activity.[36] In this chapter I extend these studies by providing an analysis of change for artists and architects between 1970 and 1980, and incorporate into the change analysis of institutions additional types of institutions and data on NEA funding for particular art sectors.

Artists and their labor markets

For the purposes of this analysis, performing artists per capita (times 1,000) are compared with nonperforming artists per capita (times 1,000); with performers including actors, dancers, musicians, and composers, and non-performers including authors, designers, painters, and sculptors. This classification is based on the occupations that artists report in the decennary censuses and it does not permit the separation of those in the same broad category (for example, film actors from theater actors) nor does it allow a distinction between commercial and fine arts. While there are disadvantages in failing to make such distinctions, the reality is that often artists work in commercial and noncommercial settings or in different fields within the same broad area.

Given the theoretical interest in forms of inequality, major factors considered are income inequality, educational inequality, and inequalities in social class, which is defined by Duncan's index of socio-economic status (SES). While there is some conceptual overlap among inequalities in socio-economic status (SES) and inequalities in education and income, the correlations among them are not high and SES inequalities are considered to reflect differences in strata defined in global class terms, rather than specific aspects of class.[37] It is important to know that much inequality in a metropolis on any dimension often means a relatively low average or median level on that dimension.[38] The simple correlation for 1970 between income inequality and income median is −.46; that between educational inequality and median education is −.49; and that between SES inequality and median SES is −.77.

Another issue relates to the overall diversity of the population since a major assertion of the mass culturalists is that homogenization and "massification" imperil the integrity of culture. In this analysis the indication of diversity, or lack of it, is the extent to which people are more or less uniformly distributed among major occupational groups.[39]

Population size is taken into account because it indicates the potential audience for art, the level of metropolitan resources, and opportunities for employment for artists. Population change is also examined since it indicates something about the vitality of the economy and about work opportunities generally. In chapter 2 it is reported that commercial, not elite, art displays regional variation. Since many performing artists work in commercial enterprises, it is not surprising that disproportionately many of them live in west coast cities. Especially since historians and philosophers have raised the issue of the adverse effects that industrialization and the dominance of factories have had on the arts, an effort is made to take an indicator of industrialization into account.[40] The measure used, although admittedly crude, is the percentage of the labor force engaged in manufacturing.

1970 analysis for artists

The change analysis is of primary interest here because the cross-sectional analysis has already been published.[41] However, the change analysis requires a modification of the independent variables for 1970, as described above, and for this reason, the replication is presented here using 1970 independent variables that are comparable to the 1980 variables. The results obtained, as reported in table 8.1, are nearly identical to those reported earlier, which can be briefly summarized. Income inequality has a strong positive relationship with performing artists, and although it is not quite significant in the regression for nonperforming artists, it is also positive. Other parallel influences on performers and nonperformers are population size and population growth. In 1970 opportunites in labor markets for artists were greatly superior in large places and in places that were growing.

Table 8.1. *Regression analysis of performing and nonperforming artists, 1970[a]*

	Performing Artists		Nonperforming Artists	
	b (s.e.)	Beta	b (s.e.)	Beta
1 Income inequality, 1970	16.93**	.43	10.85	.20
	(4.03)		(5.50)	
2 SES inequality, 1970	26.24**	.38	−41.46*	−.44
	(6.97)		(9.59)	
3 Educational inequality, 1970	−7.59	−.15	−6.33	−.09
	(4.96)		(6.83)	
4 Occupational diversity, 1970	−83.02**	−.58	−8.99	−.05
	(11.84)		(16.31)	
5 % Manufacturing, 1970	−2.23*	−.21	3.44*	.24
	(1.06)		(1.45)	
6 Population growth, 1960–1970	.010*	.18	.015*	.20
	(.004)		(.006)	
7 West	.687**	.25	.161	.04
	(.241)		(.332)	
8 Population size (log), 1970	.311**	.23	.507**	.28
	(.105)		(.145)	
Constant	60.78		14.86	
$\hat{R}^2$	.52		.50	

*p < .05
**p < .01
[a] Sources: Appendix B, A and B.

A striking difference between performers and nonperformers is that social class (SES) inequalities appear to provide favorable conditions for performers, but not for nonperformers. Originally we interpreted this finding to mean that performing artists must live precisely in those places where there is the most demand for their work. Great class inequalities increase the demand for cultural and artistic services since attending live performances visibly draws attention to social position and, in that sense, reinforces class boundaries between different classes. On the other hand, since nonperformers do not have to be located where their cultural products are in great demand, class differences make little difference to where they work and live.

Thus, in spite of the fact that the measurement of some independent variables is slightly different in this analysis compared with the earlier one, the results obtained are quite similar. There is one exception, however. Initially we found that educational inequality adversely affects performing artists, and, to a lesser extent, nonperforming artists. It was concluded that art appreciation tends to require a considerable amount of schooling and that educational inequality creates distinct but overlapping groups, members of which share common cultural orientations and artistic tastes. However, in this analysis, although the signs for the two coefficients are consistent with the earlier results, neither is significant, indicating the single instance for which collapsing a variable (from seventeen to five categories in this case) yields a nonreplicable result.

The negative effects of occupational diversity for performing artists, but not for nonperforming artists, are also consistent with the earlier analysis. Decomposition of the diversity measure indicated that little occupational diversity means a concentration of workers in the largest occupations, specifically white collar ones,[42] which suggests that taste cultures rooted in substantially large publics with similar life styles and cultural interests are especially important for the live performing arts. In contrast, writers, painters, sculptors, and designers, who are far less dependent on the tastes of local audiences, are not so much influenced by the extent to which there is much or little occupational diversity in a place.

The remaining influences summarized in table 8.1 are also identical to those we earlier reported. For example, the negative relationship between manufacturing and artists' residence is again supported in the case of performers, who are probably unlikely to find employment opportunities in cities with a substantial industrial base. This is not the case for nonperformers, who are more likely to be living in places with a high proportion of workers employed in manufacturing. Industrial cities, it might be conjectured, attract nonperformers because they are interested in inexpensive housing and are not dependent on large audiences for their work.

We explained the pronounced attractiveness of western states for performing artists in terms of the concentration of the film and recording studios in the west, we explained the effects of population size and growth on artists' residential patterns in terms of artists' interests in the resources and opportunities that large cities and growing cities could generally offer them.

Although there are differences between the social and economic conditions that create favorable opportunities for performing artists and nonperforming artists, the most general conclusion tends to offer some support for the theoretical literature that posits a connection between inequalities and culture. That is, performing artists tend to work in places where there is relatively much income inequality and inequalities in socio-economic status.

In contrast, however, nonperforming artists tend to live in places with relatively little inequality in socio-economic status, which we considered to be the result of the fact that nonperformers are not influenced by an audience demand that is governed by differences in life style and tastes.

Occupational diversity has pronounced negative effects on performing artists, which means that a large homogenous concentration of people in a few major occupational groups that share similar cultural orientations and life styles generate markets for the performing arts. Together with the other findings it also suggests the notable effects of white collar interests in the performing arts accompany the effects of pronounced social and economic inequalities that together create conditions favorable to artists' labor markets.

Changes in artists' labor markets

Artists increased in numbers between 1970 and 1980 far more than the rate of population growth. Relative to the size of the cities in which they lived, performers increased by 30 per cent and nonperformers increased by 40 per cent, and as a percentage of the labor force the percentage change for all artists combined was 46 per cent. Given the volatility and expansion of this broad occupational category, we would expect considerable change in the features of places that attracted artists, particularly nonperformers who increased in numbers more than did performers.

The advantage that an analysis of change has over a static analysis is that it is possible to discover when conditions have persisting effects and are, therefore, more likely to be causal ones, making it possible to detect the dynamic processes that are implied in the assumption that population compositional characteristics are important in an explanation of the supply of cultural workers.

The results of the change analysis are more parsimonious than the analysis of patterns for 1970. Neither educational inequality nor the percentage of manufacturing (nor change in either) is related to the 1980 per capita numbers of performers and nonperformers, and therefore these variables are excluded from the equation. (Educational inequalities and percentage in manufacturing both diminished between 1970 and 1980 which perhaps accounts for their attenuated effects on artists' residential patterns.)

Over time there is an increasing similarity in the factors that influence both nonperformers and performers, as table 8.2 indicates. There is, in fact, a substantially higher simple correlation in 1980 than in 1970 between the numbers of performers per capita and that of nonperformers per capita,[43] which indicates the increasing concentration of artists of all kinds in the same places. Moreover, there is no significant regional variation in 1980.

Table 8.2. *Regression analysis of performing and nonperforming artists, 1980*

	Performing artists		Nonperforming artists	
	b (s.e.)	Beta	b (s.e.)	Beta
1 Income inequality 1970	27.33**	.47	26.08**	.27
	(7.19)		(8.73)	
2 SEI inequality 1970	15.66	.15	83.93**	.49
	(12.50)		(15.96)	
3 Occupational diversity 1970	−86.68**	−.41	−144.35**	−.41
	(30.49)		(32.71)	
4 ΔIncome inequality	35.30**	.33	40.38**	.23
	(10.67)		(13.58)	
5 ΔSEI inequality	28.66	.12	70.49*	.18
	(24.99)		(31.16)	
6 ΔOccupational diversity	−45.27	−.15	−138.2**	−.28
	(43.36)		(51.08)	
7 Population growth, 1979–80	−2.17*	−.21	−4.06**	−.27
	(.92)		(1.09)	
8 Population size (log), 1970	.055	.03	.168	.05
	(.183)		(.241)	
9 1970 Cultural indicator	.579**	.39	1.43**	.78
	(.144)		(.136)	
Constant	63.72		93.93	
R^2	.39		.64	

*p < .05
**p < .01

The major characteristics of urban places in 1970 and changes in them between 1970 and 1980 have consistent effects on both performers and nonperformers, although they are not always significant for performers. Most pronounced are the positive effects of income inequality and further increases in income inequality; both the lagged variable and the change score are significant in the two equations. The earlier strong positive effect of 1970 SES inequality is no longer evident for performing artists nor is an increase in SES inequality significant for performers (although both coefficients are positive). Still, 1970 SES inequality has a strong positive lagged effect on nonperformers (a reversal from 1970) and an increase in the level of SES inequality also has a positive effect on the relative numbers of nonperformers. The overall results of the change analyses support the conclusion that not only places with much inequality but also places with increasing inequality are particularly congenial for artists, apparently because they provide superior opportunities for work and employment. This supports the literature that stresses the functional significance of class difference for sustaining the vitality of the arts. Moreover, it is not inconsistent with the notion that artists need the rich as clients, patrons, and consumers, but that they also are attracted to cities with large, poor neighborhoods in which to live.

Little occupational diversity and further declines in occupational diversity promote the relative number of nonperforming artists, and though the coefficient for the change score is not significant for performing artists, the lagged effect of little occupational diversity is. These results are parallel to the 1970 cross-sectional analysis and are, if anything, stronger since three out of four coefficients are significant. Thus, cities with occupational structures composed of large and consolidated occupational strata are more attractive to artists than are cities with great occupational diversity.

The apparent paradox is that much diversity among hierarchical strata but homogeneity of large occupational groups together create attractive environments for artists. These environments are ones in which economic differences constitute fundamental class distinctions, but cross-cutting those distinctions are life style and taste communalities. Artists thrive in communities where there are many who live in penthouses and many who live in cheap apartments and, similarly, many who pay to sit in the first five rows to attend an opera or popular comedy and, still, many others who can only afford to stand in the back of the hall and pay a few dollars to attend. The point is that substantial similarities in taste that are part of the lifestyle of urban white collar workers combined with great discrepancies in economic and social classes generate sufficient variability in housing, neighborhoods, and, especially, in employment opportunities to make a city attractive to artists.

The size of the population in 1970 has virtually no effect on the supply of artists in 1980, and the results for population growth might even suggest that artists are staying in small places or moving to them. This conclusion would be consistent with the results that indicate no notable patterns of dominance by the largest United Stated cities. This would be somewhat misleading, however. The correlation between 1970 urban size (logged) and the 1970 per capita numbers of performers is .23 and that for 1970 per capita numbers of nonperformers is .45. However, the effects of urban size are attenuated because in 1970 large cities had disproportionate numbers of artists, and the presence of artists in 1970 is responsible for the spurious correlations between size and the 1980 patterns of artists' residence and work. Thus, it is not the size of the city that attracts artists but rather the size of an established artistic community which simultaneously means networks of information, promoters, agents, and presumably, the success of that artistic community in shaping community tastes and preferences. A similar explanation can account for the negative effects of population growth on the relative number of artists. Places that were large in 1970 lost population, on the average, by 1980. (The correlation between 1970 logged size and population change is $-.20$.) Because large places had disproportionately many artists in 1970 they continued to attract and to keep more artists even while they were experiencing overall population losses.

The residential patterns for nonperformers are less volatile over time than those for performers (that is, the coefficient of stability is considerably higher for nonperformers compared with performers), which probably reflects the greater tendencies of dancers, actors, and musicians to travel on tours and look for performing opportunities in different cities. Nevertheless, in spite of the lesser residential stability for performers, the factors that govern urban locations for both are more similar in 1980 than they were in 1970. All artists tend to live and work in places where there are considerable social and economic inequalities and in places where these inequalities have generally increased over time. Moreover, both tend to be located in places where there is considerable concentration of the employed population in a few major occupational groups that define the contours of a large homogeneous sector, which, in turn, implies a common public orientation to the arts and to cultural activities; indeed, it implies what the mass culturalists consider to be an undifferentiated mass of consumers.[44]

Nevertheless, artists neither define the range of culture that is available in metropolitan places nor do we expect them to respond to the same social forces that cultural institutions do. Artists are individuals who move within labor markets and respond to opportunities for jobs and for housing. Before examining the conditions of the changes in the numbers of cultural suppliers, it is useful to compare the results for artists with those for architects. Like artists, architects are involved in creative work; however, they are not so loosely connected to their labor markets as artists are but rather have relatively stable employment in organizations.

Changes in architects' labor markets

Architects did not increase in numbers as rapidly as did artists during the 1970s. Yet a growth rate of 14 per cent was greater than that for most established professions, and particularly high given the deteriorating conditions in the construction industry in the late 1960s. In interpreting this growth, Montgomery emphasizes the relative importance of the corporate sector, the population growth in the sunbelt states, and the symbolic importance of the architect-designed home for affluent families.[45] As Larson notes, architects tend to concentrate where wealthy and "interesting" clientele can be found.[46]

Because of its strong artistic component and lack of clear guidelines for establishing credentials, John Cullen suggests that the profession of architecture is much closer to that of artist than to the other established professions.[47] My own survey of over 400 architects indicates that even among those architects who work in highly specialized or technical fields, there is a strong identification with work that is creative or artistic. Of those surveyed, 98 per cent mentioned creativity as the distinctive feature of the architectural profession when compared to other professions, and when asked what, if anything, they would like to change in their work and responsibilities, 80 per cent mentioned they wanted even more opportunities for creative challenges – to have more design assignments, to be able to work autonomously, and especially, to have a greater role in the initial design stage of a project.[48] For these reasons, it is useful to compare architects with artists to see if their labor market opportunities are structured differently by social conditions owing to their tighter institutional bondedness, or in similar ways owing to their occupational identities.

The results of the cross-sectional and panel analyses fail to confirm many suppositions about the locational patterns of architects. For example, the notion that architects are concentrated in particular regions of the country is misleading. While it is the case that there were fewer architects relative to population size in the east in 1970, regional differences both in 1970 and 1980 are not large enough to be statistically significant. Although there is a positive correlation of .18 between architects per capita in 1970 and the percentage of the urban labor force engaged in construction in 1970, this relationship disappears once population size is taken into account. Furthermore, although one might suppose that urban places with much need of renovation and construction would attract architects, there is a trivial correlation between the percentage of dilapidated housing and the relative number of architects in SMSAs. It has often been said, with some bewilderment, that architectural practice does not respond in obvious ways to market forces or to building and construction activity,[49] and this is confirmed in the empirical analyses.[50]

The most important results in the panel analysis of architects' change in work and residential locations relate to the effects of changes in socio-economic inequalities. Yet in striking contrast to the results for artists, which revealed positive influences of inequalities, the results for architects demonstrate that architects are more likely to live and work in places that experienced a ten year decline in socio-economic inequality.[51] This aberration from a fairly consistent set of findings for artists raises questions about the general conclusion that culture is responsive to inequalities in the urban social structure. Nevertheless, it must be kept in mind that architects' labor markets, compared with those of artists, are far more structured around organizational arrangements and a relatively stable clientele. Architects also exhibit far more enduring attachments to their urban locations over time (as indicated by the correlation between the 1970 and 1980 per capita numbers of architects of .90). Such divergent results for occupational groups that are more or less integrated in art worlds but that work in very different types of labor markets raise questions about the meaning of differences between cultural workers and cultural suppliers, and whether or not the social conditions that govern the demand for cultural products have different consequences for artists and for institutionalized art.

Cultural institutions

Quite at odds with our findings for artists (but consistent with those for architects) we initially found that *low* levels of inequality of various kinds are related to the urban supply of cultural institutions. For example, our research indicated that for 1970 urban places with relatively little inequality in socio-economic status (SES) have more specialized museums, art museums, nonprofit theaters, dance companies, ballet companies, art galleries, theater premieres, craft fairs, and popular concerts. Low, not high, median income is also related to ballet companies, cinemas, and popular concerts, and low income inequality is related to cinemas.[52] The tentative conclusion based on cross-sectional analyses of cultural institutions was that large middle classes created a demand for cultural institutions, and that social and economic equalities are implicated in the supply of both elite and popular cultural products and events.[53] The results of a preliminary lagged panel analysis for some of the cultural institutions appeared to support that conclusion. Presented in this chapter is an extended version of that panel analysis, incorporating, when possible, information about urban arts funding for specific art sectors.[54] These results are summarized in table 8.3.

Institutions do not increase in numbers very much over a ten year period and the best predictors of how many institutions there are in 1980 in an SMSA is the number that were there in about 1970,[55] and the size of the population. However, factors related to social class composition and indications of population diversity do play a role in explaining institutional changes during

Table 8.3. *Regression analysis of cultural institutions, 1980; beta coefficients ($p < .05$)*

	Art Museums	Nonprofit Theater	Dance Companies	Ballet Companies	Ensembles	Craft fairs	Commercial theater	Popular concerts	Radio	Cinemas
SES inequality, 1970			-.12	-.13		-.19				
Education median, 1970								.13	.17	
Educational inequality, 1970										-.18
Δ Income inequality						-.26				
Δ SES inequality			-.12	-.19						
Δ Educational inequality										-.09
Employment diversity, 1970									.14	.19
Language diversity, 1970										.15
East						.25				
Art sector funds	a	.17	.21[b]							
Population size (log), 1970	.31	.25	.39	.33	.31	.33	.38[b]	.41	.15	.47
1970 Cultural indicator	.67	.51	.32	.43	.60	b	.55	.49	.67	.46
R̂²	.85	.72	.80	.61	.70	.30	.68	.74	.73	.89

[a] Not significant and deleted from equation
[b] Squared term substituted for logged term

the decade. It should be briefly noted, first, why region explains very little of the variation in the models. Craft fairs are more prominent in the northeast, as is reported in chapter 2, and while west coast cities do have more commercial theaters and cinemas, the regression results show that it is the population characteristics of these cities and not region per se that accounts for their concentration in the west.

In contrast with the results for performing and nonperforming artists, but consistent with those for architects, the general conclusion is that initial levels of low inequality and declining inequality promote institutional culture of various kinds. For example, as table 8.3 shows, ballet companies and all dance companies increase in places where there are low levels of socio-economic inequality in 1970 and further declines by 1980. Craft fairs also increase in those places where there was initially a relatively low level of social class (SES) inequality and where income inequality declined in the next decade. Cinemas increase in frequency in response to initial low levels of educational inequality as well as to declining educational inequality.

Thus, early inequalities enhance supply and declining inequalities further do so with respect to the numbers of dance companies, ballet companies, cinemas, and craft fairs. The fact that little inequality on any one of these dimensions accompanies a relatively high mean value on it as well,[56] suggests that it is a relatively affluent and well-educated middle class with proportionately few who are very poor or very rich that stimulates the demand for expanding numbers of cultural institutions. This is precisely the point made by Herbert J. Gans in his 1985 essay, "American Popular Culture and High Culture in a Changing Class Structure." A major change from the 1970s, he notes, is the "apparent emergence of a new taste culture that seems in some ways to cut across and blend upper and lower-middle culture, and which, for want of a better term, I will label middle culture."[57]

In two instances it is not relative inequality in some aspect of social status but rather a high median level that promotes cultural institutions. The higher the overall level of education in 1970, the greater the increase in the number of live popular concerts and radio. This is consistent with the overall interpretation of the potent significance that a well-educated middle class has for institutionalized culture. It is also of more than passing interest that radio, which is largely commercial, and popular rock concerts, which are often viewed with considerable contempt and considered inherently inferior to "authentic" art, are benefited by a well-educated population and not by a poorly educated one.

As we have already seen, little occupational diversity and an accompanying concentration of the labor market in white-collar jobs help to account for the initial relative numbers of artists and increases of these numbers over time. Of the various forms of diversity considered, two others are important for understanding the institutional supply of culture, namely, industrial diversity and language diversity.[58]

Declining differentiation, according to mass culture theory, accompanies the homogenization of culture and the proliferation of standardized, popular culture. In fact, the results support the opposite conclusion. Radio and cinema, both commercial and widely popular types of cultural entertainment, are promoted by forms of population diversity. The greater the degree of differentiation among the population by sector of employment, the greater is the number of radio stations and cinemas. To the extent that supply is responsive to demand, the conclusion is that consumer demand for major forms of popular, commercial culture is greater when the work force is highly differentiated, suggesting that there are multiple, distinctive, and perhaps even competing taste cultures for different kinds of music stations and different kinds of films. Where there is much employment diversity there is also much occupational diversity $(r = .37)$, which supports the interpretation, even though occupational diversity does not have independent positive effects on either radio or cinemas. Nevertheless, it draws attention to the contrast between the importance of occupational homogeneity for artists' labor markets and the importance of population diversity for suppliers of popular culture.

The greater the language diversity, which is to say, the more people in a place for whom English is not the mother tongue, the greater is the supply of cinemas. A post hoc explanation for this finding is that movies (like television) provide foreign speakers with excellent opportunities for learning English.

The main point to be made here, however, is that major forms of commercial, mass culture are more in demand in cities with much differentiation or heterogeneity with respect to two dimensions of social distinction. These findings contrast with earlier conclusions about the importance of occupational consolidation for artists' labor markets, and they also contrast with the polemical argument of mass cultural theory. It appears not that "the great mass of consumers now determines what is to be produced" and that "the average of tastes . . . grows accordingly" as Ernest van den Haag wrote,[59] but rather that distinct, articulated groupings of people who are different in major respects generate demands for a variety of popular culture.

An incomplete, but nevertheless important, indicator of public support for a city's cultural enterprises is the dollar amount of grant monies awarded by the National Endowment of the Arts to its institutions. It is possible to match NEA categories of institutional funding for museums, theaters, and dance companies.

In one case, namely museums, the influences of public support are negligible. This is not particularly surprising, however, because funds are not available for construction purposes.[60] However, NEA directly or indirectly promotes the creation of new theater and dance companies. In the case of dance it provides performance and personnel grants, and in the case of theater, it funds training programs, personnel salaries, playwright commissions, and development grants. Independent of urban size and initial numbers of theater and dance companies in the early 1970s, the effect of funding on the sheer numbers of theaters and dance companies in the 1980s is significant and positive. The multiplicative effects of funding in the case of dance companies are, in fact, stronger than the linear effects of the simple logged dollar amount, which is why the squared term is used instead of the logged term in the equation. Of special interest is the effect of each of these funding factors on the relationship between the 1970 level variable and the 1980 level variable in both these regressions. In the case of dance companies, the beta of the lagged (1970) dependent variable is reduced from .42 to .32 when the funding variable is added to the regression equation, and in the case of theater companies the beta of the lagged dependent variable is reduced from .61 to .51.

Thus, federal funding not only increases the total supply of dance and theater companies in urban places, but it also reduces the significance of earlier institutional patterns on present ones; that is, public funding helps urban places that initially have few institutions more than those with many. Since the amount of funding does not modify the influences of other variables, these results suggest that funding does not disrupt the "normal" forces that govern the relation between demand and supply, and that it accelerates the process of cultural development, especially in those places that were initially disadvantaged.

Conclusions

In strains of cultural analysis, social conservatism and aesthetic progressivism became so intertwined that it is difficult to disentangle the modernist values of progress and creativity from values of authority and hierarchy. The assumption that aesthetic standards require distinguishing "good" art from "bad" art is used to justify the claim that elite standards and traditional values are essential for preserving the basis on which this distinction is made. "Good art," it is often assumed, requires good taste, a liberal education, the right sort of social background, while "bad" art – hack work, kitsch, commercial products – can be left to those who may not care, namely, those with boring jobs, a poor education, and undiscriminating tastes. In this way, social and economic inequalities become linked with the distinction between authentic culture and mass culture and the possibility of either a universal or a highly pluralistic culture is denied within this modernist perspective. No less misleading is a simplistic marxist version of modernism that views popular culture as the casualty of class differences. Instead, findings of this study suggest that both institutionalized popular and elite culture are governed by about the same social and economic conditions.

The modernist assumptions – whether they be embedded in a marxist or a conservative framework – are rooted in two sets of observations, one involving what people tend to like and dislike and the second involving an historical record. What individuals tend to like and dislike and the consequences of subtle differences in preferences for social worth are of little relevance for understanding patterns on a large scale. An accounting of the historical conditions that gave rise to great cultural epochs and major artistic contributions cannot be extrapolated to contemporary times. What may have influenced the development of art in the past several centuries in aristocratic societies may not be the same as what influences it in a capitalistic society where art no longer depends primarily on rich patrons but on large numbers of people who are middle class.

The conditions that are conducive to the development of high culture are not that different from those that are conducive to the development of popular culture, and while these conditions differ in interesting and specific detail they do so in ways that are contrary to what cultural theories would predict. Low and declining levels of inequalities are conditions that are favorable to the growth of the supply of elite culture and, in numerous instances, to that of popular culture as well. High – not low – levels of education create favorable conditions for both popular concerts and radio. Major forms of social diversity – not homogeneity – are particularly important for several kinds of popular culture. In general terms, markets for both elite and popular culture are defined by urban populations with little class inequality and markets for popular culture are also characterized by much population diversity. Class structures do have a bearing on culture – at least on the supply of institutional culture – but in ways that are the opposite of what is conventionally expected.

Artists' opportunities for jobs and employment are governed by social and economic conditions that are very different from those that govern the institutional supply of culture. The urban conditions that affect artists are, in fact, very little different from those that characterize firms and big businesses: workers' lives are structured by career ladders, departments, and job titles. That is, artists' labor markets are largely defined by inequalities and hierarchies – that is, by great class differences – and this becomes increasingly

Table 8.4. *Independent variables: means and standard deviations*

	Mean	Std dev
1 Income inequality 1970	.3426	.0277
2 SES inequality 1970	.2931	.0159
3 Education median 1970	11.5304	.4399
4 Education inequality 1970	.1651	.0200
5 Δ Income inequality	.0152	.0153
6 Δ SES inequality	−.0202	.0070
7 Δ Education inequality	.0235	.0110
8 Occupational diversity 1970	.8850	.0076
9 Industrial diversity 1970	.8728	.0244
10 Language diversity 1970	.3079	.1079
11 Occupational diversity	−.0009	.0055
12 % Manufacturing 1970	.2597	.1055
13 Pop. change 1960–70	.1999	.1885
14 Pop. change 1970–80	.1339	.1592
15 Ln pop. size 1970	8.7609	.8194
16 Ln size squared 1970	.6660	1.1566
17 East	.2240	.4186
18 West	.1920	.3955
19 Theater funds (Ln)	2.0829	2.4158
20 Dance funds (Ln squared)	4.4846	6.9444

N = 125

pronounced over time. Both labor markets and institutions interlock with the social structure, but they do so in quite different ways. Labor markets are always notoriously imperfect markets, and we would expect that artists' labor markets are especially so since networks, luck, and gossip about jobs are more critical for artists than for most workers. Places with notable affluence, considerable poverty, and great inequalities attract artists.

In contrast, large consumer markets and institutionalized suppliers operate in sluggish ways. Statistical profiles of the average audience member, surveys by market research groups, and the known successes and failures of other institutions all help to provide cultural institutions with information about markets and control over them. And, institutionalized suppliers of all kinds rely less on a few patrons or a few investors than they do on a broad based following. Places with large critical masses – not classes – are congenial for the growth and development of cultural institutions.

Table 8.5. Correlations among all independent variables

	1	2	3	4	5	6	7	8	9	10	11	12	13	14	15	16	17	18	19
1 Income inequality 1970																			
2 SES inequality 1970	.02																		
3 Education median 1970	.01	−.41																	
4 Education inequality 1970	.62	.21	−.49																
5 Δ Income inequality	−.68	.02	−.07	−.26															
6 Δ SES inequality	−.58	−.07	−.15	−.35	.40														
7 Δ Education inequality	−.38	.32	−.46	−.15	.30	.46													
8 Occupational diversity 1970	.39	.44	.12	.23	−.25	−.44	−.18												
9 Industrial diversity 1970	.55	−.16	.02	.32	−.27	−.41	−.22	.37											
10 Language diversity 1970	−.11	−.05	.14	−.06	.26	.10	.29	−.19	−.10										
11 Δ Occupational diversity 1970	−.53	.20	−.49	−.05	.33	.65	.48	−.57	−.49	.08									
12 % Manufacturing 1970	−.58	.20	−.40	−.14	.28	.47	.50	−.30	−.67	−.04	.66								
13 Pop. change 1960–70	.15	−.18	.39	−.23	−.13	−.20	−.30	−.01	.12	.07	−.34	−.39							
14 Pop. change			.24	.04	.22	.37	.39	.26	.34	.02	.38	.59	.71						

15 Ln pop. size 1970	.06	−.53	.14	−.06	.14	.00	.04	−.18	.15	.24	−.16	.03	.03	−.20					
16 Ln size 1970 squared	.08	−.24	.09	.01	.13	.05	.12	−.18	.06	.24	−.02	−.01	−.09	−.21	.64				
17 East	−.26	−.03	−.29	−.01	.13	.24	.48	−.39	−.17	.38	.37	.43	−.32	−.43	.10	.11			
18 West	.04	.02	.40	−.29	.12	−.13	−.14	.17	.22	.31	−.23	−.44	.45	.47	.04	.02	−.26		
19 Theater funds (Ln)	−.01	−.49	.16	−.10	.04	−.04	−.02	−.25	.14	.16	−.16	−.03	−.02	−.24	.67	.48	.20	.01	
20 Dance funds (Ln squared)	.06	−.40	.15	−.05	.06	.04	−.01	−.29	.10	.16	−.03	−.06	−.05	−.18	.62	.75	.14	.06	.53

Notes

1 *From Graven Images* (New York: Columbia University Press, 1983), p. 180.
2 See, for example, Cesar Graña, *Fact and Symbol* (New York: Oxford University Press, 1971).
3 *The Waning of the Middle Ages* (New York: Anchor, 1954 [1942]), p. 244.
4 See Frederick Antal, *Florentine Painting and Its Social Background* (London: Routledge and Kegan Paul, 1947); Francis Haskell, *Patrons and Painters* (New York: Knopf, 1963); Arnold Hauser, *The Social History of Art*, Vol. 2 (New York: Knopf, 1968 [1951]).
5 See Paul DiMaggio, "Cultural Entrepreneurship in Nineteenth-Century Boston," *Media, Culture and Society* 4 (1982), 33–50; Neil Harris, *The Artist in American Society* (New York: Simon and Schuster, 1966); Lillian B. Miller, *Patrons and Patriotism* (Chicago: University of Chicago Press, 1966); Janet Minihan, *The Nationalization of Culture* (New York: New York University Press, 1977).
6 (Cambridge MA: Harvard University Press, 1984), pp. 372–385.
7 Paul DiMaggio and Michael Useem, "Cultural Democracy in a Period of Cultural Expansion," in Jack B. Kamerman and Rosanne Martarella, eds., *Performers and Performances* (South Hadley MA: Bergin and Garvey, 1983).
8 Chris Rojeck, *Capitalism and Leisure Theory* (London: Tavistock, 1985), p. 107.
9 Antonio Gramsci, *Selections from the Prison Notebooks* (London: Lawrence and Wishart, 1971); also see Patrick Brantlinger, *Bread and Circuses* (Ithaca: Cornell University Press, 1983); Sharon Zukin, "Art and the Arms in Power," *Theory and Society* 11 (1982), 423–451.
10 The arguments summarizing this position are in articles by Ernest van den Haag, Leo Lowenthal, and Bernard Rosenberg in Bernard Rosenberg and David Manning White, eds., *Mass Culture* (Glencoe IL: Free Press, 1957). A more recent summary is provided by Edward Shils, "Mass Society and its Culture," pp. 200–229 in P. Davison, R. Meyersohn, and E. Shils, eds., *Literary Taste, Culture and Mass Communication* (Teaneck NJ: Somerset House, 1978).
11 For example, S. Hall and T. Jefferson, eds., *Resistance Through Rituals* (London: Hutchinson, 1976); Dick Hebdige, *Subculture* (London: Methuen, 1979); Iain Chambers, *Popular Culture* (London: Methuen, 1986).
12 Roy Rosenzweig, *Eight Hours for What We Will* (Cambridge: Cambridge University Press, 1983).
13 "Art as Collective Action," *American Sociological Review* 39 (1974), 767–776.
14 In a critical review of research on cultural capital, Michele Lamont and Annette Lareau make this point in "Cultural Capital in American Research," *Working Papers and Proceedings of the Center for Psychosocial Studies* (Chicago, 1987). Also see Herbert J. Gans., "American Popular Culture and High Culture in Changing Class Structure," pp. 40–57 in Judith H. Balfe and Margaret J. Wyszomirski, eds., *Art, Ideology and Politics* (New York: Praeger, 1985).
15 *The Civilizing Process*, Vol. 1, trans. Edmund Jephcott (New York: Pantheon, 1978 [1939]).
16 Georg Simmel, *The Problems of the Philosophy of History*, trans. and ed. Guy Oakes (New York: Free Press, 1977), p. 91.

17 For a summary see Joseph Bensman and Bernard Rosenberg, "Mass Media and Mass Culture," pp. 166–186 in Philip Olson, ed., *America as a Mass Society* (New York: Macmillan, 1963).

18 See note 9; also see Janet Minihan, *The Nationalization of Culture* (New York: New York University Press, 1977); Peter Dobkin Hall, *The Organization of American Culture, 1700–1900* (New York: New York University Press, 1984).

19 For a clear discussion see Ronald C. Kessler and David F. Greenberg, *Linear Panel Analysis* (New York: Academic Press, 1981).

20 U.S. Bureau of the Census, *1970 Census of Population and Housing – Geographic Identification Codes* (Washington DC: GPO, 1972). The only instances for which precise geographical matches were not possible were for indicators obtained from the 1972 and 1977 Censuses for Selected Services for which the smallest geographical unit reported is the SMSA. To estimate how the effects of changed boundaries would alter the results for commercial theaters and cinemas, the analysis was also carried out using per capita variables. Except for the different coefficients obtained for population size the results are the same.

21 There is no original reference for the 1970 data since they were aggregated from the Public Use Sample to the SMSA level by the Bureau of the Census. These data were originally obtained by Peter M. Blau and employed by him and Joseph Schwartz in a study of intermarriage. Further descriptions of the data set are provided in their book, *Crosscutting Social Circles* (New York: Academic Press, 1984). A summary of categories for the 1980 census is reported in U.S. Bureau of the Census, *Users' Guide*, Part C, *Index to Summary Tape Files 1 to 4* (Washington DC: U.S. Bureau of the Census, 1980).

22 For variables used in computing change scores the correlations based on raw data and 1970 categorized data are: income inequality (.85), educational inequality (.85), occupational diversity (.93). See text for discussion of SES inequality.

23 The original index is described by Otis Dudley Duncan in his 1961 article in Albert J. Reiss, ed., *Occupations and Social Status* (Glencoe IL: Free Press); scores that are based on 1970 occupational characteristics were obtained from Robert M. Hauser and David L. Featherman, *The Process of Stratification* (New York: Academic Press, 1976).

24 To take into account the weights in the sampling procedure and to estimate values for grouped data the following formula is used:

$$\text{Gini} = 1 - [\Sigma \text{Value}_i \ \text{Freq}_i \ (\text{Freq}_i + 2(N - \text{Cumulative Frequency}_i))/N^2(\text{Mean}_i)]$$

25 Revised occupational reclassifications are reported in U.S. Bureau of the Census, *Detailed Occupations of the Experienced Civilian Labor Force by Sex for the United States and Regions: 1980 and 1970, Supplementary Report* (Washington DC: GPO, 1984).

26 The correlation between the 1970 SES Gini coefficient for detailed occupations and the 1970 SES Gini coefficient for major occupations is .96, providing sufficient justification to use the latter in the change analysis.

27 See chapter 7, note 37.

28 For example, suspecting a directory of museums was not comprehensive, two other

sources for museums were coded. As it turned out, the directory is not as comprehensive as the others but high correlations among urban totals indicate that it is not biased. Specifically, the correlations among variables B, C, C-1, and D from Appendix B range from .64 (A and C-1) to .89 (between A and C).

29 See chapter 2, note 25.

30 The reason why relatively few (ten) can be considered is that while many advocacy and professional associations compiled directories in the early 1970s – probably in response to the heightened level of public funding – few did in the later period. Directories for the later period could not be located for chamber music, theater premieres, and opera workshops; it was considered unlikely that opera companies and symphony orchestras increased very much over the decade. Information on bands and commercial orchestras was not used because definitions for them were revised by the Census for Selected Services; all dance companies (rather than modern and ballet companies) are compared so that the effects of funding could be analyzed.

31 A logit procedure, which is generally recommended for dichotomous dependent variables, cannot be employed in a change analysis, but a logit regression and an OLS regression for 1970 yielded identical results.

32 There were minor changes in the definitions of the categories within types of artist occupations; for example, window dressers were classified as designers in 1980 but not in 1970, and theater directors were added to the category of actors in 1980; see National Endowment for the Arts, "Artist Employment in 1983," *Journal of Cultural Economics* 9 (1985), 86–90. To test whether these changes would have systematic effects on the results, all analyses were replicated after removing outliers on the z scores of the absolute differences between 1970 and 1980. It was concluded that these minor changes in occupational definitions have random rather than systematic effects since the results are unaffected by removing the outliers.

33 The cohort and age effects reported in chapter 3 are spurious here, owing to the positive relations between the age categories and other urban characteristics, notably population size. Divorce rate and percentage change in blacks are significantly related to two 1980 dependent variables, as reported in Peter M. Blau, Judith R. Blau, Gail Quets, and Tetsuya Tada, "Social Inequality and Art Institutions," *Sociological Forum* 1 (1986), 561–585. These turned out to be spurious, owing to population change between 1970 and 1980, although population change itself does not yield significant coefficients in the regressions. Other influences identified as significant in cross-sectional analysis are not in the lagged analysis. For example, the relation between the percentage of women (lagged) and 1980 popular concerts (.22) is destroyed due to its contemporaneous relation with 1970 popular concerts (.35).

34 The actual categories used are: (1) museums; (2) dance; and (3) theater. Program funding grants by NEA are reported at the institutional level in its *Annual Reports*, so dollar amounts were coded by city or place location of the institution and aggregated to the SMSA level. The Foundation Center reports contributions in its annual *Foundation Grants Index*, but the cultural categories of recipients are sufficiently ambiguous in many instances to preclude analysis of SMSA differences in funding for specific arts. Efforts were also made to obtain reports from State Art

Councils. While agencies were very co-operative, reports vary so much that coding them to obtain SMSA estimates of funding proved to be impossible.
35 Correlations among funding amounts in different years range from .67 to .85.
36 Judith R. Blau, Peter M. Blau, and Reid M. Golden, "Social Inequality and the Arts," *American Journal of Sociology* 91 (1985), 309–331; Judith R. Blau, "The Elite Arts, More or Less de Rigueur," *Social Forces* 64 (1986), 875–905; Peter M. Blau *et al.*, "Social Inequality and Art Institutions."
37 Income inequality (and median) is based on 1970 and 1980 family income. Although income data for 1980 is reported with $75,000 and above as the upper limit, the 1970 upper category was $50,000 and above. To obtain measures that would be comparable, the upper two categories of family income are combined. Education measures are based on data for persons 25 years and older and 1980 categories are used to collapse 1970 data. For a description of procedures used to compute SES measures see notes 24 and 26.
38 There is a lack of mathematical independence between any Gini coefficient and the mean of that variable since the mean is in the denominator.
39 See chapter 7, note 37.
40 See Herbert Read, *Art and Society* (New York: Schocken, 1966); John Dewey, *Art as Experience* (New York: Putnam's, 1958 [1934]), pp. 9–10.
41 Judith R. Blau *et al.*, "Social Inequality and the Arts."
42 The relative size of four major occupational groups – professionals, clerks, operatives, and service workers – is largely responsible for the influence of occupational heterogeneity.
43 The simple correlation for performers and nonperformers for 1980 is .63; for 1970 it is .26.
44 See note 10.
45 Robert Montgomery, "The Recent Rapid Expansion of American Architecture Employment," paper presented at the Conference on the History and Sociology of Architectural Practice, Princeton University, June 1985.
46 Magali Sarfatti Larson, "Emblem and Exception," pp. 49–86 in Judith R. Blau, Mark E. LaGory, and John S. Pipkin, eds., *Professionals and Urban Form* (Albany NY: State University of New York Press, 1983).
47 "Structural Aspects of the Architectural Profession," pp. 280–289 in *Professionals and Urban Form*.
48 Judith R. Blau, *Architects and Firms* (Cambridge MA: MIT Press, 1984), p. 49.
49 Mary E. Osman, "Survey of Firms Charts Decline In Employment," *American Institute of Architects Journal* 66 (1975), 41–42.
50 The detailed results are summarized in my chapter in Paul L. Knox, ed., *The Design Professions and the Built Environment* (London: Croom Helm, 1988), pp. 127–146.
51 The unstandardized coefficient for the SEI difference score is −10.81 and its standard error is 4.34.
52 Empirical results reported in Peter M. Blau *et al.*, "Social Inequality and Art Institutions," and Judith R. Blau, "The Elite Arts, More or Less de Rigueur."
53 Urban elites, as identified from social registries, are found to be important for museums, but only when characteristics of the central city are considered. See Judith

R. Blau, "High Circles, High Art," *Empirical Studies of the Arts* 5 (1987), 79–86.

54 There are a few trivial differences reported here and in earlier published papers, owing to the addition of the funding variables and some trimming of the model that this change warranted.

55 Overall, there is not a dramatic increase in the average number of any type of cultural supplier. While the means for museums, dance companies, craft fairs, and radio are all higher in the later period than in the earlier one, the means for other suppliers, notably, theater companies, ensembles, legitimate theater, and cinemas, are slightly lower in the later period compared with the earlier one. In some instances such a decline actually conceals an increase in the number of SMSAs that acquire an institution of a given kind during the period. For example, the mean for legitimate theater is slightly lower in 1977 compared with 1972 (5.5 and 5.7, respectively), but the numbers of SMSAs with at least one commercial theater increased from 89 to 99. As noted in the text, the decline in the mean numbers of live popular concerts is considerable, and is attributed to the increasing use of large arenas.

56 When both the Gini and a measure of central tendency are entered into the equation, the Gini is usually significant and the mean or median is not.

57 Herbert J. Gans, p. 44.

58 The extent to which the members of the population are more or less evenly distributed among sixteen industrial sectors defines the measure for employment diversity. There are two categories for language, whether English or another language is spoken at home, and a high value indicates a linguistically heterogeneous population, which means that relatively many persons have a mother tongue other than English.

59 "Of Happiness and Despair We Have no Measure," pp. 519, 520.

60 However, funding data were coded only for 1971–72 for museums, yielding a measure of support somewhat inferior to those for theater and dance.

9 The transformation of American culture

> The entropy of a gas of particles in equilibrium is easy to calculate; according to statistical mechanics it is proportional to the total number of particles. The more particles in the gas, the messier it can become, the larger its entropy.
>
> Heinz R. Pagels, *Perfect Symmetry* (1985)

The second law of thermodynamics states that a closed system can become more disordered (or stay the same), but it cannot become less disordered. The entropy of a gas reaches its maximum in its equilibrium state when the particles are random both with respect to the distribution of their positions and to their velocities. Under such "messy" conditions, observing an unusual combination of particles or any interesting configuration is rare. The first deal in a game of poker (that is, with one deck of cards that are thoroughly shuffled) is unlikely to yield a winning hand. There is a smaller probability of a chance encounter with a sociology colleague on a vacation than at the annual sociology meetings. Most people, in fact, arrange their lives to maximize the probabilities of interesting configurations. Social arrangements are, by definition, nonrandom. On varieties of social, economic, and political dimensions, cities have relatively much structure and they vary in the composition of people who live in them. However, on dimensions of culture we find that American cities vary surprisingly little, and that cultural patterns are not so highly structured.

Structural bases for cultural production

Spatially, culture exhibits a relatively ubiquitous pattern. Cultural institutions that sponsor traditional or elite art are widely dispersed throughout the nation so that opportunites to attend the ballet, the opera, or the theater are about the same in any large American city, while, in contrast, commercial cultural institutions do exhibit some geographical concentration. Judging from the temporal changes of demand by people in different age groups, it was inferred

175

that interests in culture have silted through the population. That is, there is no distinctive market and no conspicuous process of cross-generational transmission that might insure a source of prominent demand for the supply of culture. It is only one single, aging cohort that carries with it over time a "taste" for what is most unusual and innovative in cultural worlds.

Suppliers of popular culture increase lockstep with increases in the population as the number of popular culture institutions has a linear relation with the size of the metropolitan place. The process underlying the increase in the supply of elite culture institutions is different, but it suggests a potential outcome of saturation that would occur at very high population threshold levels. Specifically, once a critical mass is reached, high culture "takes off," increasing at a rate faster than that of population size.

In these circumstances it is hard to conceive of persisting localized domains of culture that are governed by community members' distinct preferences and traditions. There is additional evidence to support this conclusion. For instance, the specialized, traditional art museum that once presumably flourished in provincial enclaves is, apparently, being replaced by the cosmopolitan public-spirited museum – an all-purpose variety that suits diverse interests. For another, the proverbial uniqueness of New York as a haven for the theatrical avant-garde, which is generally attributed to New York's special affinity for the unconventional and daring, can be better explained in nonlocal, "noncultural" terms. Populations with relatively affluent residents, as is the case for New York, are likely to support innovative theater. The paradoxical conclusion is that the activities and products of cultural institutions are increasingly liberated and exempted from culture – culture, that is, in its generic and anthropological sense.

As contradictory as it might at first appear, such conclusions are not inconsistent with those of art critics, who are concerned with the transformations of meaning in contemporary art. Writing not about the urban supply of art, but rather about what art signifies, Hal Foster notes, "Meanwhile, the conventions of art are not in decline but in extraordinary expansion. This occurs on many fronts: new forms, whose logic is not understood, are introduced, and old codes, with the 'decorum' of distinct mediums broken, are mixed. Such art can pose provocative contradictions, but more often the mix is promiscuous and, in the end, homogeneous."[1]

When cities teem with cultural producers of every stripe and there are cultural products for every conceivable public, and when art conventions are cheek by jowl, it is not so inexplicable that art forms are unchaste and that the codes of art are impure and highly decorated. Post-modernism may be the symbolic expression of abundant supply – or its consequence. To contend that cultural institutions are impervious to distinctive traditions, customs, values and beliefs – culture in the generic sense – and also that cultural supply is expanding as a direct function of population demand points to the equality of opportunity, and not necessarily to the homogenization of style and convention. Nevertheless, the very ubiquity of all forms of cultural institution provides a partial explanation for the loosening of fixed conventions, the mobile meanings of art, cross-over styles, and broken codes that are described in contemporary analyses of art. As Jameson observes, a feature of postmodernism is "the effacement . . . of some key boundaries or separations, most notably the erosion of the older distinction between high culture and so-called mass or popular culture."[2] It is hardly surprising that styles, intentions, techniques, and conventions intermingle as cultural producers of all kinds proliferate in a given community.

There is another structural explanation – besides the one that deals with the sheer amount of cultural supply and cultural producers – that might also account for the increasing convergence of artistic conventions. This relates to a principle stated by Robert Duverger in *Political Parties*,[3] an analysis of the relation between parties and partisanship. In a highly segmented and stratified society a large number of distinctive parties compete with one another, each promulgating its unique political ideology and cultivating the support of well defined groups. Political culture, under these circumstances, is contentious and highly pluralistic. In the absence of well defined groups, political parties "play the game" of consensus politics,[4] and, as a result, political culture is a loose amalgam of diverse, but not very distinctive, ideological convictions; there is a minimum of radical purity and instead a hodgepodge of adulterated orientations and a rhetoric of compromise. The few major parties generate increasingly similar ideological conventions as they must compete for the centrist majority.

Both popular culture and elite culture are rooted in similar ways in the social and economic matrix. Cities with relatively little inequality and a substantial middle class have more culture of all kinds. It is highly plausible to posit that the very milieu in which culture flourishes, namely one with homogeneous and nonsegmentalized markets, with a broad middle class and a diminutive social elite, will encourage much cross-fertilization and homogeneity. If cultural producers are to survive they must, after all, compete for the middle, and in the process pilfer from others whatever is – at the time – provocative or tasteful, exemplary or marketable.

How these macro-level processes influence those at the individual level is not well understood. However, recent work sheds some light on the ways by which cultural tastes are diffused through neighborhoods and cities. Although it is true that a person's education and income are among the best predictors of attending a ballet, the cinema, an opera, or any other cultural event, the average education and income of the neighborhood residents' also increase the likelihood of a person attending such events, regardless of his or her own education and income. This means that an interest in culture is partly acquired through the influences of community characteristics above and beyond the person's own status and resources. Additionally, certain personal characteristics that are related to cultural interests have stronger effects in those communities in which many residents share these same characteristics (such as high educational attainments) and in communities where there are considerable cultural opportunities.[5]

Thus, community influences have independent effects on individuals' cultural preferences and reinforce the effects of personal background characteristics on these preferences. This denotes a process of contagion of taste and the public diffusion of cultural interests.

Cultural organizations

The findings hardly support the notion that strong interdependencies exist among cultural suppliers. Nor do they suggest that there are specialized taste cultures in urban places. For if there were either strong interdependencies or specialized taste cultures there would be high probabilities of co-occurring suppliers of similar types of culture, which there are not. There are very few dyadic ties that can be explained in terms other than those of chance. The few dyadic combinations that do occur make little sense until more complex configurations are examined. A large critical mass virtually ensures the existence of an opera company, which in turn generates the conditions for co-occurring institutions. It was concluded that it is not so much the nature of the cultural product that the organization supplies, but rather its uncommonness that empowers the rare organization to establish integrative bonds among many other organizations. Thus, an initial condition of prominent outcropping and low entropy easily converts into one of uniform structure and high entropy.

As cultural organizations grow and prosper, their configurations change in counterintuitive ways. For example, the response of a performing arts organization to a munificent environment is to divest itself of administrators. This could mean that the tasks of co-ordination, management, and supervision – that is, *internal* administrative functions – are carried out more efficiently by relatively few administrators when there are plentiful resources than when there are few. But this is not the reason since the proportion of administrators declines with organizational size regardless of the character of the environment. The more likely possibility is that munificence dramatically alters the relation of the arts organization to the *external* environment that includes government agencies, arts funding agencies, philanthropists, and publics. It was argued that under such conditions arts organizations become submerged, co-opted, and integrated into a larger organized cultural sphere, in which more powerful forces pre-empt local administrative functions. While the implications for centralized control and thoroughgoing systematic co-ordination by external agencies and foundations could only be a matter for speculation here, the evidence does indicate that there is a loosening of the boundaries between arts organization and the larger environment. We could view this as resulting in the lesser autonomy of the local arts organization.

At the same time, public funding for the arts increases innovation and also increases the sheer number of arts organizations over time, particularly in places that initially had relatively few organizations. Such support, I concluded, hastens the process of democratization of the arts and also promotes artistic innovation, contrary to the view that the arts benefit in competitive free markets.

Artists

Cultural workers, to the extent I am able to investigate their activities and urban presence, leave traces that contradict the themes of this book and belie its premises. (This is, perhaps, no cause for surprise, but rather a confirmation of our beliefs about the contrariness of artists.) Professional artists are, for example, prominently present in the smallest arts organizations, whereas there are proportionately few of them in large arts organizations. Artists are replaced in organizations by amateurs and the larger the organization the greater the tendency to recruit amateur artists instead of professional artists.

The endeavors in which artists are engaged – whether it be dancing, making music, or acting – have ramifications for the way in which the organization is itself structured. For example, the initial differences in organizational structure among music, dance, and drama groups increase as organizations grow in size; thus, the small music group has relatively few administrators compared with the small dance or theater group, and for its size the large music group is uncharacteristically nonbureaucratic, which is not the case for the large dance or theater group.

Although the production of art and the demand for art are rooted in a broad middle class, and cultural suppliers of all kinds thrive in cities with small class differences, artists' work opportunities are greatest in places where there is relatively much inequality, that is, with extremes of rich and poor. It could be said that producers respond to universal markets, whereas artists' labor markets respond to particularistic conditions rooted in class differences.

The historical dimension

The analysis of meaning in the social sciences is sometimes called structural sociology when one refers to the work of, say, Roland Barthes or Claude Lévi-Strauss; the analysis of social configurations, such as ones produced by networks of relations or forms of differentiation, is also called structural sociology. Let us call the first interpretation and the second explanation, which would be consistent with Alfred North Whitehead's early formulation of their contrasting assumptions[6] and with E. H. Gombrich's application of these two approaches. The two structuralisms have little in common except both posit that there are concommitant variations or discernable relationships in a system, whether these relationships are parallelisms and pertain, for example, to myth and kinship structure; or are causal and pertain to, for example, economic differentiation and the distribution of power. Still, it may be permissable to cast anchor in both intellectual currents while speculating about the historical development of culture.[7]

I have employed a set of data that is essentially cross-sectional and I have discussed the outcome of an historical process without describing the genesis of change from which present conditions are still driven. A broad sketch of the contours of the American historical transformation is necessary to make the present conditions understandable, and since it is a story with which everyone is familiar, it can be brief. What will be emphasized here, which was not in earlier chapters, is the extent to which this transformation was comprehensive, involving economic and social changes as well as cultural ones.

The quite extraordinary artistic achievements in twentieth century America would never have been predicted by early observers. De Tocqueville assessed American art to be inferior in quality and generally cheap and tasteless.[8] Mrs. Trollope, while probably more preoccupied with what she considered to be the detestable manners of Americans, also commented on the generally low quality of artistic productions.[9] Nevertheless, Mrs. Trollope was impressed with the wide availability of art, however low its quality: "trash which penetrates into every cot and corner of the country, and which is greedily sucked in by all ranks, is unquestionably one great cause of its inferiority."[10] And American artisans, commented de Tocqueville, endeavor "to bring their useful productions within the reach of the whole community."[11] Thus, in spite of a certain availability, cultural products in American society in the early nineteenth century on all accounts were of trifling quality.

This is hardly remarkable in view of the fact that Americans were fully antagonized by European aristocratic and courtly traditions. Even for the well-to-do, strong Puritanical traditions dictated simplicity. "The fine arts," as the Congressional minutes in 1815 record, "are the foppish instruments of the devil."[12] There are other considerations: around 1830, only about 37 per cent of school age children were actually enrolled in school and probably about one-quarter of American adults were literate.[13] Three out of every five workers were engaged in agriculture, and the average workday was about thirteen hours.[14] Under such conditions there was little time for the cultivation of taste and edifying leisure. Nor were the rich and educated much predisposed to cultivating the arts.

Within a few decades there were quite extraordinary changes, and by the end of the century great fortunes were invested by Americans in art, cultural institutions, Grand Tours abroad, and, as Thorstein Veblen observed, in vulgar and ostentatious display of costly possessions.[15] The circumstances that shifted the balance from equality in the enjoyment of shoddy but simple entertainment in the 1830s to great inequality in leisure and taste by the end of the century are related to the profound economic and social changes in the intervening decades.

The greatest increase in the concentration of wealth, according to economic historians, occurred during the nineteenth century and probably did not decline until the 1930s recession. For example, Gallman's estimate is that in 1860, the richest 1 per cent of the population owned about 24 per cent of the wealth,[16] while Soltow's analysis indicates that one-tenth of 1 per cent owned 15 per cent of the wealth.[17] Whichever figures are used, economic and social inequalities obviously were considerable. What changed during the twentieth century was not so much the decline in the proportions at the bottom and at the absolute top, but rather substantial declines in the proportions of the near rich, so that the middle 60 per cent increased their share of income.[18]

It was precisely during the ascendancy of a wealthy elite that the rural and foreign poor were immigrating in unprecedentedly large numbers to American cities,[19] providing the substantial base for a vital vernacular culture – burlesque, vaudeville, music halls, dime museums, and professional sports. Barth describes these new forms of culture as the response to nineteenth century social and economic problems:

Fashioned freely by and for large numbers of people, they marked the culmination of the process of creating ways of life out of new social and economic institutions. Modern city culture boldly answered the mounting need of diverse people for a common urban identity that also left enough room for each individual's dreams and aspirations. Its expressions spoke to and for the average individual, without putting artists and writers, architects and philosophers, on pedestals.[20]

Demographic, economic, and social transformations of the late nineteenth century and early twentieth century were of an extraordinary magnitude. By 1890 64 per cent of school age children were in school;[21] transportation improvements reduced great regional disparities in population composition, economic and commercial activities, and incomes;[22] real earnings for nonfarm employees rose 63 per cent between 1900 and 1929.[23] Accompanying these socio-economic changes in the early part of the twentieth century was the displacement of local forms of amusement – vaudeville, burlesque, and music halls – by national ones – radio, the cinema, and later television – creating universal realms of cultural participation.[24]

It is still true that not all Americans visit museums, go to rock concerts, attend baseball games, or go to the ballet. Such opportunities are sufficiently commonplace, however, so that they are all within the realm of the possible for most urban Americans. At the same time it is still true that participation in any of these activities, as Pierre Bourdieu observes, reflects a judgement of taste on which others make judgements, yielding classifications that reinforce status differences. "Taste classifies, and it classifies the classifiers."[25]

But such classifications would not be possible at all if cultural realms were not universally understood and there were not widespread knowledge about the difference between styles and genres. It is only when there is widely shared knowledge and broad public understanding that fine distinctions can be made that are socially meaningful. Culture functions as a common currency because it provides near equivalent social meaning throughout a complex and differentiated social order.

Notes

1 *Recordings: Art, Spectacle, Culture Politics* (Port Townsend WA: Bay Press, 1985), p. 19).
2 Frederic Jameson, "Postmodernism and Consumer Society," pp. 111–125 in Hal Foster, ed., *The Anti-Aesthetic* (Port Townsend WA: Bay Press, 1983), p. 112; also see Rosalind E. Krauss, *The Originality of the Avant-Garde and Other Modernist Myths* (Cambridge MA: MIT Press, 1986); Iain Chambers, *Popular Culture* (London: Methuen, 1986).
3 (New York: Wiley, 1974).
4 I have taken some license in interpreting Duverger's structural theory; he did not put great emphasis on the a priori importance of status groups, but rather on the number of political parties *per se*.
5 Judith R. Blau, *The Role of Social Context: Working Paper* (New York: Center for the Social Sciences, Columbia University, 1987); Peter M. Blau, *Social Inequality, Cultural Opportunities: Working Paper* (New York: Center for the Social Sciences, Columbia University, 1987).

6 *Science and the Modern World* (New York: Macmillan, 1925).

7 This is justified according to some traditions. See, for example, Norbert Elias, *The History of Manners*, Vol. 1, *The Civilizing Process* (New York: Pantheon, 1978).

8 Alexis de Tocqueville, *Democracy in America*, Vol. 2 (New York: Knopf, 1945 [1835]).

9 *Domestic Manners of the Americans*, Vol. II (London: Whittaker, Treacher, 1832).

10 *Domestic Manners of the Americans*, p. 119.

11 *Democracy in America*, p. 53.

12 Quoted in Stuart Bruchey, *The Roots of American Economic Growth* (New York: Harper and Row, 1965), pp. 198–99; also see David E. Shi, *The Simple Life* (Oxford: Oxford University Press, 1985).

13 John B. Folger and Charles B. Nam, *Education of the American Population*, U.S. Bureau of the Census Monograph (Washington DC: U.S. Government Printing Office, 1967).

14 Relative size of the agricultural labor force is reported in Stanley Lebergott, *Manpower in Economic Growth* (New York: McGraw Hill, 1964); sources of productive income, including agricultural, are reported in Robert K. Martin, *National Income in the United States, 1799–1938* (New York: National Industrial Conference Board, 1939).

15 *Theory of the Leisure Class* (London: Allen and Unwin, 1925 [1899]).

16 Robert E. Gallman, "Trends in the Size Distribution of Wealth in the Nineteenth Century," pp. 1–24 in Lee Soltow, ed., *Six Papers on the Size Distribution of Wealth and Income* (New York: National Bureau of Economic Research, 1969).

17 Lee Soltow, "The Wealth, Income and Social Class of Men in Large Northern Cities of the United States in 1860," pp. 233–276 in James D. Smith, ed., *The Personal Distribution of Income and Wealth*, Studies in Income and Wealth, Vol. 39 (New York: National Bureau of Economic Research, 1975).

18 See Robert J. Lampman, *The Share of Top Wealth-Holders in National Wealth, 1922–56*, A Study of the National Bureau of Economic Research (Princeton NJ: Princeton University Press, 1962); Simon Kuznets, *Shares of Upper Income Groups in Income and Savings* (New York: National Bureau of Economic Research, 1953). Stanley Lebergott, *The Americans*, p. 72, n. 42; p. 498. Authors advise caution in trying to estimate long term trends since most of the studies for the nineteenth century distribution are based on personal and property wealth, while studies of the twentieth century distributions are based on income. As Lester C. Thurow observes, income data greatly underestimates the financial resources of the rich (*The Zero-Sum Society*, New York: Basic Books, 1971), p. 168.

19 E. P. Hutchinson, *Immigrants and Their Children, 1850–1950*, Census Monograph Series (New York: Wiley, 1956).

20 Gunther Barth, *City People: The Rise of Modern City Culture in Nineteenth-Century America* (Oxford: Oxford University Press, 1982), p. 229.

21 Folger and Nam, *Education of the American Population*.

22 Simon Kuznets, Anne Ratner Miller, and Richard Easterlin, *Population Redistribution and Economic Growth United States, 1870–1950*, Vol. 2, *Analysis of Economic Change* (Philadelphia: American Philosophical Society, 1964).

23 Stanley Lebergott, *The Americans*, p. 379.

24 Realism and naturalism in the arts and architecture undoubtedly played a role, too, in promoting incorporation of all communities and classes into universal cultural conceptions (see Peter Dobkin Hall, *The Organization of Culture*, New York: New York University, 1984). Granted, the conservative decades of the early twentieth century tended to reinforce cultural distinctions through its anti-immigration policies, pronounced reverence for property and wealth, and anti-union legislation which slowed the process of cultural fusion. Yet, after the Depression, expanding educational opportunities, combined with the battering that the privileged had taken, played important roles in accelerating this fusion. See, for example, James MacGregor Burns, *The Workshop of Democracy* (New York: Alfred A. Knopf, 1985).

25 *Distinction,* trans. Richard Nice (Cambridge MA: Harvard University Press, 1984), p. 6.

Appendix A
List of SMSAs and 1970 population

Akron	630,800
Albany–Schenectady–Troy	723,800
Albuquerque	318,900
Allentown–Bethlehem–Easton	542,600
Anaheim–Santa Ana–Garden Grove	1,420,000
Appleton–Oshkosh	275,700
Atlanta	1,387,700
Augusta	276,000
Austin	299,900
Bakersfield	331,900
Baltimore	2,068,000
Baton Rouge	286,400
Beaumont–Port Arthur–Orange	317,200
Binghamton	299,200
Birmingham	732,800
Boston	3,703,000
Bridgeport	791,100
Buffalo	1,348,100
Canton	370,700
Charleston	307,500
Charlotte	409,000
Chattanooga	310,100
Chicago	6,945,100
Cincinnati	1,385,700
Cleveland	2,061,000
Columbia	324,600
Columbus	920,600
Corpus Christi	285,800
Dallas	1,548,500
Davenport–Rock Island–Moline	362,000
Dayton	847,300
Denver	1,223,900
Des Moines	285,600
Detroit	4,187,400
Duluth–Superior	263,500

El Paso	358,200
Erie	261,100
Flint	493,600
Fort Lauderdale–Hollywood	617,300
Fort Wayne	680,300
Fort Worth	762,900
Fresno	410,800
Gary–Hammond–East Chicago	629,300
Grand Rapids	538,400
Greensboro–Winston–Salem–High Point	601,500
Greensville	302,200
Harrisburg	408,700
Hartford	811,800
Honolulu	764,500
Houston	1,991,600
Huntington–Ashland	252,400
Indianapolis	1,1094
Jackson	2,608
Jacksonville	5,298
Jersey City	6,067
Johnstown	2,623
Kansas City	12,592
Knoxville	4,039
Lancaster	3,198
Lansing	3,769
Las Vegas	2,756
Little Rock–North Little Rock	3,248
Lorain–Elyria	257,200
Los Angeles–Long Beach	7,018,700
Louisville	825,200
Madison	291,000
Memphis	767,300
Miami	1,267,000
Milwaukee	1,400,600
Minneapolis–St. Paul	1,814,100
Mobile	379,000
Nashville–Davidson	542,700
New Haven	744,100
New Orleans	1,045,900
New York	11,538,400
Newark	1,851,400
Newport News–Hampton	292,300
Norfolk–Portsmouth	678,100
Oklahoma	638,100
Omaha	540,000
Orlando	427,700

Oxnard Ventura	376,900
Paterson–Clifton–Passaic	1,359,800
Peoria	340,400
Philadelphia	4,802,100
Phoenix	960,500
Pittsburgh	2,405,300
Portland	1,013,900
Providence	765,700
Reading	299,700
Richmond	513,600
Rochester	876,900
Rockford	270,900
Sacramento	799,700
St. Louis	2,355,100
Salinas–Seaside–Monterey	248,300
Salt Lake City	553,600
San Antonio	865,900
San Bernardino–Riverside–Ontario	1,144,200
San Diego	1,354,700
San Francisco–Oakland	3,111,700
San Jose	1,063,700
Santa Barbara	262,800
Seattle–Everett	1,423,900
Shreveport	294,500
South Bend	276,000
Spokane	286,900
Springfield–Holyoke	457,500
Stockton	287,800
Syracuse	637,800
Tacoma	407,600
Tampa–St. Petersburg	1,010,800
Toledo	686,500
Trenton	307,200
Tucson	349,500
Tulsa	477,100
Utica–Rome	338,000
Washington	2,853,300
West Palm Beach	350,800
Wichita	390,100
Wilkes–Barre–Hazelton	341,900
Wilmington	500,100
Worcester	634,700
York	325,300
Youngston–Warren	536,300

Source: 1970 Public Use Sample

Appendix B
Sources and descriptions of cultural indicators: means and standard deviations

A Performing artists per 100,000 population, 1970
Includes actors, musicians and composers, and dancers. Source: Public Use Sample of the 1970 U.S. census, 5% and 15% county-group files.

$$\bar{x} = 1.59 \quad \text{s.d.} = 1.09$$

AA Performing artists per 100,000 population, 1980
Includes actors and directors, musicians and composers, and dancers. Source: see A.

$$\bar{x} = 2.06 \quad \text{s.d.} = 1.62$$

B Nonperforming artists per 100,000 population, 1970
Includes authors, designers, painters, and sculptors. Source: see A.

$$\bar{x} = 2.71 \quad \text{s.d.} = 1.48$$

BB Nonperforming artists per 100,000 population, 1980
For definition see B. Source: see A.

$$\bar{x} = 3.76 \quad \text{s.d.} = 2.71$$

C1 Performing arts groups
Includes groups and companies for all types of performing arts. Source: Beatrice Handel, ed., *The National Directory of Performing Arts and Civic Centers*, 3rd ed., (New York: Wiley, 1975).

$$\bar{x} = 7.34 \quad \text{s.d.} = 12.58$$

C2 Performing arts buildings
Includes theaters, halls, civic centers, churches, university centers, and auditoriums that house performing arts groups and events. Source: see C1.

$$\bar{x} = 5.59 \quad \text{s.d.} = 10.18$$

D Art museums and specialized museums
Those listed as art museums are distinguished from other specialized museums (such as history, natural history, ethnography, children's, folklore museums) or from those with specialized collections (such as classical antiquities, crafts and decorative arts). Source: Helmut Rouschenbusch, ed., *International Directory of the Arts*, Vol. 1, 11th ed., (Berlin: Deutsche Zentraldruckerei Ag: 1971/72).

188

D1 Total museums
$$\bar{x}=9.81 \quad \text{s.d.}=17.45$$

D2 Art museums
$$\bar{x}=2.05 \quad \text{s.d.}=2.96$$

D3 Specialized museums (excludes other)
$$\bar{x}=6.87 \quad \text{s.d.}=49.39$$

E Art museums, 1975
The total number of museums listed or cross-listed under the category of art museums are coded. Source: American Association of Museums, *Official Museum Directory* (Chicago: National Register Publishing Co., 1975). An earlier directory was not coded because procedures used in 1975 for compiling information are different from those used earlier but are the same for those used at a later date. Also see chapter 7.
$$\bar{x}=3.43 \quad \text{s.d.}=5.60$$

EE Art museums, 1985
Source and descriptions: see E.
$$\bar{x}=4.46 \quad \text{s.d.}=6.77$$

F Galleries
Galleries are described by type. Those listed as art (paintings, graphic arts, sculpture) are distinguished from other specialized galleries (including furniture, numismatics, oriental, porcelain, reproduction, tapestries, antiquities, decoration, jewelry). Galleries with art and other specialties coded as art galleries. Source: Helmut Rauschenbusch, ed., *International Directory of Arts*, Vol. 2, (Berlin: Deutsche Zentraldruckerei Ag, 1971/72).

F1 Total galleries
$$\bar{x}=19.57 \quad \text{s.d.}=90.81$$

F2 Art galleries
$$\bar{x}=12.70 \quad \text{s.d.}=43.34$$

F3 Specialized galleries
$$\bar{x}=6.87 \quad \text{s.d.}=49.39$$

G Theater premieres
Number of premieres for a two year period summed over an SMSA's listed theaters. Source: Donald W. Fowle, ed., *Notable Names in the American Theater* (Clifton NJ: James T. White, 1976).
$$\bar{x}=41.18 \quad \text{s.d.}=368$$

H Nonprofit theaters, 1977–78
Number of nonprofit professional theaters. Source: Theater Communication Group,

Theater Profiles 4 (New York: TCG, 1979). Also see chapter 7.
$$\bar{x} = 1.40 \quad s.d. = 5.38$$

HH   Nonprofit theaters, 1981–82
See H. Source: *Theater Profiles 6* (New York: TCG, 1983).
$$\bar{x} = 1.20 \quad s.d. = 3.70$$

I   Dance premieres
Number of premieres for 1974–75 season summed over an SMSA's dance companies.
Source: John Willis, ed., *Dance World* (New York: Crown Publishing, 1976).
$$\bar{x} = 4.54 \quad s.d. = 16.19$$

J   Dance companies, 1974
Number of dance companies grouped by categories. Source: Heidi von Obenauer, ed.,
Dance Magazine Annual (New York: Danad Publishing Company; 1974).

J1   Total dance companies
Modern, ballet, children's, ethnic and folk, historical, jazz, mime, solo, tap.
$$\bar{x} = 3.88 \quad s.d. = 18.10$$

J2   Ballet companies
$$\bar{x} = 1.45 \quad s.d. = 2.72$$

J3   Modern dance companies
$$\bar{x} = 1.14 \quad s.d. = 6.92$$

JJ   Dance companies, 1984
See J.

JJ1   Total dance companies
$$\bar{x} = 6.11 \quad s.d. = 28.10$$

JJ2   Ballet companies
$$\bar{x} = 1.98 \quad s.d. = 3.58$$

JJ3   Modern dance companies
$$\bar{x} = 2.33 \quad s.d. = 14.34$$

K   Opera companies
Listing of opera companies. Although the date of the publication is 1983, a list of
founding dates supplied by the Central Opera service indicates no change since 1970.
Source: Central Opera Service, *Opera Directory* (New York: COS, 1983).
$$\bar{x} = .34 \quad s.d. = .58$$

L   Opera workshops
Numbers of workshops and festivals combined. Source: Central Opera Service, *Opera*

Companies and Workshops in U.S. and Canada (New York: COS, 1977).

x̄=2.05   s.d.=3.01

M   Symphony orchestras

Numbers of orchestras by following categories, the first five of which are defined by minimum annual income (in parentheses): major ($2m), regional ($600,000), metro ($150,000), urban ($60,000), community (maximum $60,000), college, youth, other. Source: American Symphony Orchestra League, "North American Orchestra Directory," *Symphony Magazine* 31 (December 1981). This is the first published directory but founding dates indicate high stability since the early 1970s.

M1   Total orchestras

x̄=2.42   s.d.=2.95

M2   Major orchestras (first two categories)

x̄=.44   s.d.=.66

M3   Nonmajor orchestras (remaining categories)

x̄=1.98   s.d.=2.50

N   Chamber music groups

Primarily quartets and quintets, although some larger groups (with nine or eleven members) included. Source: Chamber Music America, *Directory* (New York: CMA, 1985).

x̄=2.53   s.d.=12.87

O   Contemporary ensembles, 1975

Performance of contemporary music is the criterion for inclusion in the directory. All groups perform at least some experimental music, multi-media works or electronic compositions. The groups range in size from duets to chamber orchestras, but no soloists or orchestras are listed. Source: The American Music Center, *Contemporary Music Performance Directory* (New York: AMC, 1975).

x̄=2.92   s.d.=13.03

OO   Contemporary ensembles, 1985

See O, with name of directory changed to *Performing Ensembles Directory*. Editors report no change in criteria for inclusion.

x̄=2.54   s.d.=12.47

P   Craft fairs, 1971, 1972, 1973

Calendars for all bimonthly issues for three years coded. Craft exhibits at galleries and museums and one person shows not included. Source: American Craft Council, *Craft Horizons* (New York: ACC, 1971, 1972, 1973).

x̄=.97   s.d.=1.74

PP   Craft fairs, 1981, 1982, 1983
See P. Same except that magazine's name changed to *Craft Horizon*.
$$\bar{x} = 2.34 \quad \text{s.d.} = 4.02$$

Q   Music festivals
Bluegrass and ole' time country music festivals coded. Each SMSA credited for its state's festivals. Source: Bluegrass Unlimited, "Festival Guide Issue" (Burke, Va.: BU, 1975).
$$\bar{x} = 15.55 \quad \text{s.d.} = 10.95$$

R   Cinemas, 1972
Commercially operated conventional or "four wall" theaters and drive-in theaters engaged in the exhibition of motion pictures, with payroll. Source: U.S. Bureau of the Census, Census for Selected Service Industries (Washington, D.C.: Bureau of the Census, 1972) SIC code 783.
$$\bar{x} = 45.51 \quad \text{s.d.} = 59.28$$

RR   Cinemas, 1977
See R.
$$\bar{x} = 42.88 \quad \text{s.d.} = 51.84$$

S   Legitimate theaters, 1972
Establishments with payroll primarily engaged in presenting live theatrical productions in legitimate theaters; primarily for-profit. Source: See R, SIC code 7922 part.
$$\bar{x} = 5.72 \quad \text{s.d.} = 24.68$$

SS   Legitimate theaters, 1977
See S.
$$\bar{x} = 5.50 \quad \text{s.d.} = 21.02$$

T   Commercial orchestras, 1972
Orchestras, string instrumental, and related groups with payroll organized for the presentation of music or dance. Primarily commercial groups but also includes non-profit groups that charge fees. Source: See R. SIC code 7929 part.
$$\bar{x} = 2.54 \quad \text{s.d.} = 6.27$$

TT   Commercial orchestras, 1977
Commercial orchestras are included under two sub-categories of SIC 7922 in 1977, and those classified in the sub-category, "Other music and entertainment" could not be separated from other establishments in that sub-category and are not included in these counts. See T.
$$\bar{x} = .679 \quad \text{s.d.} = 1.85$$

U   Bands, 1972
Dance bands, orchestras (except symphonies), combos, quintets, and similar instrumental organizations presenting popular music on a contract or fee basis for

restaurants, night clubs, radio and television programs, etc. with payroll. Source: See R, SIC code 7929 part.

$$\bar{x} = 18.86 \quad \text{s.d.} = 36.41$$

Note: there is no comparable category for 1977.

V   Variety entertainment, 1972
Entertainers (other than orchestras, dance bands, or other similar organizations) who perform in restaurants, night clubs, on radio, or television, etc., on a contract or fee basis. Burlesque and vaudeville are included. With payroll. Source: See R, SIC code 7929 part.

$$\bar{x} = 12.44 \quad \text{s.d.} = 41.83$$

Note: there is no comparable category for 1977.

W   Dance halls, 1972
Establishments engaged in operating dance halls, studios, schools. Source: see R, SIC 791.

$$\bar{x} = 13.34 \quad \text{s.d.} = 24.67$$

Note: there is no comparable category for 1977.

X   Popular music concerts, 1975
Live concerts. Types distinguished in Chapters 3 and 7. Source: *Rolling Stone*, biweekly calendars (San Francisco, Ca.: Straight Arrow Publications, 1975).

$$\bar{x} = 16.02 \quad \text{s.d.} = 18.78$$

XX   Popular music concerts, 1983
Source: see X.

$$\bar{x} = 6.91 \quad \text{s.d.} = 8.30$$

Y   Television viewing
Estimates on audience size or the proportion of television households reached by network programming during an average 15 minute period during specified parts of the day. The translation from geographical units, "designated market areas" into SMSAs was carried out by Steven Messner who made these data available to me. Source: A. C. Nielsen Co., *Unpublished data for fall season, 1982* (New York: A. C. Nielsen).

$$\bar{x} = 28.47 \quad \text{s.d.} = 3.67$$

Z   Radio stations, 1974
Formats were coded regardless of whether one station had more than one format or not and regardless of number of hours of broadcasting time. This was considered the preferred strategy since the prime interest is the demand for given types of programs. News, religious programs, and formatted discussion programs were not coded. Source: *Directory of Radio Stations in the United States and Canada* (Washington DC: Broadcasting Publications, 1974).

$$\bar{x} = 19.36 \quad \text{s.d.} = 14.24$$

ZZ Radio stations, 1983
Source: see Z.

$$\bar{x} = 25.23 \text{ s.d.} = 16.08$$

Appendix C
Log transformation*

Most cultural indicators and other variables based on counts are highly skewed. A standard procedure for dealing with this is to transform the indicator using a logarithmic transformation. However, a nontrivial number of zeros in a data set creates problems because the logarithm of zero is negative infinity. The usual solution to this problem is to add a constant to the variable before taking its logarithm. Rather than add an arbitrary fixed constant (e.g., 0.5, 0.17 or 1, constants that have been suggested for particular statistical applications) before taking logarithms, the solution used throughout this book is to allow the constant to depend on the distribution of the indicator being transformed. The solution employed is to add to the observed value the proportion of cases in the data set that have a non-zero value, prior to taking the natural log of the variable. Thus:

$$Y = \log_e [Y + (1 - n/N)]$$

where n is the number of cases with a value of zero and N is the total number of cases (usually 125)

The log transformation shrinks differences among high scores while expanding differences among low scores. By adding a larger constant before taking logarithms, one reduces the expansion of differences among low scores. If Y has very few zeros, the above displaced logarithmic transformation ensures that these zeros will not dominate the variance of Y (leaving most of the variance to reflect differences among the non-zero cases). On the other hand, if there are many zeros then the variation in Y primarily reflects the distinction between zeros and non-zeros and the displaced logarithmic transformation will emphasize this distinction, making Y closely approximate a dichotomous variable.

A second rationale for using the displaced logarithmic transformation is that Y is a stochastic variable that can only be observed as an integer value. In all analyses, one uses the observed variable as an indicator of the expected number of events (for example, performing art centers) that a unit (SMSA) with certain characteristics has. This expected number is positive (though possibly less than one) and therefore the observed zeros necessarily underestimate this expected number, E(Y). (Non-zero scores can be underestimates or overestimates of the expected number of events.) The optimal strategy would be to take the logarithm of the expected number of events, but this expected value is unknown. Nevertheless, it is intuitively clear that the more zeros

* This solution was developed by Joseph E. Schwartz.

an indicator has, the lower the expected value is likely to be. Assuming one cannot explain a very high proportion of the variance of this variable, a conservative estimate of the expected number of events is the proportion of cases having at least one event. It is this value which is used as the constant for the displaced logarithmic transformation.

In summary, when the distribution of Y has many zeros, this tranformation concentrates the variance in the distinction between zeros and non-zeros, effectively making Y essentially a dichotomous variable. When there are few zeros, a larger constant is added to ensure that the zeros do not become outliers of the transformed variables.

Appendix D
Polynomial term*

One conventional method for estimating the multiplicative effect of an independent variable is to include its square in a regression equation. Such an effect is of substantive interest in this book in the case of three variables: population size, organizational size, and public funding for the arts at the SMSA level. In each case, however, there is strong multicollinearity between the natural log of the variable and its natural log squared. An alternative quadratic term is therefore employed, specifically, the square of the residuals or deviations from the mean:

$$(Ln\ X - mean\ Ln\ X)^2$$

When both the log of the variable and the squared term for the logged variable are included in the equation, the first estimates the linear effect, and the second estimates the curvilinearity of the relationship.

*This solution was developed by Joseph E. Schwartz.

Index of authors

Index of subjects

Other books in the series

J. Milton Yinger, Kiyoshi Ikeda, Frank Laycock, and Stephen J. Cutler: *Middle Start: An Experiment in the Educational Enrichment of Young Adolescents*

James A. Geschwender: *Class, Race, and Worker Insurgency: The League of Revolutionary Black Workers*

Paul Ritterband: *Education, Employment, and Migration: Israel in Comparative Perspective*

John Low-Beer: *Protest and Participation: The New Working Class in Italy*

Orrin E. Klapp: *Opening and Closing: Strategies of Information Adaptation in Society*

Rita James Simon: *Continuity and Change: A Study of Two Ethnic Communities in Israel*

Marshall B. Clinard: *Cities with Little Crime: The Case of Switzerland**

Steven T. Bossert: *Tasks and Social Relationships in Classrooms: A Study of Instructional Organization and Its Consequences**

Richard E. Johnson: *Juvenile Delinquency and Its Origins: An Integrated Theoretical Approach**

David R. Heise: *Understanding Events: Affect and the Construction of Social Action*

Ida Harper Simpson: *From Student to Nurse: A Longitudinal Study of Socialization*

Stephen P. Turner: *Sociological Explanation as Translation*

Janet W. Salaff: *Working Daughters of Hong Kong: Filial Piety or Power in the Family?*

Joseph Chamie: *Religion and Fertility: Arab Christian–Muslim Differentials*

William Friedland, Amy Barton, Robert Thomas: *Manufacturing Green Gold: Capital, Labor, and Technology in the Lettuce Industry*

Richard N. Adams: *Paradoxical Harvest: Energy and Explanation in British History, 1870–1914*

* Available from the American Sociological Association, 1722 N Street, N.W., Washington, DC 20036.

206

Mary F. Rogers: *Sociology, Ethnomethodology, and Experience: A Phenomenological Critique*

James R. Beniger: *Trafficking in Drug Users: Professional Exchange Networks in the Control of Deviance*

Andrew J. Weigert, J. Smith Teitge, and Dennis W. Teitge: *Society and Identity: Toward a Sociological Psychology*

Jon Miller: *Pathways in the Workplace: The Effects of Race and Gender on Access to Organizational Resources*

Michael A. Faia: *Dynamic functionalism: Strategy and Tactics*

Joyce Rothschild and J. Allen Whitt: *The Co-operative Workplace: Potentials and Dilemmas of Organizational Democracy*

Russell Thornton: *We Shall Live Again: The 1870 and 1890 Ghost Dance Movements as Demographic Revitalization*

Severyn T. Bruyn: *The Field of Social Investment*

Guy E. Swanson: *Ego Defenses and the Legitimation of Behaviour*

Liah Greenfeld: *Different Worlds: A Sociological Study of Taste, Choice and Success in Art*

Thomas K. Rudel: *Situations and Strategies in American Land-Use Planning*

Percy C. Hintzen: *The Costs of Regime Survival: Racial Mobilization, Elite Domination and Control of the State in Guyana and Trinidad*

John T. Flint: *Historical Role Analysis in the Study of Religious Change: Mass Educational Development in Norway, 1740–1891*

DATE DUE